SERVICE SECTOR IN INDIAN ECONOMY

SERVICE SECTOR IN INDIAN ECONOMY

Edited by
Talluru Sreenivas
MBA, M Com, M Phil, Ph D.
Reader, Department of Management Sciences
RVR & JC College of Engineering
Guntur 522 019 (Andhra Pradesh)

Foreword by
Dr. R Murali Babu Rao
Professor of Cardiology on special duty
Guntur General Hospital, and Guntur Medical College
Guntur 522 004 (Andhra Pradesh)

DISCOVERY PUBLISHING HOUSE
NEW DELHI-110002

First Published-2006

ISBN 81-8356-050-4

Published by

DISCOVERY PUBLISHING HOUSE
4831/24, Ansari Road, Prahlad Street,
Darya Ganj, New Delhi-110002 (India)
Phone: 23279245 • Fax: 91-11-23253475
E-mail:dphtemp@indiatimes.com

Printed at
Arora Offset Press
Laxmi Nagar, Delhi–92

Dedicated to

Dr. Maddineni Gopalkrishna
Secretary
Nagarjuna Education Society and
Secretary & Correspondent
RVR & JC College of Engineering
Guntur, Andhra Pradesh

Where the mind is without fear and the head is held high,
Where knowledge is free,
Where the world has not been broken up into fragments
by narrow domestic walls,
Where words come out from the depth of truth,
Where tireless strying stretches its arms towards perfection,
Where the clear stream of reason has not lost its way
into the dreary desert sand of dead habit,
Where the mind is led forward by thee
into ever-widening thought and action
into that heaven of freedom, my father, *let my country awake.*

–Rabindranath Tagore

FOREWORD

In the recent decades, Indian planners and scientists have been looking ahead visualising what India can aspire to be in the foreseeable future, say by 2020. As a nation with rich traditions and cultural values and with steady pattern of growth of economic and social aspects of development, India has been striving hard to overcome structural limitations in various spheres, and lay the foundation for sustained acceleration for growth with equity. For the large populous nation, with innumerable diversities and historical legacies, development path has not been as smooth and steady as visualised. The revered President of the Indian Republic, Dr. A.P.J. Abdul Kalam, has in a recent statement conceptualised the future of India as a developed nation by 2020 by stating as follows:

"A developed India by 2020 or even earlier, is not a dream. It need not even be a mere vision in the minds of many Indians. It is a mission we can all take up and succeed."

It is the missionary zeal with which India can channelise its human capital and physical resources with determination, and with the required mindset, work culture, commitment and dedication, that can help Indians to collectively work towards the cherished goal. This will enable us to feel proud of being citizens of a modern and resurgent India, a developed nation in the not too distant future.

Human and social aspects of development have assumed greater importance in recent years, compared to economic and technological aspects, as they are aimed at improving people's welfare. On the human development front, prominent reports highlighting national level data are the United Nations Development Programme's (UNDP's) *Human Development Report* released annually, *Human Development in South Asia Report* released annually by the Human Development Centre for South Asia in Islamabad (Pakistan), and the first *India - National Human Development Report 2001* released in 2002 by the Planning Commission, Government of India. The latest available volumes for the first two publications are of 2004. they deal with cross-country comparisons, whereas the Indian volume of 2001 of Government of India deals with state level analysis for 1981, 1991 and 2001. the findings of all these volumes on the present position of India on various socio-economic indicators are really revealing; and many keep referring to these findings in various contexts. It is worth recalling select highlights of these volumes.

As per the latest UNDP Report 2004, Human Development Index (HDI) for India improved from 0.416 (1975) to 0.443 (1980), 0.481 (1985), 0.519 (1990), 0.553 (1995), 0.590 (2001), and 0.595 (2002). In the ranking of 2001 and 2002, India's position is shown as 127 out of 177 countries for which ranking was attempted. China stands at rank 94 in 2002. India has moved to the position of a country with medium level of development, showing steady growth in the value of the index over years. Human Poverty India (HPI) is 33.1%, with rank 53. Population below the poverty line as per national analysis is 28.6% in 1999-2000, and as per international poverty line for the same year, population earning below one US $ per day is 34.7% with porvery gap between urban and rural areas as 8.2%, and below two US $ a day is 79.9%, with poverty gap between urban and rural areas as 35.3%. Population under the age of 15 as percentage of total population in 2001 is 35.3, which will be of the productive citizen's category by 2015. Growing younger work force is an advantage for the nation. Total fertility rate per woman is 3.1 by 2001. Gender Development Index (GDI) is 0.572 in 2002, with India's rank as 103 out of 144 countries. Life expectancy at birth in 2002 for females is 66.9 years, and for males 63.9 years ; the average for males and females being 65 years ; in comparison with the figure for China as 71 years, and for Sri Lanka as 74 years.

The index and the ranking for India given above are arrived at through a composite value of various relevant social indicators.

Progress in the country in respect of education, health, gender development, work participation, and a number of other sectors is analysed. These indicators are monitored regularly for improving the performance at national, state and district levels. It is well recognized that improvement in health status of population is both an important means of increasing productivity and economic growth as well as an end in itself. The importance of improvement in health is also acknowledged in the Millennium Development Goals of the UNDP, which call for a dramatic reduction in poverty, and improvements in health, especially of the poor. Ensuring good health of the vast majority of poor population in particular is a challenging task. The *National Health Policy 1983* set some targets for 1985, 1990 and 2000. A comparison of the goals with actual achievements reveals the real picture. We are nowhere near targets, except for life expectancy, crude death rate and polio immunisation.

A comprehensive study of the Indian health sector was undertaken in 2000 to provide valuable inputs into the work of The Commission on Macroeconomics and Health, appointed by the World Health Organisation (WHO), and coordinated at the national level by the Indian Council for Research on International Economic Relations (ICRIER), New Delhi. The findings of the study are brought out in *India Health Report* authored by Rajiv Misra et al.(2003) published by Oxford University Press, New Delhi. The principal objective of the study is to assess the importance of investing in health to promote economic development and reduce poverty in the third world. The findings of the study have been utilised in the formulation of the *National Health Policy 2002* of Government of India. The study examines the reasons for poor health scenario in India, and challenges in the provision of health care in the country. Several recommendations made by the study are under implementation at present. These relate to control of communicable diseases, the rising threat of non-communicable diseases, reduction of infant and maternal mortality, the emerging threat of the proliferating HIV/AIDS infection, financing of healthcare systems (both public and private), drug policy and regulations, health research, and Indian systems of medicine.

Communicable and infectious diseases constitute a major cause of premature death in India, killing over 2.5 million children below the age of five, and an equal number of young adults every year. Despite significant progress achieved in the overall quality of life, and reduction in absolute poverty, the proportion of total deaths on account of communicable diseases, maternal and parinatal conditions, and nutritional deficiencies continues to be unacceptably high at 42 per cent of total deaths due to various diseases, the balance being 48 per cent due to non-communicable diseases (NCDs), and 10 per cent due to injuries. While current efforts will ensure elimination of leprosy and polio within the next five years, environmental and social factors impose severe constraints on the eradication of malaria, TB, or HIV/AIDS. Thus, efforts will have to be aimed at reducing disease transmission, minimising drug resistance, and reducing mortality and morbidity; this is an economic imperative as it is the poor who suffer the most. Improvement in the general levels of health through larger allocations and more effective implementation of communicable and non- communicable disease programmes, changes in the pattern of assistance and implementation, and greater focus on tertiary health care have received special attention. In pursuance of the concept of convergence, a National Vector Borne Disease Control Programme has been started from 2003-04 through the convergence of three ongoing programmes (Malaria, Kala-azar and Filaria), and inclusion of Japanese Encephalitis and Dengue. The main objective of the programme is prevention and control of vector borne diseases, and pursuance of the goals set under the National Health Policy 2002.

The focus of the health sector programmes has so far been largely on control of communicable diseases. Some programmes for non-communicable diseases (NCPs) such as blindness, iodine deficiency, and cancer are also under implementation. However, prevalence of NCDs like cardiovascular diseases (CVDs), mental disorder, cancer and trauma has been rising due to various factors. During the Tenth Plan (2002-07), efforts are being made to improve preventive, curative and rehabilitative services for NCDs throughout the country at all levels of care.

Cross-sectional studies in India have revealed the prevalence of coronary artery disease (CAD), which is several-fold higher than that in developed countries. Projections based on Global Burden of Disease study estimate that by the year 2020, the burden of atherothrombotic cardiovascular disease (CVD) in India would surpass that in any other region in the world. The mortality attributable to CVD in India is expected to rise by 103 per cent in men, and by 90 per cent in women from 1985 to 2015. This predilection to coronary artery disease (CAD) is attributed to a clustering of various traditional and non-traditional risk factors, which are believed to constitute the atherogenic phenotype characteristic of Indians. From 1990 to 1995, the prevalence of CAD in adults increased from 3 to 10 per cent among urban Indians, and from 2 to 4 per cent among rural Indians, with women having rates similar to men. Although the prevalence of CAD in rural India is half that of urban India, this is still two-fold higher than the overall CAD rates in the U.S., and several-fold higher than in rural China. In 1990, there were 783,000 deaths due to CAD in India, and this is projected to double by the year 2015, primarily due to affluence and urbanisation. CAD is the leading cause of death in women. Health care providers need to be sensitive to gender differences in presentation, prognosis and responsiveness to treatment of CAD.

The key to combating the increasing incidence of CAD among Indians, is, therefore, the control of known risk factors by a population-based strategy aimed at comprehensive risk factor reduction. The relatively low levels of conventional risk factors in rural populations, and the concurrent low prevalence of CAD in these communities presents a window of opportunity for primordial and primary prevention.

Clarifying the role of the state in health is only the first step. A major effort to mobilise resources from both external and domestic sources is required to achieve the necessary higher levels of state investment. Meanwhile, a comprehensive health-sector reform initiative should direct resources to priorities, and raise utilisation efficiency. This would need reform not only at the central and state level to provide the management and institutional frameworks to carry out the assigned functions but also the involvement of local bodies such as panchayats and municipalities as indicated in the 73rd and 74th amendments of the Indian Constitution (1992). Initiatives need to be taken at all levels. High level of political support and popular participation is required to make this exercise a success. Involvement of non-government organisations (NGOs) and charitable institutions, with private sector involvement will go a long way in improving the delivery system. As the programme essentially involves bringing about awareness and education among people at large, at various levels of delivery system, commitment, discipline and dedication to growth with equity, and to make health policy adequately pro-poor and pro-senior citizen become imperative. Role of bureaucracy and political leadership at different levels, including local level in villages and towns needs to be improved to a great extent to ensure high quality of health care for the society.

Based on our own and international experience, we are convinced, that there is indeed no alternative to strong state intervention for improving public health as well as health care of the poor in our situation. Role of the state in the liberalised environment has to be even more aggressive compared to earlier years. In the Tenth Plan, and in the National Common Minimum Programme (NCMP) of the Union Government, emphasis given to health care is quite significant to tackle health–related issues. Adoption of the Millennium Development Goals by the UN and deliberations in various Global Summits have created a favourable health–related donor assistance. A vigorous follow-up of the Commission on Macroeconomics and Health (CMH) is planned by WHO, which promises to significantly improve the donor support for health while generating an informed debate on the best strategies to accelerate progress towards global health goals. It is hoped that these steps will help in generating political and public support for higher investment in health coupled with wide-ranging reforms.

I am delighted to learn of the importance given to social aspects of development including education, health and gender development in the National Seminar organised by RVR & JC College of Engineering, Guntur, on Emerging India – Challenges and Opportunities, during March 2004. I would like to congratulate the management of the college, and in particular Dr. Talluru Sreenivas, Reader in the Department of Management Sciences who undertook the responsibility for organising the National Seminar, and bringing the papers and proceedings of the Seminar in the form of a publication.

This publication covering papers on social aspects of development, along with the keynote address from Prof. D.L.

Narayana, Chairman of the Andhra Pradesh State Third Finance Commission brings out a plethora of viewpoints and research efforts at one place to stimulate thinking among well-informed persons. I have great pleasure in recommending this publication to policy matters and administrators associated with social aspects of development, scientists, academics and researchers for pursuing the thread from the coverage of recommendations evolved in the Seminar. Efforts should be made by all quarters to stimulate thinking and action for the welfare of the Indian Society at large.

Guntur
June 1, 2005

Dr. R. Murali Babu Rao
Professor of Cardiology on special duty
Guntur General Hospital, and
Guntur Medical College
Guntur 522 004 (Andhra Pradesh)

PREFACE

Social sectors occupy a prominent place in the economic well-being of the citizens of the country. Ongoing economic reforms and the National Common Minimum Programme (NCMP) of the United Progressive Alliance (UPA) Government at the Centre attach high priority to the development of social sectors to enable people to participate in and contribute fully to the development process, and at the same time benefit more from higher economic growth and development. Sustained economic growth guarantees social sector development in a tangible manner. Adverse macroeconomic imbalance and high inflation, on the other hand, affect the poor, and vulnerable segments of the population adversely. For social sector development, it is therefore important that the high growth rate of the economy is sustained over a longer period.

The Union Government in its NCMP has given due recognition to social sector development, especially in areas such as health, education, employment generation, and poverty alleviation programmes. Expenditure on these sectors has also increased substantially during the recent years. But this is still considered inadequate compared to the need. Higher levels of expenditure on the social sectors could be sustained through reprioritisation of expenditure by the states and the Centre. Similarly rationalisation of subsidies would release resources which could be better targeted to the poor through specific social sector programmes.

Availability of resources alone cannot guarantee social sector development. The efficacy of a large number of government programmes on the ground would have to be vastly improved through various measures. An efficient management and improved delivery of these programmes are essential to implement most social sector programmes through the decentralised system of Panchayat Raj Institutions (PRIs) with the full participation of the people. This would also ensure transparency in implementation which would effectively check leakages in these programmes.

There are wide differentials across states and within each state on the health and education scenario. The health indicators of Kerala are comparable to those of middle - income countries, while those of Uttar Pradesh, Madhya Pradesh and Orissa are almost at the level of sub-Saharan Africa. There are huge disparities between urban and rural areas, and between developed and relatively remote areas inhabited by the marginalised sections of the society.

As per India's National Human Development Report 2001, HDI for India has improved from 0.302 (1981) to 0.381 (1991), and 0.472 (2001). The indicators used for analysis in this report are far more detailed and relevant to the Indian situation, and amenable for state-wise analysis. In the latest year, Kerala and Punjab stand first and second respectively among the 15 major states, with HDI (i) for Kerala as 0.500 (1981), 0.591(1991), and 0.638 (2001) ; and (ii) for Punjab as 0.411 (1981), 0.475 (1991), and 0.537 (2001). HDI for Andhra Pradesh with rank as 10 among the 15 states is as follows: 0.298 (1981), 0.377 (1991), and 0.416 (2001). A few states with rank of HDI in 2001 that deserve special mention are : Tamil Nadu (rank 3), Maharashtra (rank 4), Haryana (5), Gujarat (6), Karnataka (7), West Bengal (8), and Rajasthan (9). States with lowest ranks are Orissa (11), Madhya Pradesh (12), Uttar Pradesh (13), Assam (14), and Bihar (15). Inter-state variations as noticed from this analysis are very large. Human Development Reports have also been prepared for over ten states in India by the respective state governments. These reflect sharp district level variations for various indicators, and also for the combined index for each district. These sharp differences deserve close study for evolving appropriate action strategies for looking ahead to improve the socio-economic conditions of the people of different regions in the country, and for bridging the gap across districts over a period. India's Tenth Plan (2002-07) and Eleventh Plan (2007-12) provisions incorporate the Millennium Development Goals set by the UN.

In the global scenario in the era of liberalisation, constant monitoring of the performance of India in comparison with a number of other countries - developed and developing - is important. In South-East Asia, South Korea and China, efforts put in during the recent two decades on developing social opportunities have been stupendous. India has to go a long way in achieving these levels in social indicators. For overcoming regional disparities in economic and social development, and also disparities among vulnerable sections including low income women members, Indian efforts have to be stepped up manifold. What has been achieved so far is quite limited.

Considerable progress has been achieved in the socio-demographic parameters over the last two decades. However, the country continues to lag behind several other countries in the region. The Tenth Plan targeted a reduction in Infant Mortality Rate (IMR) from 63 per 1000 live births in 2002 to 45 by 2007, and 28 by 2012; reduction in Maternal Mortality Rate (MMR) from 5.4 per 1000 live births in 2000 to 2 by 2007, and 1 by 2012; and reduction in decadal growth rate of population between 2001-2011 to 16.2 per cent from 21.34 per cent between 1991-2001. The National Population Policy 2000 aims at achieving replacement levels of total fertility rate by 2010 through vigorous implementation of inter-sectoral operational strategies. The long term objective is to achieve population stabilisation by 2045, at a level consistent with the requirements of sustainable economic growth, social development, and environmental protection.

The NCMP envisages raising public spending on health to at least 2 - 3 per cent of GDP with focus on primary health care. It also lays emphasis on stepping up public investments for control of communicable diseases, and providing leadership for control of AIDS efforts. Special attention will be paid to poorer sections, in the matter of health care. The basic objective of achieving an acceptable standard of good health amongst the general population of the country as set out in the National Health Policy (NHP) 2002, and reiterated in NCMP continues to be the focus. Central Government has announced the creation of a National Investment Fund in May 2005. The proceeds of this fund will not be reflected in the nation budget. Funds accruing to the Centre out of divestment of Government equity in Central Public Sector undertakings will be deposited in the newly created fund. 75 per cent of the fund will be utilised to finance the health and education schemes, and the balance will be used for supporting revivable public sector units.

The broad policy framework for the development of education, and eradication of illiteracy is provided in the National Policy on Education (NPE) 1986, which had set a goal of expenditure on education at 6 per cent of GDP. As against this target, the combined total expenditure on education by the Central and state governments was 3.74 per cent of GDP in 2003-04. High priority has been accorded to this sector in the Tenth Plan period (2002-07).

The papers presented at the National Seminar on Emerging India : Challenges and Opportunities organised during March, 2004 by RVR & JC College of Engineering, Guntur, incorporated in this publication refer to education, health and a few other social sectors. The other sectors covered include service sector in its totality, improving service quality and insurance. In addition to select papers received for the seminar, efforts have been made to include a few more special contributions from prominent professionals and researchers on themes relevant for the publication. Special care has been taken in these papers to examine the past trends at micro level in a number of cases, apart from district and state levels in particular, to bring out lessons for focussing attention on each aspect in future. Conclusions and recommendations brought out by the authors deserve special consideration of the policy making and implementing organisations. These will be equally relevant for everyone including researchers associated with or actively participating in the respective programmes. The editor acknowledges the valuable contribution of the authors, and recommends the suggestions for adoption extensively in the concerned sectors.

Guntur **Talluru Sreenivas**

June 1, 2005

ACKNOWLEDGEMENT

Inspired by the article which I co-authored recently with my Research Director, Professor G Prasad, Department of Commerce and Business Administration, Acharya Nagarjuna University, entitled, Health Care in India – Strategies for Globalisation, I embarked on the humble venture of organising a National Seminar on the very fascinating topic, dearest to our young minded, dynamic first citizen of our country, his Excellency Bharat Ratna Dr. A.P.J. Abdul Kalam, Emerging India – Challenges and Opportunities. The present publication is the outcome of the proceedings of the seminar held under the editor's secretaryship during March 2004 at RVR & JC College of Engineering, Guntur (Andhra Pradesh).

Sizeable number of papers on different functional areas and in different sectors were received from academics, research scholars, and practitioners. These papers deal with various topics which were taken up for discussion in different technical sessions. The sessions were captioned as : (i) Is India Emerging?, (ii) Industry, Infrastructure and Agriculture, (iii) Service Sector and Developed India, and (iv) Human Resources as a strategic strength. In addition to select papers received for the seminar, efforts have been made to include a few more special contributions from prominent professionals and researchers on themes relevant for the publication. The Seminar organisers are highly indebted to all the contributors for their painstaking efforts to make the presentation highly thought-provoking and instructive. We would like to convey our gratefulness to all of them, and look forward to their bringing out greater insight on these themes in future. These papers are distributed over four publications : (i) Service Sector in Indian Economy, (ii) Perspectives of Indian Agriculture, Industry and Infrastructure, (iii) Banking Sector and Human Resources – Changing Scenario, and (iv) Globalisation and Emerging India.

I acknowledge with gratitude the help I received from Professor D Dakshina Murthy, Former Dean, Faculty of Commerce and Business Administration, Acharya Nagarjuna University, who currently heads the Department of Management Sciences of our College, and all other colleagues in our Department for their constant guidance, encouragement and support.

It gives me great pleasure to place on record my indebtedness to Professor G Prasad, whose guidance gave me the strength and courage to bring out this publication. His scholarly guidance and encouragement are responsible for my success in this venture. He has been a continuous source of inspiration to me.

I would like to convey my gratefulness to a number of elders and well wishers for the substantial encouragement and support given to me on various occasions. These include Dr KRR Mohan Rao, former Vice-Chancellor, Acharya Nagarjuna University, Guntur; Professor P Murali, former Vice-Chancellor, Sri Venkateswara University, Tirupati; Professor V Balamohan Das, Vice-Chancellor, Acharya Nagarjuna University, Guntur; Professor L Venugopal Reddy, Vice-Chancellor, Andhra University, Visakhapatnam; Professor GN Brahmanandam, Dean, Faculty of Commerce & Management Studies, Acharya Nagarjuna University, Guntur; Professor DAR Subrahmanyam, Principal, Mahatma Gandhi College, Guntur; Dr K Chandrasekhara Rao, Head, Department of Commerce, Pondicherry University, Pondicherry; Professor PS Sankara Rao, Andhra University, Visakhapatnam; and Professor NV Narasimham, School of Management Studies, IGNOU, New Delhi.

It gives me pleasure to thank Dr R Murali Babu Rao, Professor of Cardiology on special duty, Guntur General Hospital, and Guntur Medical College, Guntur, for writing the foreword to this work in spite of his busy schedule. I am highly obliged to Professor DL Narayana, Chairman, Third Finance Commission of Andhra Pradesh for delivering the keynote address at the Seminar, and enlightening all the delegates with his extensive research highlights.

It is my privilege to express deep sense of gratitude to the Management of RVR & JC College of Engineering, particularly to our beloved President, Dr K Basavapunnaiah, and our dynamic Secretary & Correspondent, Dr M Gopalkrishna, Sri R Gopala Krishna,

Treasurer, and Professor K Pameswara Rao, Principal, Professor B Ravindra Babu, Vice-Principal, PS Somayajulu, Registrar, NV Srinivasa Rao, Administrative Officer, G Anantha Narayana, Office Manager, and other senior faculty in the College for providing me conducive work environment to organise this mega event. I specially acknowledge the support of Sri DSR Anjaneyulu and Sri SV Rattaiah who helped me in the completion of this gigantic task.

I am greatly indebted to Dr C Ramachandra Prabhu, faculty of Department of Physics, RVR & JC College of Engineering, Dr D Nagayya, former Director, National Institute of Small Industry Extension Training (NISIET), Hyderabad, and Professor S Krishna Sharma, formerly of the Dept. of English, Acharya Nagarjuna University, Guntur for the encouragement, help and support extended to me while working on this publication.

My special thanks are due to the Management of Discovery Publishing House, New Delhi for bringing out this publication in an elegant manner in record time.

I also want to thank a number of personal friends for their solid support and involvement in a variety of ways in my academic ventures. These include : Smt & Sri GS Ram Prasad, Smt & Sri K Shyam Babu, Smt & Sri G Subrahmanyam, Smt & Sri M Subba Rao, Smt & Sri Y Durga Prasada Rao, Smt & Sri PN Uday Kumar, Smt & Sri R Vasu, Smt & Sri V Srinivasa Rao and Smt & Sri M Venkateswara Rao.

All my family members have patiently borne the inconvenience due to my involvement in a number of academic activities including the release of this publication, and encouraged me a great deal. I acknowledge their silent and valued contributions.

Talluru Sreenivas

LIST OF CONTRIBUTORS

Dr. Bhaskara Rao Digumarti
Reader, RVR College of Education
JKC College Road
Guntur - 522 006

Professor Brahmanandam GN
Dean, Faculty of Commerce
Dept. of Commerce & Business Administration
Acharya Nagarjuna University
Nagarjuna Nagar - 522 510

Dr. Chandrasekhara Rao K
Head, Department of Commerce
Pondicherry University
Pondicherry - 605 014

Smt. Deepthi K
Research Scholar
Dept. of Business Management
Bharatiar University
Coimbatore

Dr. Jayasree K
Faculty member, St. Joseph's College of Education
Naaz Centre, Guntur - 522 001

Dr. Jyothi Kumar NVR
Reader, Dept. of Business Management
Mizoram Central University
Aizwal - 796 012, Mizoram

Sri Kishore Babu M
Lecturer, Dept. of Business Studies
Mahatma Gandhi College (PG)
Guntur - 522 019

Dr. Koteswara Rao MVS
Reader, Dept. of Political Science
Acharya Nagarjuna University
Nagarjuna Nagar - 522 510

Sri Kumar Ch HKS
Assistant Professor, Dept. of Science and Humanities
Alhabeeb College of Engineering and Technology
Hyderabad

Dr. Nagayya D
Former Director
National Institute of Small Industry
Extension Training (NISIET)
Hyderabad

Professor Narayana DL
Chairman
Third State Finance Commission
Andhra Pradesh

Professor Prasad G
Dept. of Commerce & Business Admn.
Acharya Nagarjuna University
Nagarjuna Nagar - 522 510
Guntur, Andhra Pradesh

Dr. Prasad KVR
Apollo Institute of Hospital Management
Jubilee Hills
Hyderabad

Sri Prasada Rao YVS
Lecturer, PG Dept. of Management Studies
TJPS College
Guntur - 522 006

Dr. Ramachandra Prabhu C
Dept. of Physics
RVR & JC College of Engineering
Guntur - 522 019

Dr. Ramakrishna AS
Reader, RVR College of Education
JKC College Road
Guntur - 522 006

Sri Rama Krishna NS
Cotton Corporation of India
Guntur - 522 002

Ms Ratna DLK
Executive Director
Mahatma Gandhi College
Guntur - 522 006

Mr. Ravi Kumar U
MBA Student
RVR & JC College of Engineering
Guntur - 522 019

Sri Sastry GEP
Senior Lecturer, DIET
Boyapalem, Guntur Dist.

Dr. Sivaram Prasad R
Faculty of Management
Dept. of Computer Applications
Acharya Nagarjuna University
Nagarjuna Nagar, AP

Dr. Sreenivas Talluru
Reader, Dept. of Management Sciences
RVR & JC College of Engineering
Guntur - 522 019

Dr. Srinivasulu Y
Sr. Lecturer, Dept. of Management Sciences
RVR & JC College of Engineering
Guntur - 522 019

Professor Subrahmanyam DAR
Principal
Mahatma Gandhi College
Guntur - 522 006

Dr. Surya Prakasha Rao BK
Reader, Dept. of Management Sciences
RVR & JC College of Engineering
Guntur - 522 019

Dr. Venkateswara Rao Malapati
Professor and Head
Dept. of Chemical Engineering
RVR & JC College of Engineering
Guntur - 522 019

Sri Vinith V Dani
Faculty Member
Dept. of Management Studies
TKR College of Engg. & Technology
Hyderabad

CONTENTS

SECTION–I
KEYNOTE ADDRESS

1

EMERGING INDIA
*CHALLENGES AND OPPORTUNITIES**

Professor D.L. Narayana**

"The twentieth century will be chiefly remembered not as an age of political conflicts or technical innovations, but as an age in which human society dared to think of the welfare of the whole human race as a practical objective".

–Arnold Toynbee

1. Social Science Theories

Laws of science are exact but the laws of social sciences are tendencies governed by a wide range of micro and macro variables. Indeed laws of social sciences are most complicated as compared to science or technology. According to Eric Roll as stated in his "History of Economic Thought", "Economic theories are always, though often, tortuously related to economic practice". Theories emerge from the speculation of fertile human mind on the basis of conditions of life over time and space. Many ideas in the past heed their roots in institutional arrangements, in the relation between different economic groups and in their conflicting interests. But the longevity of social laws depends on the wide range of changing and differing conditions. Social laws which hold good at certain times may become obsolete

---

* Keynote address delivered at the National Seminar on 'Emerging India: Challenges and Opportunities', organised by the Department of Management Sciences, RVR & JC College of Engineering, Guntur – 19, March 11-12, 2004.

** Chairman, Third State Finance Commission, A.P.

and irrelevant and again giving life and relevance under a new pattern of social, political and economic circumstances. Social laws are not permanent laws.

China and India account for about 36 percent of World's population. China's population by the middle of 21st Century may be at about the level of 1.5 billion population - equal to World's population at the beginning of 20th century. Accordingly, by 2050 both India and China will have the 1901 dimension of World's population. Indeed China and India are the most populous countries in the world today.

The following are the intellectual tides in Economics for growth.

1. Adam Smith Tide: 1776-1889
   Laissez-faire free market for advancing wealth and capitalism through industrial revolution.
2. Marxian Tide: 1917-1985
   Totalitarian economic planning for acceleration of economic growth with complete Government control to usher in socialism.
3. Hayak Tide since 1980s
   Liberalization and privatization with a decline of State in planning for the emergence of market and prosperous capitalism.
4. Asian Tigers Tide since 1950
   Resurgence of State and Market for high economic growth rate and evolution of welfare state.
5. The Human Development Tide since 1990
   Crucial role of State for people's welfare with welfare capitalism to reach the goal of welfare state.
6. Globalisation Trend
   Evolution of international set up to strengthen policies and action for human welfare.

In the words of Alfred Marshall, the author of Classic text book in economics, "Nearly the founders of modern economies were men of gentle and sympathetic temper, touched with the enthusiasm" of humanity. They cared little for wealth for themselves, they cared much for its wide diffusion among the masses of the people.... They were without exception devoted to the doctrine that well-being of the whole people should be the ultimate goal of all private effort and all public policy..... The rights of property, such, have not been venerated by those master minds who have built up economic science".

2. Quality of Indian Human Resources

India is a vast country of diverse regions, religions and cultures. Although free India planned economic development, its average growth rate was about 3.5 per cent for over 30 years up to 1980s, and it was characterized by one of the past Planning Commission members as "Hindu growth rate" with an ironical tinge. After 1980, the growth rate improved a bit, and since 1990, it shows variation between 4.5 and 6 per cent as compared to the South East Asian Countries, which had a sustained growth rate of about 8 to 10 per cent. India's population was 34 crores at the time of Independence which has gone up by three times in 2001 to 103 crores.

The macro-economic inefficiency of India since Independence has no relationship with the micro-competence of Indians in different walks of life. Indians proved their great potential for productivity and development. In a sense the caliber of Indians is next to none in the world either in terms of historical past or the present.

According to Mark Twain, India is the cradle of human race, the birth place of human speech, the mother of history, the grand-mother of legend, and the great grand mother of tradition. Our most valuable and most constructive materials in the history of man are treasured up in India only.

Some of these facts are worthy of note:

- India never invaded any country in her last 10,000 years of history.
- India invented the Number System. Zero was invented by Aryabhatta.
- The world's first university was established in Takshasila in 700 B.C.
- The art of Navigation was born in the river Sindh, 6000 years ago. The word Navigation is derived from the Sanskrit word "Navgatih". The word navy is also from Sanskrit "Nou".

All the above is just the TIP of the iceberg, the list could be endless. But, if we don't see even a glimpse of that great India in the India that we see today, it clearly means that we are not working upto our potential and that if we do, we could once again be an ever shining and inspiring country setting a bright path for the rest of the world to follow.

Even in the contemporary world Indians are the best. There are 3.22 millions in America.

38 per cent of doctors in America are Indians.

12 per cent of the Scientists in America are Indians.

36 per cent of NASA employees are Indians.

28 per cent of the IBM employees are Indians.

34 per cent of Microsoft employees are Indians.

Indians have made a mark the world over in the most promising field, Information Technology as innovators whose details may occupy two or three full pages.

3. Diversities in India

India is the world's largest democracy with 31 States and largest number of political parties. According to the Election Commission, India has 680 Regional Parties and 54 National Parties. It possesses 800 languages and dialects that evolved their diverse heritages and cultures. Hindi is the single majority language. The country has 3743 castes according to the Mandal Commission Report (Vol. III, pages 173-225) with vast social inequalities without any comparison in the World. It is the home of several religions in which Hinduism constitutes the predominant religion evolved with rich spiritualism and the largest possible divine diversity in the world facilitating personal autonomy and choice. The significant diversities not to speak of others, create complications for the development of Corporate spirit required for national progress and social development. Indeed people in the country are more conscious of their aspirations today than ever before in the history of India. Consequently agitation for every grievance, small or big, has become a regular feature in different parts of the country involving several deleterious consequences. After fifty five years of Independence the country is facing serious problems associated with bootlickers, boot-leggers, black-marketeers, bitter politics and politicians apart from the wide prevalence of parallel economy. Thus India has emerged as a difficult country to govern. The only silver lining in the situation is the survival of democracy without its collapse. A developed country like Italy experienced the change of the government for more than three dozen times since the Second World War.

Predominance of politicization, casteism, communalism, corruption, regionalism, poor work motivation and dutifulness, soft government, dominant bureaucracy without responsive management, perpetuation of nepotism and favoritism, laissez-faire approach to people's problems, ineffective administration and the wide prevalence of terrorism are adversely influencing law and order, and proper functioning of society, jeopardizing security in its different ramifications. Social pollution is undermining the socio-economic progress with its multifarious ramifications.

Unlike the emergence of the Asian Tigers since 1950, India to-day has emerged as an Asian Tiger in population explosion, poverty explosion and unemployment explosion. The significant diversities in social conditions have undermined social solidarity, which in turn undermined political solidarity. Consequently Indian politics have become a business enterprise involving the seeking of votes of different groups of people at the time of elections either for State Legislatures or for Parliament. Consequently power politics has emerged. The elected people are inevitably seeking ways and means of gaining economic strength to survive in public life. Consequently social service has become a by-product of power politics in a large number of cases of elected representatives.

4. Human Development

Since 1990, UNDP has been publishing an annual report on Human Development. The opening lines of the first report state that the real wealth of a nation is its people. The purpose of development is to create an enabling environment for people to enjoy long, healthy and creative lives. This simple but powerful truth is too often forgotten in the pursuit of material and financial wealth. All the Human Development Reports are about people and their growing inter-dependence in to-day's globalising world.

The first HDR introduced the new concept of Human Development Index (HDI) designed to measure economic and social progress. HDI takes into account three basic elements of human well being–longevity, knowledge and the access to resources for decent living, measured respectively by life expectancy, adult literacy and real per capita income adjusted for purchasing power. Literacy is a catalytic agent for understanding and utilization of opportunities for personal and family welfare. Female literacy is quite complementary for family welfare. Life expectancy can cover the impact of nutrition, sanitation, health care, medical care and safe drinking water supply. Per capita income covers the other aspects of standard of living. GNP per capita was used for long as an index of economic growth. A single variable index like the per capita income is inadequate to portray the changing economic and social phenomena, as it depicts one of the many social dimensions. The HDI has displaced the per capita index, as human development is the end, economic growth is only a means. It constitutes a significant innovation for the measurement of human progress.

The human development experience over the last three decades reveals outstanding lessons. High levels of human development can be achieved at modern income levels as long as governments put people at the center of the policies. There is no automatic link between economic growth and human progress. Growth with equity is the best recipe for accelerated human development. Equitable income growth must go a long way in well-structured state policies of intervention in the form of across-the-board provision of health and education services. People must be at the center of all development programmes to accelerate human progress. The worldwide spread of privatization revolution does not dilute the case for intensive public policy for countries because of its vital importance in social development. The significant success of human development in facilitating social development with low level of per capita income is an eloquent testimony to the benevolent role of government public policies in some of the third world countries.

The HDI is a new yardstick of comparative human development among the different countries of the world. It is not a standard scale for the absolute measurement of human development in each country. The HDI is classified into three levels: low level below 0.500, medium level 0.500 to 0.799 and high level above 0.800.

Although the ranks of different countries show variation over years as regards the human development, it is quite instructive to know the new perspectives in the measurement and analysis of development. The HDI study of the first HDR produced surprises. Most of the Oil rich countries are not nearly as well off as they appear. A number of developing countries are doing far better on their human development ranks than on their income ranking, showing that they have directed their economic measures towards some aspects of human progress. The people of Bolivia, China, Sri Lanka, Tanzania and Zambia are much better off according to the new index, instead of measuring living standards as per the conventional methodology. The People of Algeria, Angola, Iran, Kuwait and Saudi Arabia are among those who are much worse off inspite of their high level of per capita income. Costa Rica, Jamaica and Thailand are other countries that come out better off on HDI. Japan, the world's best developed nation on HDI ranks only fifth as per capita measure. Sweden and Switzerland are close behind.

One of the biggest surprises is that United States, the World's richest nation on the income measure slumps to 18th place on the new index level, with Australia and Ireland at the foot of the list of industrial nations well below Britain, Canada and West Germany and even behind Spain which has only half the U.S. income per head. Although life expectancy in the U.S. is 76 years, much the same as in the rest of industrialised nations of the world, adult literacy is only 96 per cent, while 99 per cent is quite common in other wealthy nations. Thus even developed countries do not experience the trickle-down effect of economic growth on their social well-being.

The valuable insight which the empirical findings of the HDRs are revealing on the different aspects of human progress are bound to be of substantial significance to shape the development policies of national governments with a consequential impact of the world development. The third HDR claimed that the "human development has moved to the center of global development debate". According to the 1998 HDR "The human development perspective has moved into the mainstream of the global developmental debate. The concept of human development provides an alternative to the view of development exclusively with economic growth. Human Development focuses on people. And it sees economic growth and higher consumption not as ends in themselves but as means to achieve human development·

According to HDR 1998 more than 100 countries have issued human development reports with UNDP support. There are also four regional reports each covering several countries. "This explosive growth is a clear evidence of the growing commitment to shifting development towards people centred multifaceted approaches". Although the state of human development is improving, the overall progress is marked by great inequalities between people and countries and is threatened with setbacks. It is facing new challenges and problems to be reversed. Its core approach is quite progressive and it is likely to be the most impressive intellectual tide of the twenty first century.

The speed with which the new economic and social ideas relating to human development can be translated into state policies for implementation is intractable for prediction. "There is no doubt that economic research has an influence on the development of politics and on the policy choices being made in undeveloped as well as developed countries".

HDR 1999 which was released on July, 1999 has three major components. First the HDI ranking of 174 countries along the Human Poverty Index (HPI) and the gender related Development Index (GDI) and the Gender Empowerment Measure (GEM) along with a cornucopia of comparative development statistics.

Available evidence shows that India's progress in human development leaves much to be desired. The HDI ranking for 1997 puts India at 132nd place, ahead of course of Nepal, Bhutan, Bangladesh and a constellation of highly indebted Sub-Saharan African countries. If there is some consolation for India, it is in the fact that it is bracketed within the "medium" state of human development for first time rather than in the "low human development" category in the past. Among the 94 countries which come within the "medium" bracket, India is virtually at the bottom. China is in the 98th place while Sri Lanka is even better placed at rank 90.

The India - China comparison of HDI clearly shows how much leeway India needs to make before it catches up with the other better placed "medium" countries. There is a vast hiatus in the adult literacy rate between China (82.9%) and India (53.5%). Again in gross primary school enrolment, India lags behind China (55% to 69%). The economic growth performance of China is another major factor which puts India in the shade.

Both on GDI and GEM ranking, India fared much worse than China. Here again female Adult literacy rate and female per capita income show up as India's critical deficiencies. While GEM measures capabilities of the female population GER seeks to assess opportunities. While India's rank in GDI is 112, China is ahead at 98 and Sri Lanka at 76. As per GEM, India is much behind China and much further behind South Africa. While it is a paltry 8.3% in India, female administrators and managers are a minuscule presence in India (2.3%) compared to the 6% in China and 17.4% in South Africa. To complete the tale of disparity, female professional and technical workers represent only 20.50% of the total, while the corresponding percentages in China and South Africa are 45.1% and 46.7%. Nor is the Indian record in poverty alleviation flattering with India rank in HPI placed at 59 in comparison to China's 30. In a host of deprivation indices including the access to safe water, health services and sanitation, India is laggard. The achievements of China are not a little due to its departure from the classic Marxist Economic Philosophy to "the socialist market policy" encouraging private initiative and enterprise".

Even as regards the incidence of food insecurity, India is at a great disadvantage as compared to China. The FAO's Report "The State of Food Insecurity in the World 1999" is about the extent of under- nourishment as the insufficiency in the calories consumption required to meet the basic energy requirements which is roughly the same as the definition of poverty which the official statistics in India used.

The FAO statistics, based on the India data place the number of malnourished Indians in 1995-1997 at 204 million, which constitute the largest number of undernourished people in the World. Indeed the number of Indians suffering from chronic food insecurity is more than all people in all of sub-Saharan Africa. In 1997, China has 164 million suffering from malnourishment. Although more than 200 million Indians are categorized as undernourished, it is equivalent to 22 per cent of its population classified as "moderately high undernourishment" as compared to "very high undernourishment" when the rate crosses 35 per cent.

Comparison of the incidence of food insecurity in India with that of China reveals that the positive progress in China is more than that of India. The incidence of food insecurity in India was 38% during 1979-81, 26% in 1990-92 and 22% during 1995-97 as against 30%, 17% and 13% of China in the respective periods. As compared to the developing world as a whole, the incidence of food undernourishment is higher in India as those countries had only 29%, 20% and 18% in the respective periods.

The FAO estimates that the number of malnourished in the world has declined from 30 billion in 1990-92 to 799 million in 1995-97. This is only a fall in the number of malnourished by about 8 million a year. The pace is too slow to realize the goal of halving the global number to 400 million by 2015. If the present rate continues, there will be 638 million consuming inadequate amounts of food by 2015 in the world.

It is obvious from the above comparison that there is an alarming hiatus between India and China as regards the achievements in human development. Most of the backwardness of human development of India is due to the inadequacy of basic needs and services required by the rural people for survival. There is an imperative need to accelerate rural development in the country in conformity with the 73rd Constitutional Amendment by strengthening the third tier Government, the local-self Government of rural areas by appropriate plan programmes. Adequate devolution of funds from the State Governments is a crucial requisite for accelerating the rural development.

Without rural development, there can be no national development in underdeveloped countries. As rural development is sine qua non of human development in Indian circumstances, the dynamic Chief Minister of Andhra Pradesh (1995-1999) initiated a number of programmes for peoples' welfare acquitting the state as a model one in the country for advancing human development.

The theoretical and empirical analysis of the evolution and evaluation of the role of State and Market in economic postulates synthetic approach on the part of the public and private sectors to pursue favourable attitudes for the advance of human development. Welfare State Policy and Welfare Capitalism constitute the foundations for human development in the developing countries. Availability of appropriate public leadership to provide such State governance and management is an essential requisite.

The Human Development Reports constitute a mine of knowledge relating to social and economic development for close study by public leaders to shape government policies, administrators at State and Central Government levels to formulate and pursue the required policies and by social scientists to disseminate the knowledge among university students and generate new knowledge by their research programmes. Human Development is emerging as a new school of thought.

According to Prof. Amartya Sen, "Nothing is as important today in the political economy as social participation and leadership of women". While a large part of the world continues to look at women's issues in terms of paternalism and well-being, the concept of women's empowerment in the social, political and economic order in terms of pre-requisites of human development is hardly given the priority that it deserves. Moreover concentration on women's well-being, which is perhaps a progressive turning away from the encrusted social and cultural tradition of subordination of women to an inferior status, is not the same thing as the recognition of women as change-agents in society. That development policy itself would be flawed unless it is anchored in the "agency" role of women not only needs to be understood but what is strategic even if it is complex is the pragmatic translation of such a policy into programmes in different areas of the social process.

The development experience of many western countries establishes the casual relationship between women empowerment (through education, property entitlement and the dismantling of gender discrimination in employment and in the holding of public and political offices and those in the professions and particularly in the judiciary) and economic growth in its totality encompassing capital formation, human resource development, technology advancement and professional managerial competencies.

The East Asian "economic miracle" with all its aberrations and setbacks is not a little due to the replication of the Western development through deliberate governmental policies intended to reserve the traditional deprivation of women and the female child in such areas as nutrition, education, health and employment; these countries have succeeded in their developmental tasks unlike other countries still mired in poverty and gross gender discrimination.

The World Development Report (WDR) 2000-01 lists all the debilities of societies that continue to be afflicted with massive poverty which has much to do with gender inequality as a historical legacy. Not only are the predominant cultural attitudes in these societies obstacles to the emergence of women as active agents or instrumentalities of progress, but the economic process is such that women, and more so poor women, are often outside the system of distribution of public goods and services. Women's lack of access to resources, to the system of decision-making and to the over-all domain of public life is a grim reality that will not dissolve merely because the rate of growth of the economy is pushed up through liberalization. The persisting gender inequality threatens such societies with the continuing spectre of high infant mortality, maternal mortality, nutritional deficiency and the resultant adverse impact on cognitive development of the child and so forth. Unless these societies put gender justice in the forefront of their national agenda, the chances of their graduation into the higher stages of development can only be precarious.

While a certain degree of optimism seems justified in terms of how India has grappled with the age-old incubus of gender injustice through legal reforms, spreading of the reach of education and the expansion of the system of public health, it cannot be said that even in a progressive State such as Kerala, the development paradigm has distinctly recognized women as the agents of social and economic transformation. Progress there has been but not empowerment of women, notwithstanding the Constitutional amendments providing for one-third reservation for women in elected positions in village Panchayats and nagarapalikas.

According to data published in the Human Development Report (HDR) 2000, female adult literacy in India is only 65 per cent of the male adult literacy rate which itself is perhaps hovering around 55 per cent. School enrolment for female children, which was 71 percent at the primary stage (in 1997), was distinctly lower at the secondary stage at 48 per cent. At the tertiary level, hardly five out of 1,000 females made it to the university. Female "work participation" has no doubt grown according to Indian official data from 19.7 percent in 1981 to 22.3 per cent in 1991. But according to the HDR, "female economic activity rate" in India in 1998 was only 41.8 per cent, not even half that of the male population. This figure excludes the massive phenomenon of female child labour (below the age of 15).

Firm action is required in India to advance human development to eradicate poverty and deprivation while accelerating economic growth.

Government has to do more to raise literacy levels and provide greater access to basic health services. It has a particularly critical role in spreading literacy and access to primary health care so that all can participate in a meaningful manner and benefit fully from India's economic transformation. Much higher levels of literacy could be achieved through creative use of Information Technology, better school attendance and other policies with a clear focus on inclusion of girls and other traditionally disadvantaged groups. The economic and social returns from such an initiative would be huge. Evidence from across the world suggests that high levels of literacy have helped raise economic growth rates and reduce fertility rates. Public health campaigns are also required to combat major infectious diseases especially the incipient AIDS epidemic.

Expenditure on educating girls is perhaps one of the most productive investments. It helps bring down both fertility and infant mortality rates. The impact on the former is seen to be significant and similar in most Indian States. Besides, higher female literacy would be instrumental in raising the status of women in society. The Central Government has to provide enhanced transfer payments to the States to help support primary health and education. This may be done on a matching grant basis so that State Governments are given an incentive to increase their own effort in these areas. In addition, some part of the privatization revenues could be earmarked for primary health and education. In fact, a reorientation is required in the Government's social policy with high priority for human resource development.

5. State and Market in Economic Policy

After the First World War, the Marxian Doctrine of socialism with proletariat dictatorship inspired U.S.S.R. to embark on totalitarian planning, which yielded good success in the early decades of its implementation as analysed by leading lights like Sydney Webb, Beatrice Webb and Mawrice Dobb of U.K.

The Marxian tide promoted the rise of socialism and economic planning after the First World War in U.S.S.R. and the spread of economic planning later, especially after the Second World War to a large number of countries in the world.

The Second World War and its aftermath witnessed the rise of European democracies and the Chinese Revolution. Several colonial countries achieved independence. Since 1950's economic planning got spread among the developing and developed countries rapidly. The four decades of democratic planning in the world and seven decades of totalitarian planning in U.S.S.R. revealed their limitations for further dynamic growth by accumulating their own problems that are standing in the way of their reaching their goals of higher economic growth and welfare.

Despite the phenomenal impact of Soviet Economic Development, the totalitarian planning in U.S.S.R. undermined economic freedom and individualism. The Gorbachev Revolution with Perestroika and Glasnost polices initiated changes towards privatization and liberalization coinciding with the emergence of New Economic Policy in the World since 1980s. The new Economic Policy has crystalised into five basic principles of liberalisation, privatisation, modernisation, marketisation and globalisation.

Contemporary Russia displays many symptoms of the free market. It has entrepreneurs, stock exchanges and banks; but the Russian businessman is unlike his counterparts elsewhere. Because of the indolence of the state police, he is forced to deploy a private army, and because of lack of coherent laws, he is forced to bribe officials. The officials like it so much that they are in no hurry to establish a consistent legal system.

Russian entrepreneur is legally bound to pay a good proportion of his profits to the state treasury and the percentage may rise or fall depending on the goodwill of individual officials. Additional taxes payable to the Mafia are unavoidable, so the businessman has no alternative but to offer to the official a sweetener for interpreting the law in his favour.

Hence, what Russia is having today is a bandit capitalism. It is a unique grafting together of indigenous black market gangsterism, party clientism, ethnic nepotism along with Mafia lines and western joint ventures. The system operates in the twilight world of the hard currency zone, and like all forms of criminal capitalism, it generates large amount of inequality and growing amount of political corruption, it is capitalism, red in tooth and claw.

Today, a growing number of Russians have realized that decades of systematic suppression of initiative and enterprise have left a mindset that will take a generation to alter.

Indeed according to the Transparency International, Berlin, study of corruption among 85 countries, Russia was always a top index contender along with the Colombia, Bolivia and Nigeria. Its rank is 76th during 1998 out of the 85 countries as for per capita occupation index.

Under the determined leadership of Deng, China switched over to Socialist market policy since 1978 achieving outstanding results as analysed in detail later.

While the World Bank is advocating market friendly approach for economic growth among the different countries of the World, UNDP since 1990s has been emphasizing people's friendly approach for human development and economic growth, involving Government intervention in the developing countries in particular. There is a growing realisation that ideology driven prescriptions of either of interventionist variety or free market variety may not deliver the goods. An appropriate synthesis of State and Market with innovative cooperation and coordination holds the key for World economic development today. The experience of Asian Tigers ranging from Japan to South Korea and China bear testimony to the purpose.

David F. Burton, after evaluation of the challenges of newly industrialised countries as competitors to America asserted that the distinguishing feature of "East Asian Economic performance is not the dominance of free enterprise but the higher effective collaboration between the private and public sectors. Shared goals and commitments together with a high degree of professionalism in the service of national economic development have characterized the region's economic strategy. Market forces and Government intervention are not at odds with each other but carefully coordinated for national economic gain".

Competent policy advisers are now inclined to focus on appropriate combination of markets and State intervention. It is now generally recognized that apart from maintaining macro economic stability, governments in developing countries must also strongly intervene in sectors like health care, education, development of physical infrastructure such as roads, transportation, power and communications as well as anti-poverty programmes and protection of environment. The State has to intervene to minimize government failure and market failure, so that social objectives can be achieved at minimum social cost.

What development requires is good governance and public intervention which supplements rather than supplants the market mechanism. Hundreds of years ago, Kautilya's Arthasastra postulated: "In the interest of the prosperity of the country the King should be diligent in foreseeing the possibilities of calamities, try to avoid them before they arrive, overcome those which happen, remove all obstructions to economic activity and prevent loss of revenue to the State".

The three hundred years of industrial civilization witnessed the resurgence of market for accelerating economic growth with an intervening phase of totalitarian planning in U.S.S.R. and intensive democratic planning world war. Free market does not mean the withering of the State. Appropriate coexistence of State and Market with suitable pursuit of economic activities constitutes the enlightened path for high economic development. The State and market have to adopt innovative cooperation and coordination to generate high economic growth like the dutiful husband and wife to promote the growth of their family. Hence the case is for an appropriate synthesis of State and market for high rate of economic growth for accomplishing welfare State sooner than later for the rapidly growing world population. A crucial requisite for the emergence of the world welfare state is the commitment of the public sector and private sector for advancing the welfare of the people in their decision making and management of the economy without undermining efficiency.

6. China's Miracle of Economic Growth

Today, there are nine Asian Tigers: Japan, Hongkong, Singapore, Taiwan, South Korea, Indonesia, Malaysia, Thailand and China. While Japan is the classic tiger of Asia known for its rapid growth after the Second World War, China's pragmatic policies of achieving one child family in population planning, market friendly approach and effective mobilization of capital from foreign countries enabled it to emerge as the most dominant Asian tiger in size since 1970.

In view of their high economic growth rate, the Asian tigers are having high per capita income as compared to that of India. According to the HDR 1999, the per capita of India in 1997 is only \$ 498 as against \$ 25,084 of Japan, \$ 12,438 of Hongkong, \$ 3,387 of Malaysia, \$ 1970 of Thailand and \$ 785 of Indonesia. During 1998, the GNP of China was \$ 929 billion as against \$ 440 billion of India. While GNP of China is higher by 2.8 times over that of India, per capita income is higher by 2.4 times. The disparity in GNP and per capita income of India and China must have further increased by now with greater advantage to China.

The World Bank conducted a study of the East Asia miracle under the leadership of John Page[3]. The study found that the Asian tigers, have the world's fastest growing areas for the past 30 years. The high performing eight nations excluding China grew since 1960 twice as best as East Asia and Latin America countries. China's southern region has been growing fast, but this is a recent phenomenon since 1978. The World Bank organized a separate study of China. The miraculous growth of Chinese economy is highlighted at the end of this section in view of the special importance for economic policy for development.

The essence of the World Bank study of Asian tigers is that most of East Asia's extra-ordinary growth flowed from a reservoir of physical and human capital they built over the years and allocated to highly productive sectors in much better way than other countries. They also invested in the acquisition of modern technology.

The East Asian experience poved that the acquisition of physical and human capital is the engine and motive force of economic growth. The eight countries spent 7 to 10 percent of G.D.P. more than in other countries on education and training. "People in these countries worked harder and saved more than people in other countries". As the state played positive contributive role to economic development in some of these countries, the study found that state intervention is not bad. While the world-wide spread of privatization and the erosion of the role of State in economic policy in developed countries undermined the importance of Government intervention in economic policy for development, the extraordinary economic growth rate achieved by Asian tigers has gone a long way to strengthen the case for resurgence of state and market for economic development. East Asia's fastest growth rate is based on several governing factors which are quite significant in visualizing the scope and nature of contemporary economic development, although they vary among the different countries in relation to the stage of their development. They are listed out hereunder.

1. Political stability
2. Investment in human capital
3. High rate of saving
4. Attracting foreign investment of a high order
5. Imported technology for catching up process and progress
6. Selective industrial policies involving state intervention
7. Effective implementation and management
8. Importing professionalism
9. Low fiscal deficit and stable macro economic policy
10. Aggressive export development
11. Pursuit of principles of shared growth emphasized and followed by leadership to benefit the middle class and the poor to get the benefit of growth
12. Educated labour force and its active cooperation

13. The impact of Diaspora in the case of China since 1978 with liberal economic policy
14. Dominant role of private entrepreneurship
15. Close cooperation between Government and private business on creation of public enterprises with high start-up costs and externalities as components of strategy
16. Pursuit of middle path with external extreme and drastic policies
17. Influence of Buddhist and Confucius thought on society contributing to corporate spirit and social efficiency in economic activity

China's miraculous economic growth is a reflection of two stabilities - political stability and economic stability. China rose to great height in advancing economic development with the dynamic role of diaspora whose perception is one of loyalty. Loyalty has a far deeper moral contribution governing Chinese development that is behind China's miracle. China is having one of the most sweeping historical dramas not only of the 20th century but perhaps of all time. According to Fredric R. Clairmont "No economy in the world, it would appear, is so favourably poised to meet the competitive challenges of the 21st century as China today"[4]. The Chinese developmental experiment reveals that it revised its original philosophy and vision of creating a new China as an alternative system of classless and stateless communism. Its pragmatic and successful efforts for social and economic development are quite revealing and inspiring about which a detailed note is provided in this section.

China has emerged as a country of rapid economic growth with its vigorous programme of economic reform of 1978. After years of State Control of all productive assets, it encouraged the formation of rural enterprises and private business, liberalized foreign trade and investment, released State Control of some prices and investment in industrial production and the education of its work force.

As compared to the annual growth rate of 6 per cent a year in pre-1978 China, the post-1978 China witnessed average real growth of more than 9 per cent a year. During the peak years, Chinese economy grew more than 13 per cent. Per capita income has nearly quadrupled in the last 15 years, 1985-2000. A few analysts are predicting that the Chinese economy will be larger than that of U.S.A. in about 20 years. Its growth compares favourably, as compared to 7-8 per cent during the last 15 years.

An important lesson of Chinese development experience for countries with a large segment of population underemployed in agriculture, is inspiring the growth of rural enterprises and not focusing exclusively on the urban industrial sector that has successfully moved millions of workers off the farms into factories without creating an urban crisis, as a large proportion of China's explosive industrial growth took place in township, village enterprises (TVEs). TVEs grew in strength and in 1995-96 they produced 61% industrial output and facilitated take-off in China. TVEs are collectively owned by the respective township and villages. Their surpluses accrue to the township and village authorities and not to individual capitalists. As they are located on land owned by local authority itself, they need not pay any rent for land.

Capital in China is substantially cheaper than in India. China's saving rate is more than 40 per cent as compared to India's 23 per cent.

As compared to price advantage of land and capital, the most outstanding feature of China's competitiveness is the dynamic advantage of higher labour productivity or labour efficiency. Indeed China's recent productivity performance is quite remarkable. While the productivity of Asian Tigers hovered around 2 per cent, China's rate of about 4 per cent puts it simply in a class by itself.

Moreover China's open door policy has spurred foreign investment into the country apart from the Diaspora. The foreign investment has added power to economic transformation as it facilitated the building of factories, creation of jobs and linking China to international market. It helped the important transfers of technology with greater advantage for a dozen open coastal areas where foreign investors enjoy tax advantages. Further economic liberalization boosted exports, which rose to 19 per cent a year during 1981–94. Strong export growth, in turn, appears to have fuelled productivity growth in domestic industries.

China's strong productivity, growth, spurred by the market-oriented reforms, is the leading cause of China's unprecendented economic performance.

The absence of land market, production for export, educated labour force and greater identification of labourers in a large number of enterprises, i.e, TVEs with result of their labour are some of the factors accounting for China's higher productivity and its competitiveness in the World market. Thus, Chinese economy has become a market socialist economy. It may be noted that China achieved a GDP growth rate of 13.3 per cent during 1991-92 to 1995-96 as against 5.3 per cent of India.

In fine China's miracle of employment and economic growth is an illustration of the policy of market socialism, which constituted a successful experiment in effective implementation of the collaborative effort of State and market.

It may be further noted that against the annual growth rate of 6 per cent in pre-1978 China, post-1978 China witnessed average real growth of more than 9 per cent a year. During the peak years Chinese economy grew more than 13 per cent. Per capita income has nearly quadrupled in the last 15 years, 1985-2000. A few analysts are predicting that the Chinese economy will be larger than that of USA in about 20 years. Probably, China is destined to make world history for achieving highest economic growth rate.

Although East Asian Countries experienced foreign currency account deposit problem since 1997 on account of inadequate foreign exchange reserves in relation to short term external liabilities, China, like Japan, Taiwan and Singapore, inspite of some financial turbulence, maintained surplus in their current account. Consequently they did not experience any recession and unemployment as in the case of Latin American countries. (Mihir Rakshit: "The East Asian Currency Crisis", 2002).

The following table reveals the comparative superiority of China over India as regards some important economic indicators.

Some Economic Indicators of Contrast between India and China

	Description	India	China	Remarks
1.	Saving Rate	23 per cent of GDP	45 per cent of GDP	approximately double that of India
2.	Annual F.D.I. Flow	$2.16 billion	$ 40 billon	About 19 times over India
3.	Power Generating Capacity	90,000 MW	1.6 lakh MW	About 3 times over that of India
a)	Transmission and Distribution loss in Power	6.8 percent	1.8 percent	Cost of loss of power India is 3.5 times over that of China
b)	Power cost per 100 Kwh	$ 7.83	14.3	India is nearly twice that of China
c)	Per capita consumption	350 Kwh	1000 Kwh	About 3 times over that of India
4.	Agricultural productivity per hectare in Kg			
	Paddy	2,195	6,331	About 2½ times over that of India
	Maize	1,594	4,481	About 2½ times over that of India
	Groundnut	998	2,574	About 3 times higher than of India.
	Cotton	311	943	About 3 times over that of India
	Wheat	Lower in China by 54 per cent over that of India		
	Sugarcane	Lower in China by 10 per cent over that of India		

Source: *The Hindu,* Chennai, 4-10-2001.

It is obvious from the table that China possesses outstanding superiority in the availability of capital, electricity generation and utilization and agricultural productivity of important crops like paddy, maize, groundnut and cotton.

7. Resurgence of Indian Economy

(a) Growing Economy of India

The five years of stability and careful governance provided by the National Democratic Alliance (NDA) have paved the way for India to emerge as a growing economy. According to the Central Statistical Organisation (CSO), Indian economy is poised to grow at 8.1 per cent in 2003-04 as a consequence of 9.1 per cent increase in agriculture and 7.1 percent in manufacturing. The expected growth rate this year is more than double the four per cent growth recorded in 2002-03. The gross domestic product (GDP) is expected to be Rs. 14,24,507 crores against the estimated GDP of Rs. 13,18,821 crores for 2002-03. The growth in per capita income is estimated to be 6.6 percent during the current financial year against previous years' estimate of 1.8 per cent. The per capita income in real terms (at 1993-94 prices) is estimated to attain a level of Rs. 11,864 during 2003-04, higher than Rs. 10,964 estimated for 2002-2003.

Accordingly India is considered as one of the best performing economies in the world. Only China is doing better. Hence, the sentiments expressed are 'feel good', and 'India is shining'. India shining does not mean that all problems of Indians have disappeared from 1991. India's foreign reserves have lamenated to $795 millions, the nation has to ship part of its gold reserves as collaterals to avoid debt default. Now the foreign reserves have zoomed to the $ 105 billion mark. Moreover food production is estimated to reach 212 million tons giving a food surplus to the economy.

According to the Deputy Chaiman, Planning Commisiion, K.C. Pant, India is also on the way to achieving the Millennium Development goals as they were built into Tenth five Year Plan and were closely being monitored. India is likely to achieve all the social targets set for the current plan period and also indicated that most of the targets for the Tenth Plan were more ambitious than Millennium Development goals.

The Prime Minister, Atal Bihari Vajpayee said, "The country is stronger than ever on the security and development fronts. We launched many ambitious development programmes in the last five years and the National Highway Development Project (NHDP) is one among them''. ''This will be over the entire nation, particularly State capitals and trading centers in a comprehensive way with four lane high ways''.

''Roads are the lines of India's destiny. We are waiting for the day to travel on these world class highways across the length and breadth of the country''.

Optimistic and pessimistic views may not be free from some bias. Realistic interpretation of events in social sciences ar complicated.

The acceleration of growth during 2003-04 is very much a recovery from the low level of last year, it is being driven by the good monsoon of 2003. There has been a spurt in the past in growth, wherever an agricultural good year has followed the drought. The double digit growth of 1988-89 by 10.1 per cent came after the 1987 drought. Hence, it is premature to claim that economy has broken through the growth barrier.

In the words of Alok Mukherjee, "A growing economy, low inflation, increasing consumer choice, a rising stock market, no major scams, no major droughts or floods, no external tension, an enhanced international profile-all this came in 2003-2004. So it was okay to feel good as long as the going was good. No one said the situation was permanent''.

(b) Jobless Growth

As population is increasing rapidly in India crossing the one billion mark today, work force is also increasing.

Recent experience has proved that the GDP is increasing at about 8 percent, employment has increased by only 1 percent. Consequently unemployment has emerged as a national problem.

When India got Independence in 1947, there were only 26 Universities. Now the number of Universities is about 300. Along with the growth of Universities, there must have been corresponding growth of colleges and high schools. Although Indian economic development since Independence has been of moderate level, there is a good growth of middle class people seeking employment opportunities.

According to latest data available from the Statistical Abstract of 2003, the number of registrations with employment exchanges in India is 4,19,95,000 or 4.20 crores. Only a negligible few of them get job opportunities through the exchanges.

Jobs in India are available in the Defence and Railway departments. When the railways advertised for 30,000 jobs, seven lakh persons have applied. Most of them possess higher qualifications than those required by the railways. This instance illustrates the problem of unemployment in India.

As the job opportunities are not available for the job-seekers in India, many of them are seeking jobs in foreign countries through private agencies, some of which are functioning as bogus organizations subjecting the job-seekers to several difficulties including loss of huge amounts.

Unemployment has emerged as a major problem in India.

(c) Population Control

An effective Population Control Policy might have moderated unemployment and under-employment in the rural sector of India. It is a sensitive policy for the rich spiritualism of Hindus and intensive religious feelings of Muslims who advocate secularism not to interfere with religious values. Population control was an election issue only in the post-emergency 1977 elections. People have expressed their annoyance at the emergency excesses in the family planning programme. The Government elected to power put the programme on hold. The scope of action could have been taken after the constitutional amendment of 1976, vesting the Central Government with concurrent responsibility of population control and family planning. But it remained unexplored.

There is a strong case for population control in India. Population increased from 34 crores at the time of Independence to 103 crores in 2001. Per capita availability of agricultural land declined from about one acre in 1951 to 0.4 acre in 2000, not to speak of the decline in the availability of water and food grains per capita.

India's population density of 324 persons per sq.km. is very high, compared to the global density of 45, Asia's 116 and China's 133. The overcrowding in India is so great, it needed population control more urgently than China. In the 1960s both India and China had the same rate of population growth of 2.2 per cent per annum. By adopting two child norm per family in 1990, it enacted one child population control law in 2002. India's population continued to stagger at 1.9 per cent per annum. China is close to stabilizing its population. For India it is a distant goal. By 2030 India may overtake China's population.

Although India adopted two child norm of small family, it is not administered effectively. The Supreme Court recently provided for a uniform civil code. As such India has a mandate for uniform family size. Only through electoral mandate, can India adopt that law.

(d) Social Challenges

According to Asian Development Bank (ADB) latest report, the social challenges which India is facing are analysed apart from the jobless growth.

In the health sphere, the maternal mortality rate has remained more or less stagnant and the proportion of assisted deliveries would have to double at least to reach the Millennium Development Goal (MDG) targets set by the United Nations. The National Family Health Survey-2 has revealed that more than one third of the women in the age group of 15-49 were undernourished. It also revealed considerable disparities in the health status across States and between socio-economic groups. Under-5 and infant mortality rates continued to be high and changes in the population structure have resulted in a larger growing population as per the latest 2001 census, which impacts on human development. The spread of AIDS/HIV and other infectious diseases, stress and population - all pose new challenges to human development, the ADB report said.

There were also a variety of persisting disparities across gender, regions and different social groups which are undermining social cohesion. Gender impartiality in secondary education is far from being achieved. The juvenile sex ratio has recorded sharp decline, highlighting the vulnerable status of the girl child and women. There is also accentuation of regional disparities with the southern and western regions doing much better than the northern and eastern regions. Human poverty indices based on health, literacy, income and social exclusion factors place some States such as Gujarat, Haryana, Kerala, Maharashtra, Punjab and Tamil Nadu on the top rung while Assam, Bihar, Madhya Pradesh, Orissa, Rajasthan and Uttar Pradesh are on the lowest rung, says the report.

Going further on the social challenges, the report points out that rural-urban and gender disparities continue to exist between and within States. Significant inequalities also exist in the distribution of interpersonal consumption and levels of living, even within States.

Studies have revealed that the intensity of poverty was the highest among landless wage earners, marginal farmers, scheduled castes, scheduled tribes and indigenous populations, the report said.

(e) Swaraj

India got Swaraj in the sense of freedom from foreign rule. According to Gandhiji, Swaraj means freedom from poverty and hunger. Even today 26 crores of Indians are considered to be below poverty line. Most of them are living in villages. The greatest need of these villages is food security and clean drinking water supply.

India today is fortunate to have favourable circumstances to tackle the problem of the basic needs. India has three million members of Panchayat bodies, $ 107 billion dollars of foreign exchange and food surplus of about 50 million tons in godowns with a favourable annual agricultural production of 212 million tons during the current year.

Dr. Swaminathan arranged for the release of food insecurity atlas of Rural India on 24 April, 2001 by our Prime Minister, Atal Bihari Vajpayee, who called for concerted action to achieve substantial freedom from hunger by August 15,2007, which will be the 60th anniversary of India's Independence.

Right for nutritious food and clean drinking water constitute the basic rights of humanity. Food with human dignity should be the basic approach. The poor should not be subjected to a patronage approach and referred to as beneficiaries. They should be attached as partners in achieving the aim of ensuring that every child, woman and man in the country has an opportunity for a productive and healthy life. The right to adequate food and clean drinking water should be regarded as a basic right. Successful provision of such an opportunity for the poor is by no means an easy task. It needs a wide-ranging institutional setup to tackle the problem in all parts of the country. The following steps are to be taken.

1. Guiding principles for converting goods into accomplishments:
   (a) Decentralisation
   (b) Life cycle approach
2. Initiation of a National Food for Social Capital Programme.
3. Monitoring and Evaluation.
4. Consultative Group for freedom from Hunger.
5. Standing Committee of National Development Council (NDC)
6. Immediate action during 2003-2004.
7. Information, Education and Communication
8. Household entitlement card
9. Asset Building and Community Development
10. No time to relax on Food Production.

The Agenda of 2007: Hunger Free Area Programme" should bear Gandhiji's advice given before his death.

"Forget the past. Remember every day dawns for us from the moment we wake up. Let us, evey one, wake up now".

According to Transparency International, Berlin Institute, which is publishing annual report on the incidence of parallel economy in the world, India is one of the top ten countries in the parallel economy, which automatically promotes bureaucratic administrative set up. Both problems contribute challenges for tackling gradually.

The enclosed Appendix further illustrates the problems which the Indian democracy is facing.

The outbreak of terrorist destruction is an important problem of democracy.

APPENDIX

8. India's Social Trends are Becoming Liabilities and Drawbacks for Development

1. Politics without principles;
2. Democracy without discipline;
3. Wealth without work;
4. Commerce without ethics;
5. Knowledge without character;
6. Education without merit;
7. Science without humanity;
8. Worship without sacrifice;
9. Pleasure without conscience;
10. Rights without duties;
11. Administration with accountability
12. Power without responsibility;
13. Social order without normal moral fabric;
14. Social chaos without political perception;
15. Rampant corruption without control;
16. Increasing tax evasion without limit;
17. Increasing accumulation of black money that is threatening the normal working of the economy;
18. Democracy without a functional bureaucracy;
19. Corporate practices without ethical values;
20. Political and commercial nexus without ethical basis;
21. Increasing pressure of private corporate sector for tax incentives;
22. Audit reports without adequate response and responsibility from State Government and Central Government;
23. Government without effective law and order;
24. Government without required stability;

25. Government without solidarity of the political parties;
26. Power corrupts, fear of losing power corrupts more;
27. Corruption trends to be followed without exposure;
28. Democracy without discipline, and the functional efficiency;
29. Democracy cannot be sustained without responsibility;
30. Governance without vibrant discourse and discussion undermines the capacity for democracy;
31. Grab-as-much-as you can syndrome accounts for the governing bodies without the exercise of vibrant discourse;
32. Elimination of MLAs and MPs from the scope of prevention of Corruption Act will aggravate the parallel economy;
33. People's representatives at different levels are indulging in self service rather than in social service;
34. Denigrating Mahatma Gandhi as Father of Nation by indulging in rival names exposes political bankruptcy on account of greed for power and riches;
35. Total prohibition in any country or region never attained success;
36. Indian Solidarity and nationhood is not complete in spite of fifty years of Independence;
37. Evolving social anarchy abandons the future of a nation to chance;
38. Without rural development, there is no national development in a country of villages;
39. As our cities are turning into urban nightmares with many people in too little space, there is a need for a promotion of balanced urbanization, in particular the control of mega cities;
40. The functioning of democracy bristles with a number of distortions. Political power has become an end in itself.
41. Politics has become a visible profession in the country.

42. The MPLAD Scheme providing Rs. 2 crore for each Parliamentary Constituency as a catalyst of local development is an ill-conceived and unhealthy measure as its impact on a few preferred pockets divides the political base of the MP.

43. Ever-increasing "Bandhs" and "Dharnas" without rule and rhyme are disturbing and dislocating civic life involving violence, deaths and loss of property.

44. Gunnar Myrdal's provocative "Asian Drama: An enquiry into poverty of Nations", rightly pointed out that Asian countries including India have become soft states.

45. Since independence all castes have become more conscious of their needs and aspirations consequently their organizations are increasing their militancy, resulting in frequent Bandhs and Dharnas leading to violence, deaths and loss of property.

46. With increasing pressure of population, underground waters are decreasing paving the way for incidence of droughts.

47. Due to crop failures, farmers are committing suicides.

48. With increasing poverty, unemployment and under-employment, social crime in India is getting accelerated.

49. Without mandate from the electorate, Government in India is not likely to take stringent steps for family planning with a common code.

50. It has become easy to incite the poor and unemployed persons for terrorism to play a destructive role in the society.

51. Government in India is a Soft State, according to Gunner Myrdal, Adam Smith of poverty of Nations.

52. Gender irregularity is a prime feature of Indian society.

53. Persons with established criminal records are to be excluded from elections to assembly and Parliament.

9. Opportunities for Development

Public leadership with political solidarity, continuity, commitment and social capital is likely to advance development. The background problems and resources of a country provide the opportunities that can be utilized for development. The following areas of development indicate the scope of opportunities.

I. Human Development

(a) Effective Family Planning

(b) Universal literacy

(c) Good Public Health Policy

II. Economic Reforms

(a) Improved Infrastructure

(b) Export promotion

(c) Reduction of Fiscal Deficit

(d) Strengthening of economic and financial investment with the support of overseas Indians.

(e) Increased investment and development to reduce unemployment.

III. Effective Decentralisation

(a) Rural Development to secure Swaraj and better amenities in villages to reduce migration to towns.

(b) Shelter development to village settlers in cities.

IV. Improvement of Science and Technology

(a) Second Green Revolution to improve further productivity as the per capita land is declining.

(b) Commitment to Information Technology

V. Disaster management like droughts, famines and floods

VI. Tackling of Environmental Pollution.

10. Goldman Sachs Prediction

According to Goldman Sach's significant study, "Dreaming with BRICs", comprising Brazil, Russia, India and China are identified as the fastest growing economies over the next 50 years, 2000 to 2050. The study is based on the World Bank statistics of gross national product in terms of nominal as well as purchasing power parity (PPP) of the various economies. According to the study, India had a nominal GNP of $ 477 billion and a PPP and GNP of $ 2,913 billion in 2001.

In PPP terms, India was already the fourth largest economy in 2001 after the US, China and Japan although India's per capita income continues to be abysmally low, both in nominal and PPP terms. The study predicts GDP of seven countries including US, Japan and Germany along with the BRIC countries whose PPP is higher than their GDP.

The Goldman Sachs study basically uses a growth model in terms of labour, capital stock and the level of technical progress or total factor productivity to arrive at growth projection. Further the model of real exchange rates is calculated from the prediction of labour productivity growth. This is because currencies tend to rise as higher productivity leads economies to converge on PPP exchange rates.

The following two tables provide the projected US # GDP in $ billion and the projected US $ GDP per capita.

Projected GDP in US $ Billion

Country	*2000*	*2015*	*2025*	*2040*	*2050*
Brazil	762(5)	952(7)	1,695(6)	3,740(6)	6,074(5)
China	1,078(4)	4,754(3)	10,213(2)	26,439(2)	44,453(1)
India	469(6)	1,411(5)	3,174(4)	12,367(3)	27,803(3)
Russia	391(7)	1,232(6)	2,264(5)	4,467(5)	5,870(6)
Japan	4,176(2)	4,858(2)	5,567(3)	6,039(4)	6,673(4)
USA	9,825(1)	14,786(1)	18,340(1)	27,229(1)	35,165(2)
Germany	1,875(3)	2,386(4)	2,604(7)	3,147(7)	3,603(7)

Projected GDP Per Capita in US $

Country	*2000*	*2015*	*2025*	*2040*	*2050*
Brazil	4,338(4)	4,664(5)	7,781(5)	16,370(6)	26,592(5)
China	854(6)	3,428(6)	7,051(6)	18,209(5)	31,367(6)
India	468(7)	1,149(7)	2,331(7)	8,124(7)	17,366(7)
Russia	2,675(5)	8,736(4)	16,652(4)	35,314(4)	49,646(3)
Japan	32,960(2)	38,626(2)	46,391(2)	55,721(2)	66,805(2)
USA	34,797(1)	45,835(1)	52,450(1)	69,431(1)	83,710(1)
Germany	22,814(3)	29,111(3)	32,299(3)	40,966(3)	48,952(4)

Source: *The Hindu*, dated 29-12-2003, P-16. The figures in brackets indicate the ranks calculated.

China will be a country with the highest national income in 2050 and India will be the third country while USA gets the second rank in the growth of GDP.

In per capita GDP USA will be having the first rank throughout the period, Japan the second rank, with India taking the seventh rank. According to the prediction of the report, it is to be noted that the largest economies of the world may not be richest in terms of the per capita income.

At present economic powers are mainly the US, the European Union countries and Japan. In view of the size of population the BRIC countries with their long economic success would also have major impact on power equations in the world.

A basic assumption of the study is that BRIC countries maintain policies and develop institutions that are supportive of growth. These include some macro-economic policies and a stable macro-economic background (low inflation, supportive government policies, sound public finance and well managed in exchange rate), stable political institutions, openness and high level of education.

China which is three times bigger than India in area is maintaining the policies required in economic growth. Consequently it will take the first rank among the countries by 2050.

Given the comparative advantage of skilled work force available at low costs, backed by huge foreign exchnage reserves and food grain surplus, India has historical opportunities to fulfill BRIC report predictions.

Nevertheless, many things can go wrong even with reasonable predictions. In underdeveloped countries, human development advocates rightly stress on the advancement of education, health improvement and provision of nutrition for poor people. Human development is quite conducive for improvement of productivity of work force. But human development without balancing economic development to create employment opportunities to the workforce results in jobless growth which arrests social development. Hence in India both Government and Private sector have to increase investments.

India bristles with several social problems that undermine governance. India lacks political stability. There are about 53 National Parties and 680 regional parties. At present NDA is managing national political scene under the leadership of its Prime Minister. There are about four thousand castes which have become more conscious of thier needs and aspirations since the days of Independence. The rampant casteism is increasing the political and social conflict undermining the required corporate spirit. There is also adverse communalism involving the conflict between the Hindus and Muslims not to speak of other communities. Regionalism is creating its own deleterious tendencies. There are about 800 languages with dialects, black economy is a well-known fact. The prevalent black economy in the country is an important social complication. Thus the innumerable differences are undermining the corporate spirit for effective functioning of the Government. Hence India may not be in a position to reach the third place in GDP growth as predicted by Goldman Sachs. Indeed social environment bristles with significant diversities in India. Hence it is no wonder that Indians in general shine better in foreign countries than in their own country. As China is free from this type of problems its miraculous growth facilitates its emergence as the dominant currency in the world by 2050.

India and China are the most populous countries in the world. The latest statistics also reveal the favourable position of China over that of India.

China's population is 130 crores as against 108 crores of India. The growth rate of China's population is 0.87%. It is effectively administering one child norm per family as against the two child norm of India administered less effectively. India's population growth is 1.51% per year. In the case of India the poor people account for 25% as against 10% in China. Foreign investment in India is only $ 340 crores as against $4420 crores in China. The Chinese in foreign countries are about 6 crores as against 2 crores of Indians in foreign countries. As regards urbanization China is having 35% of its population which is higher than that of India with about 28 per cent.

It is to be further noted that in the case of India about four crores of people have registered with employment exchanges, which are more or less unemployment exchanges as things stand today.

SECTION–II
EDUCATION

2

HUMAN RIGHTS EDUCATION

Dr. Digumarti Bhaskara Rao*

The United Nations adopted the Universal Declaration of Human Rights (UDHR) in the UN General Assembly Session on 10 December 1948. This powerful instrument continues to exert an enormous impact on people's lives all over the world. 58 member states of the UN adopted it at that time. The Declaration has inspired a large number of subsequent human rights instruments, which together constitute the International Law of Human Rights. Two Protocols to the Convention have been adopted in 2000. At the World Conference on Human Rights held in Vienna, Austria in 1993, as many as 171 countries reiterated the universality, indivisibility and interdependence of human rights, and reaffirmed their commitment to the Universal Declaration of Human Rights. They adopted the Vienna Declaration and Programme of Action. The UN General Assembly proclaimed the period 1995–2004 as the UN Decade for Human Rights Education.

Human Rights Education is one of the key activities for popularising the practice of Human Rights by all concerned by educating people about its content. Education, training and information dissemination among the public receive priority in implementing the Declarations. The paper presents details of a comprehensive and effective national strategy for infusing human rights education into the educational systems, at various levels, beginning from the primary stage. Main aspects covered for implementing the programme of education presented here are: content

* Reader, RVR College of Education, JKC College Road, Guntur-522 006.

of teaching, rights and responsibilities, teaching and preaching, techniques and modalities of teaching, teaching methods, and practice in the school environment. In the concluding section, importance of periodically evaluating the teaching methods, modalities used, and the impact on children, teachers and the society at large is also suggested. Human Rights education should become part and parcel of education in every school; and everyone should practise the rights and responsibilities extensively, and evolve models for implementation.

Introduction

Human rights may be generally defined as those rights, which are inherent in our nature and without which we cannot live as human beings. Human rights and fundamental freedoms allow us to develop fully and use our human qualities, our intelligence, our talents and our conscience, and to satisfy our spirituality and other needs. They are based on humankind's increasing demand for a life in which the inherent dignity and worth of each human being are accorded respect and protection. Their denial is not only an individual and personal tragedy but also created conditions of social and political unrest, sowing the seeds of violence and conflict within and between societies and nations.

The Development of the Human Rights Framework

The history of human rights has been shaped by all major world events and by the struggle for dignity, freedom and equality everywhere. Yet, it was only with the establishment of the United Nations that human rights finally achieved formal, universal recognition.

The turmoil and atrocities of the Second World War and the growing struggle of colonial nations for independence prompted the countries of the world to create a forum to deal with some of the war's consequences and in particular to prevent the recurrences of such appalling events. This forum was the United Nations.

When the United Nations was founded in 1945, it reaffirmed the faith in human rights of all the peoples taking part. Human rights were cited in the founding Charter as central to their concerns and have remained so ever since.

One of the first major achievements of the newly formed United Nations was the Universal Declaration of Human Rights (UDHR), adopted by the United Nations General Assembly on 10 December 1948. This powerful instrument continues to exert an enormous impact on people's lives all over the world. It was the first time in history that a document considered to have universal value was adopted by an international organization. It was also the first time that human rights and fundamental freedoms were set forth in such detail.

There was broad-based international support for the Declaration when it was adopted. Although the fifty-eight Member States that constituted the United Nations at that time varied in terms of their ideology, political system, religious and cultural background, and patterns of socio-economic development, the Universal Declaration of Human Rights represented a common statement of shared goals and aspirations - a vision of the world as the international community would like it to be.

The Declaration recognizes that the "inherent dignity of all members of the human family is the foundation of freedom, justice and peace in the world" and is linked to the recognition of the fundamental rights to which every human being aspires, namely, the right to life, liberty and security of person; the right to an adequate standard of living; the right to seek and to enjoy in other countries asylum from persecution; the right to own property; the right to freedom of opinion and expression; the right to education; the right to freedom of thought, conscience and religion; and the right to freedom from torture and degrading treatment, among others, These are inherent rights to be enjoyed by all inhabitants of the global village (women, men, children and all groups in society, whether disadvantaged or not) are not "gifts" to be withdrawn, withheld or granted at someone's whim or will.

The Declaration has inspired a large number of subsequent human rights instruments, which together constitute the international law of human rights. These instruments include the International Covenant on Economic, Social and Cultural Rights (1966) and the International Covenant on Civil and Political Rights (1966), treaties that are legally binding on the States that are parties to them. The Universal Declaration and the two Covenants constitute the International Bill of Rights.

The rights contained in the Declaration and the two Covenants have been further elaborated in other treaties such as an International Convention on the Elimination of All Forms of Racial Discrimination (1966), which declares dissemination of ideas based on racial superiority - or hatred as being punishable by law, and the Convention on the Elimination of All Forms of Discrimination against Women (1979), prescribing measures to be taken to eliminate discrimination against women in political and public life, education, employment, health, marriage and the family.

Of particular importance to anyone involved with schools is the Convention on the Rights of the Child's that lays down guarantees of the child's human rights. Adopted by the General Assembly in 1989, the Convention has been ratified by more countries than any other human rights treaty. In addition to guaranteeing children protection from harm and abuse and making special provision for their survival and welfare through, for example, health care, education, and family life; it accords them the right to participate in society and in decision-making that concerns them. Two Protocols to the Convention have recently been adopted, the Optional Protocol on the sale of children, child prostitution and child pornography and the Optional Protocol on the involvement of children in armed conflict (2000).

Promoting Human Rights

Since the adoption of the Universal Declaration of Human Rights, human rights have become central to the work of the United Nations. Emphasizing the universality of human rights, Secretary General Kofi Annan stated on the fifteenth anniversary of the Declaration that "Human rights is foreign to no country and native to all nations", and that "without human rights no peace or prosperity will ever last".

Within the United Nations system, human rights are furthered by a myriad of different mechanisms and procedures: by working groups and committees; by reports, studies and statements; by conferences, plans and programs; by decades for action; by research and training; by voluntary and trust funds; by assistance of many kinds at the global, regional and local levels; by specific measures taken; by investigations conducted; and by the many procedures devised to promote and protect human rights.

Action to build a culture of human rights is also supported by United Nations specialized agencies, programs and funds as the United Nations Educational, Scientific and Cultural Organisation (UNESCO), the United Nations Children's Fund (UNICEF), the Office of the United Nations High Commissioner for Refugees (UNHCR), the United Nations Development Programme (UNDP), the International Labour Organisation (ILO) and the World Health Organisation (WHO) and by relevant departments of the United Nations Secretariat such as the Office of the High Commissioner for Human Rights (OHCHR). Other international, regional and national bodies, both governmental and non-governmental, are also working to promote human rights.

At the World Conference on Human Rights held in Vienna, Austria in 1993, 171 countries reiterated the universality, indivisibility and interdependence of human rights, and reaffirmed their commitment to the Universal Declaration of Human Rights. They adopted the Vienna Declaration and Programme of Action, which provides the new "framework of planning, dialogue and cooperation" to facilitate the adoption of a holistic approach to promoting human rights and to involve actors at the local, national and international levels.

The United Nations Decade for Human Rights Education (1995-2004)

Not the least of these activities to promote human rights is human rights education. Since the adoption of the Universal Declaration, the General Assembly has called on Member States and all segments of society to disseminate this fundamental document and educate people about its content. The 1993 World Conference on Human Rights also reaffirmed the importance of education, training and public information.

In response to the appeal by the World Conference, the General Assembly, in 1994, proclaimed the period 1995 to 2004 the United Nations Decade for Human Rights Education. The Assembly affirmed that "human rights education should involve more than the provision of information, and should constitute a comprehensive life-long process by which people at all levels in development and in all strata of society learn respect for the dignity of others, and the means and methods of ensuring that respect in all societies".

The Plan of Action for the Decade provides a definition of the concept of human rights education as agreed by the international community, i.e., based on the provisions of international human rights instruments. In accordance with those provisions, human rights education may be defined as "training, dissemination and information efforts aimed at the building of a universal culture of human rights through the imparting of knowledge and skills, and the moulding of attitudes, and directed to:

1. the strengthening of respect for human rights and fundamental freedoms;
2. the full development of the human personality and the sense of its dignity;
3. the promotion of understanding, tolerance, gender equality and friendship among all nations, indigenous peoples and racial, national ethnic, religious and linguistic groups;
4. the enabling of all persons to participate effectively in a free society; and
5. the furtherance of the activities of the United Nations for the maintenance of peace.

The Decade's Plan of Action provides a strategy for furthering human rights education through the assessment of needs and the formulation of effective strategies; the building and strengthening of programs and capacities at international, regional, national and local levels; the coordinated development of materials; the strengthening of the role of mass media; and the global dissemination of the Universal Declaration of Human Rights.

The Process of Human Rights Education in Schools

A sustainable (in the long term), comprehensive and effective national strategy for infusing human rights education into the educational systems may include various courses of action, such as :

1. the incorporation of human rights education in national legislation regulating education in schools;
2. the revision of curricula and textbooks;
3. pre-service and in-service training for teachers to include training on human rights and human rights education methodologies;

4. the organization of extracurricular activities, both based on schools, and reaching out to the family and the community;
5. the development of educational materials;
6. the establishment of support networks of teachers and other professionals (from human rights groups, teachers' unions, non-governmental organizations or professional associations), and so on.

The concrete way in which this process takes place in each country depends on local educational systems which differ widely, not the least in the degree of discretion teachers may exercise in setting their own teaching goals and meeting them. The teacher will always be the key person, however, in getting new initiatives to work. The teacher, therefore, carries a great responsibility for communication of the human rights message. Opportunities to do this may vary: human rights themes may be infused into existing school subjects, such as history, civics, literature, art, geography, languages and scientific subjects, or may have a specific course allocated to them; human rights education may also be pursued through less formal education arenas within and outside schools such as after-school activities, dubs and youth forums.

In the classroom, human rights education should be developed with due attention to the developmental stage of children and their social and cultural contexts in order to make human rights principles meaningful to them. For example, human rights education for younger children could emphasize the development of self-esteem and empathy and a classroom culture supportive of human rights principles. Although young children are able to grasp the underlying principles of basic human rights instruments, the more complex content of human rights documents may be more appropriate to older learners with better developed capacities for concept development and analytical reasoning.

Content for Human Rights Education

The history of human rights tells a detailed story of the efforts made to define the basic dignity and worth of the human being and his or her most fundamental entitlements. These efforts continue to this day. The teacher will want to include an account of this history as an essential part of human rights teaching, and it can be made progressively more sophisticated as students mature. The fight for civil and political rights, the campaign to abolish slavery, the struggle for economic and social justice, the achievement of the Universal Declaration of Human Rights and the two subsequent Covenants, and all the conventions and declarations that followed, especially the Convention on the Right of the Child - all these topics provide a basic legal and normative framework.

The core content of human rights education in schools is the Universal Declaration of Human Rights and the Convention on the Rights of the Child. These documents, which have received universal recognition, as explained above, provide principles and ideas with which to assess experience and build a school culture that values human rights. The rights they embody are universal, meaning that all human beings are entitled to them, on an equal basis; they are indivisible, meaning there is no hierarchy of rights, i.e., no right can be ranked as "non-essential" or "less important" than another. Instead, human rights are interdependent, part of a complementary framework. For example, your right to participate in government is directly affected by your right to express yourself, to form associations, to get an education, and even to obtain the necessities of life. Each human right is necessary, and each is interrelated to all others.

However, even taught with the greatest skill and care, documents and history alone cannot bring human rights to life in the classroom. Nor does working through the Universal Declaration or the Convention on the Rights of the Child, pointing out the rationale for each article, teach the meaning of these articles in people's lives. "Facts" and "fundamentals", even the best selected ones, are not enough to build a culture of human rights. For these documents to have more than intellectual significance, students need to approach them from the perspective of their real life experience and grapple with them in terms of their own understanding of justice, freedom and equity.

Teaching *about* and *for* Human Rights

Research has shown that some upper primary and secondary school students sometimes suffer from lack of confidence that limits their ability to socialize with others. It is difficult to care about someone else's rights when you do not expect to have any yourself. Where this is the case, teaching for human rights could require going back to the beginning and teaching confidence and tolerance first. The trust exercises, in the same chapter, can be used with any group and help to establish a good classroom climate, which is crucial for human rights education. These activities can be repeated (with suitable variations) to settle students into activities that require group cooperation. They can also foster the human capacity for sympathy, which is fragile and contingent but nonetheless real, and confirm the fact that no person is more of a human being than another and no person is less.

Already implicit above is the idea that teaching *about* human rights is not enough. The teacher will want to begin, and never to finish, teaching *for* human rights. For this reason the largest part of this text consists of activities. These create opportunities for students and teachers first to examine the basic elements that make up human rights-life, justice, freedom, equality and the destructive character of deprivation, suffering and pain-and then to use them to work out what they truly think and feel about a wide range of real-world issues.

The focus of human rights education is not just outward on external issues and events but also inward on personal values, attitudes and behavior. To affect behaviour and inspire a sense of responsibility for human rights, human rights education uses participatory methodologies that emphasize independent research, analysis and critical thinking.

Rights and Responsibilities

For the basic principles of a human rights culture to survive, people must continue to see a point in defending them: "1 have a right to this. It is not just what I want, or need. It is my right. There is a responsibility to be met". But rights stand only by the reasons given for them, and the reasons must be good ones. Unless people have the chance to work out such reasons for themselves-and where better than at school? - They will not claim their rights when they are withheld or taken away, or feel responsibility to defend the rights of others. We have to see for ourselves why rights are so important, for this in turn fosters responsibility.

It is, of course, possible to proceed the other way around: to teach for human rights in terms of responsibilities and obligations first. But again, teachers will want to do more than tell students what they ought to be doing. To bring these ideas alive, they will create opportunities for students to truly understand and accept such social responsibilities. Teachers and students will then have the principles and skills required resolving the inevitable conflicts of responsibilities, obligations or rights when they arise.

Because these points of conflict can also provide useful insights, they should be welcomed. They make the teaching of human rights dynamic and relevant. Conflict offers the sort of learning opportunities that encourage students to face contrasts creatively, without fear, and to seek their own ways of resolving them.

Teaching and Preaching: Action Speaks Louder than Words

The fact that the Universal Declaration of Human Rights and the Convention on the Rights of the Child have virtual global validity and applicability is very important for teachers. By promoting universal human rights standards, the teacher can honestly say that he or she is not preaching. Teachers have a second challenge, however to teach in such a way as to respect human rights in the classroom and the school environment itself. For learning to have practical benefit, students need not only to learn about human rights but also to learn in an environment that models them.

This means avoiding any hypocrisy. At its simplest, hypocrisy refers to situations where what a teacher is teaching is clearly at odds with how he or she is teaching it. For example: "Today we are going to talk about freedom of expression-shut up in the back row!" In such circumstances, students will learn mostly about power, and considerably less about human rights. As students spend a good deal of time studying teachers and can develop a good understanding of teachers' beliefs, a teacher who behaves unjustly or abusively will have little positive effect. Often, because of a desire to please, students may try to mirror a teacher's personal views without practising them. This may be a reason, at the beginning at least, for teachers not to express their own ideas. At its most complex, hypocrisy raises profound questions about how to protect and promote the human dignity of both teachers and students in a classroom, in a school and within the society at large.

The "human rights climate" within schools and classrooms should rest on reciprocal respect between all the actors involved. Accordingly, the way, in which decision-making processes take place, methods for resolving conflicts and administering discipline, and the relationship within and among all actors constitute key contributing factors.

Ultimately teachers need to explore ways to involve students, school administrators, education authorities and parents in human rights education but also the whole community. In this way teaching for human rights can reach from the classroom into the community to the benefit of both. All concerned will be able to discuss universal values and their relation to reality and to recognize that schools can be part of the solution to basic human rights problems.

As far as the students are concerned, negotiating a set of classroom rules and responsibilities is a long-tested and most effective way to begin. Teaching practices that are compatible with basic human rights provide a consistent model. In this way a sports or mathematics teacher, for example, can also teach from human rights.

Dealing with Difficult Issues

Some times controversial and sensitive subjects come up when students begin to examine human rights. Teachers need to remain constantly alert to student discomfort and potential disagreement. Teachers should acknowledge that human rights necessarily involve conflict of values and that students will benefit from understanding these conflicts and seeking to resolve them.

Many times teachers meet resistance to human rights education on the ground that it imposes non-native principles that contradict and threaten local values and customs. Teachers concerned about resistance from administrators should meet with them in advance, share goals and plans for the class, and explain about the United Nations human rights framework and related educational initiatives (such as the UN Decade for Human Rights Education). Encourage administrators to visit a class-they may themselves benefit from human rights education!

Pedagogical Techniques for Human Rights Education

The techniques suggested below and their application in the activities offered in Chapters Two and Three illustrate how teachers can engage students' empathy and moral imagination, challenge their assumptions and integrate concepts like human dignity and quality into their everyday experience of people, power and responsibility. These techniques have proved especially appropriate for human rights education because they encourage critical thinking, both cognitive and effective learning, and respect for differences of experience and opinion, and active engagement of all participants in ongoing learning.

1. Brainstorming

This technique can be used to seek solutions to problems that are both theoretical and practical. It requires a problem to be analyzed and then solutions to be developed. Brainstorming encourages a high degree of participation, and it stimulates those involved to maximum creativity.

Following presentation of a problem, all ideas in response to it are recorded on a board or chart paper. All responses are recorded; no explanations are required and no suggestions are judged or rejected at this stage. The teacher then categorises and analyses the responses, at which stage some are combined, adapted or rejected. Finally, the group makes recommendations and takes decision on the problem.

2. Case Studies

Students in small groups work with real or fictional cases that require them to apply human rights standards. Case studies should be based on credible and realistic scenarios that focus on two or three main issues. The scenario for a study can be presented to students for consideration in its entirety or "fed" to them sequentially as a developing situation (the "evolving hypothetical") to which they must respond. This method encourages analysis, problem solving and planning skills, as well as cooperation and team building. Case studies can be used to set up debates, discussion or further research.

3. Creative Expression

The arts can help to make concepts more concrete, personalise abstractions and affect attitudes by involving emotional as well as intellectual responses to human rights. Techniques may include stories and poetry, graphic arts, sculpture, drama, song and dance. Teachers do not need to be artists themselves but to set engaging tasks and provide a way for students to share their creations.

4. Discussion

Many techniques exist for stimulating meaningful discussion in pairs, small groups or the whole class. To create an environment of trust and respect, students might develop their own "rules for discussion".

Discussion can be structured in a variety of effective ways. Some topics are appropriate to a formal debate, panel or *"Fish Bowl"* format (i.e., a small group discusses while the rest of the class listens and later makes comments and asks questions). Other topics are better suited to a *"Talking Circle"* (i.e., student's sit in two circles, one facing outward and the other inward. They discuss with the person sitting opposite; after a period the teacher asks everyone in the inside circle to move one place to the right and discuss the same topic with a new person). Personal or emotional topics are best discussed in pairs or small groups.

To engage the whole class in a topic, the teacher might use techniques like a *"Talk Around"* (i.e., the teacher asks an open-ended question like "What does dignity mean to you?" or "I feel happy when..." and each student responds by turn.

A lively method of representing discussion graphically is the *"Discussion Web"*. Students sit in a discussion circle and speak one at a time. As they do, they pass a ball of yarn along, letting it unwind in the process. Each person keeps hold of the string whenever it passes through her or his hands. Eventually a web of string links the group, clearly showing the pattern of communication that has gone on within it.

5. Field Trips/Community Visits

Students benefit from the extension of school into the community, learning from places where human rights issues develop (e.g. courts, prisons, and international borders) or where people work to defend rights or relieve victims (e.g., non-profit organizations, food or clothing banks, and free clinics).

The purpose of the visit should be explained in advance, and students should be instructed to pay critical attention and to record their observations for a subsequent discussion or written reflection following the visit.

6. Interview

Interviews provide direct learning and personalize issues and history. Those interviewed might be family and community members, activities, leaders or eyewitnesses to human rights events. Such oral histories can contribute to documenting and understanding human rights issues in the home community.

7. Research Projects

Human rights topics provide many opportunities for independent investigation. This may be formal research using library or Internet facilities or international research drawing on interviews, opinion surveys, media observations and other techniques of data gathering. Whether individual or group projects, research develops skills for independent thinking and data analysis, and deepens understanding of the complexity of human rights issues.

8. Role-plays/Simulations

A role-play is like a little drama played out before the class. It is largely improvised and may be done as a story (with a narrator and key characters) or as a situation (where the key characters interact, making up dialogue on the spot-perhaps with the help of the teacher and the rest of the class). Role-plays have particular value for sensitizing students to the feelings and perspectives of other groups and to the importance of certain issues.

Role-plays work best when kept short. Allow enough time for discussion afterwards: it is crucial for children to be able to express themselves about feelings, fears or understandings after such activities, to maximize possible benefits and dissipate negative feelings, if any. Teachers may need to discourage students from becoming their role. Participants should be able to step back from what they are doing, to comment perhaps, or to ask questions. Other members of the class should be able to comment and question too, perhaps even joining in the role-play.

Variations on role-plays include mock trials, imaginary interviews, simulation games, hearings and tribunals. These usually have more structure, last longer and require more preparation of both teachers and students.

9. Visual Aids

Learning can be enhanced by the use of blackboards, overhead transparencies, posters, displayed objects, flip photographs, slides, videos and films. As a general rule, information produced on transparencies and charts should be brief and concise, and in outline or list form. If more text is required, use handouts. However, visual aids can be over-used and should never substitute for engaged discussion and direct student participation.

Evaluation

Information content and levels of understanding of the students can be tested in standard ways. However, assessing attitudes and attitude changes is much harder because of the subjective nature of the judgements involved. Open-ended questionnaires given at repeated intervals are the simplest, but the impressions they provide are fleeting at least. It is quality difficult to evaluate whether the human rights climate of the school community has improved. However, if indicators for success are carefully defined and evaluation is done on a regular basis, changes in the school environment can be monitored and responded to. Engaging students in drawing up checklists to assess individual, classroom and school community practices in human rights terms can be an important learning activity. The human rights education should become part and parcel of every school education.

REFERENCES

Bhaskara Rao, Digumarti, editor (2000). *International Encyclopaedia of Human Rights,* 7 volumes in 13 parts. New Delhi: Discovery Publishing House.

Vol. 1 *International Instruments of Human Rights,* 2 parts

Vol. 2 *Regional Instruments of Human Rights*

Vol. 3 *Human Rights and the United Nations,* 2 parts

Vol. 4 *Fact Files of Human Rights,* 3 parts

Vol. 5 *Study Stories of Human Rights,* 2 parts

Vol. 6 *International Meetings on Human Rights,* 2 parts

Vol. 7 *Professional Training in Human Rights.*

Bhaskara Rao, Digumarti, editor (2004). *Human Rights Education,* New Delhi: Discovery Publishing House.

Bhaskara Rao, Digumarti, editor (2004). *United Nations Decade for Human Rights Education.* New Delhi: Discovery Publishing House.

3

ELEMENTARY EDUCATION IN INDIA
NOW AND THEN

G.E.P. Sastry*

The educational system in India in good olden days aimed at the building up of character, the development of personality and the preservation of the ancient culture of the motherland. The Danish Missionaries may be regarded as the torch bearers of modern education in India. The National Policy on Education, 1986 observed "Education is essentially for all. This is fundamental to our all-round development, material and spiritual. The international donor community at the Jomitien Conference, the Country saw the emergence of a large multi-state programme for Education For All (EFA) under the banner of District Primary Education Programme (DPEP). In a historic judgement in July, 1992 the Supreme Court of India declared that education is a fundamental right. Accordingly the Parliament under 93rd amendment made education upto 14 years as a fundamental right of every citizen. The Honourable Supreme Court of India, in W.P. No. 196/2001, dated 17-9-2001 directed the State Governments that hot cooked meal should be provided to all primary school classed children in Government, Government Assisted Primary Schools. The Sarva Shiksha Abhiyan as a historic stride towards achieving the long cherished goal of universalisation of Elementary Education. Inspite of all our streneous efforts Elementary Education in India has been still a promise to keep.

---

* Senior Lecturer, DIET, Boyapalem, Guntur, A.P.

Introduction

The most outstanding movement in Indian education during recent years in basic education – "the last and most precious gift to India by Gandhiji. Gandhiji held that pre basic education, therefore, in the fullest sense is the education of children under seven for a development of all their faculties, conducted by the school teachers in co-operation with the parents and community in schools, in the home and in the village. He proposed that the process of education throughout the period should centre round some form of manual or productive work , and that all other abilities to be developed and training to be given should, as far as possible be integrally related to the environment of the child.

This principle has been recognised by all famous educationists from Rousseau to Dewey. The elementary education programme in Mexico is based on work activities and vocational education rather than purely academic skills.

He also took sides in favour of adult education which is the first stage in the Nai Talim. Adult education he meant the education of the community as a whole and of every individual member for a happy, healthy, clean and self-reliant life.

The Indian National leaders urged changes in the traditional model to make Universalisation of Elementary Education feasible inspite of the limited resources available (due to level of economic development) and the poverty of the masses. The prominent among them were Gokhale, Parulekhar, Mahatma Gandhi, Acharya Vinobha, C. Rajagopalachari, B.G. Kher. Sri B.G.Kher recommended certain things as a sub – committee chairman.

The Wardha Scheme or more popularly known as the "Zakir Hussain Committee" report is the first study of elementary education on a national level. This is the outcome of the educational philosophy of Mahatma Gandhi.

In July 1937, Gandhiji wrote in the Harijan, By education, I mean an all-round drawing art of the best in child and man-body, mind and spirit......Literacy itself is no-education. I would, therefore, begin the child's education by teaching it a useful handicraft and enabling it to provide from the moment it begins its training.

This conference appointed a committee of distinguished educationists under the Chairmanship of Dr. Zakir Hussain. It was the business of the educational planning Committee to take up educational restructure at national level. The Committee report was published in March,1938. 'The Wardha Scheme of Education'. The National Congress at its Haripura sessions held in March, 1938 accepted the scheme.

Thereafter the Central Advisory Board considered reports both the sub-committees details in May 1940, and adopted most of their conclusions and recommendations. In the meantime the committee consisting of experts in education was appointed by the Central Government under the Chairmanship of Sir John Sargent, the Educational Advisory to the Government of India to draw up a post-war-development plan for education.

It was the first comprehensive educational plan formulated by the Central Advisory Board of education.

A system of universal, compulsory and free education for all boys and girls between the ages of six and fourteen. The medium of instruction should be the mother tongue of the pupils. No teacher should receive less than Rs. 20/- per mensem.

The aim of their report, whatever its imperfections, is to provide a plan for planting the men and women, without whom India can not possibly fulfill the high destiny which the Board believes to be hers.

The Post-War Educational Development Plan (1944) had proposed Universalisation of Education should be provided for all children in the age zgroup of 6-14 in a phased programme spread over 40 years (1944-84). This proposal was examined by the special committee under the chairmanship of the late Sri B.G.Khare, the then Chief Minister of Bombay, in 1950. The committee came to the conclusion that this was too long a period and recommended that the goal should be reached by 1960. This recommendation was accepted and incorporated in article 45 of the Constitution which laid down:- that "the state shall endeavour to provide within a period of 10 years from the commencement of this Constitution, for free and compulsory education for all children until they complete the age of 14 years."

Education in Free India

The Constitution of India came into force on January 26,1950. As it embodies our hopes and aspirations, it is but natural that education shared find its place in this great document.

When this is the scenario of our soil the attendance at school was made compulsory upto the age of 14 in Belgium in 1914, in England in 1918 and in France in 1936. In Germany for atleast 8 years. The republic of China stipulated the same from 6-12 years to receive free primary education. Therefore the Constitution of India stipulated the duration up to 14 years.

India has now attained independence, but her freedom has brought new problems in its wake (viz) education, agriculture and rural development, irrigation and power, transport and communication, industry, health, housing, welfare of the backward classes.

With a view to raising the standards of living the national government has put into operation three Five Year Plans (1951-56) (1956-61) and 1961-66. It allocated Rs. 170 Crores, Rs. 277 Crores, Rs. 273 Crores and the expenditure was Rs.149 Crores, Rs. 273 Crores respectively thereon towards education.

By 1950-51 there were 192 lakh children (42.6 per cent) in school in classes I to V, so also during 1955-56 there were 2.52 lakhs (52.9 per cent) and during 1960-61 there were 3.43 lakhs (61.1 per cent) estimated children in the country.

The nation fully realised that in free India education cannot be confined to a section of the population but to plan for the education of every Indian.

A new step towards 'democratic decentralisation' has been taken up by the country as a result of the recommendations of the Balwantrai Mehta Committee to take 'personal interest and make sacrifices for common good.' The Mehta Committee envisaged a three tier system of decentralisation, namely the Village Panchayat, the Panchyat Samithi and the Zilla Parishad. It felt that the Panchayat Samithi at the block level would function as an intermediary body between the Village Panchayat and the district body and it can bring primary education closer to people to achieve the target.

During 1960-61 there were 4,72,653 recognised educational institutions in the country. Of these 20.5 per cent were managed by government, 46.3 per cent by local boards, 32.2 per cent were by private bodies. (30.5 per cent aided and 2.7 per cent unaided.)

During the same period the total number of pupils in recognised institutions were 4.79 crore (3.37 crore boys and 1.42 crore girls). They were distributed as pre-primary stage 0.4 per cent, primary stage 71.2 percentage. Educational facilities available for school going children in the age group of 6-11 is 62.2 percent .

By that time the National Income per head of population was Rs. 385/-. The Government of India was able to spend Rs. 9.4 of National Income per head of population towards educational expenditure. It is the 2.4 of per head of population. Thus expenditure on education was 1.11 per cent of the national income of 1949-50.

But Kerala spent leaps and bounds of expenditure for about 40 per cent of its state revenue for education alone.

In India, for example the proportion of population in the age group of 6-14 is 20-24 per cent as against 15 per cent or so in the developed countries.

But still we couldn't achieve it till 1960. Then the Government of India took up *First All India Educational Survey between 1956-59* to locate the scenario of number of schools, enrolment, appointment of teachers to achieve the maximum effect at a minimum cost.

The Survey revealed that the country will need a total of 3,23,463 primary schools. There was also an enrolment of 70.25 per cent in class I during 1954-55 while the enrolment in Class IV during 1959-60 was 42.48 per cent. The wastage and stagnation during 1954-55 was 56.2 per cent while during1959-60 it was 58.7 per cent.

Keeping in view the scenario the Government of India constituted the Central Social Welfare Board at the instance of the union Ministry of Education, decided at its 30th meeting hold in October, 1960 to appoint a committee to prepare a comprehensive plan for the care and training of children in the age group of 0-6.

Smt. B. Tarabai headed the committee, that pre-school education must be single-mindedly devoted to the true welfare, growth and development of the human child as a vital organism, and a unit of the human species.

The pre-school programme should be based upon:-

1. Heredity and environment
2. An atmosphere which is full of joy
3. Grow up and develop in conditions of freedom
4. Activity in order to spend its energy and to expand its total capacity and abilities to contribute to its total growth and development
5. The child needs protection and assistance of parents and other competent persons.

Since the attainment of independence, the Development of Education has drawn the attention of the Government, politicians, educationists and even laymen. Therefore the Government of India appointed a 15 member Education Commission on 14th July, 1964.

This was the sixth commission in the history of education commissions in India. The report has been appropriately entitled 'Education and National Development.' The unique features of this commission are:-

1. It was not to limit its enquiry to any specific sector or aspect of education as the earlier commissions had done but to have comprehensive a review of the entire educational system.
2. Its firm belief that education is the most powerful instrument of national development.
3. Its international composition. (5 International members out of 14 members commission); Prof.D.S.Kottari, Chariman, University Grants Commission, New-Delhi-Chairman.

The commission opined that the destiny of India is now being shaped in her classrooms. The report is to identify the major programmes that can bring about the educational revolution which has 3 main aspects.

- Internal transformation so as to relate it to the life, needs and aspirations of the nation to productivity.

- Qualitative improvement so that the standards achieved are adequate, keep continually rising and, at least in a few sectors, become internationally comparable and
- Expansion of educational facilities broadly on the basis of man power needs and with an accent on equalization of educational opportunities.

It also added that education shall strengthen, social and national integration, democracy as a form of government and as a way of life; modernization, character, so also Science as a Basic Component of Education and Culture. It recommended the curriculum rounding about

Work Experience.

Vocationalisation.

Education, Social and National Integration.

Common School System.

Social, Moral and Spirtual Values

Secularism and religion

Science and Ahimsa to work Jointly.

Evaluation is a continuous process, forms an integral part of the total system of the education and is intimately related to educational objectives.

The School Complex should be established. Each higher primary school should be integrally related to 10 lower primary schools that exists in its neighborhood so that they form one complex of educational facilities. The position of GNP allocated to education to rise from 2.9 percent in 1965-66 to 6.0 percent in 1985-86.

The Commission pointed out that a good educational system should establish neighbourhood schools where each primary school would be attended by all children in the neighbourhood irrespective of caste, creed, community, religion, economic condition or social status.

The Government of India estimated 625 million children in the age group of 6-14 by 1976 and it fixed 80 per cent of them to be in schools.

The Education Commission 1964-66 recommended that the Government of India should issue a statement on the National Policy on Education which should provide guidance to the state Governments and the local authorities in preparing and implementing educational plans. In 1967 the government of India constituted a committee of members of parliament on education to prepare the draft of a statement on the N.P.E, 1968.

The policy is in the following principles:

Free and Compulsory Education:- Streneous efforts should be made for the early fulfillment of the Directive principle under Article 45, of the constitution seeking to provide free and compulsory education for all children upto the age of 14.

Regional languages. The energetic development of Indian language and literature is sine qua non for educational and cultural development.

(a) Strenuous efforts should be made to equaivalize educational opportunity

(b) Regional imbalances in the provision of educational facilities should be corrected and good educational facilities should be provided in rural and other backward areas.

(c) Efforts should be made to improve the standard of education in general schools.

(d) The education of girls should receive emphasis, not only on the grounds of social justice, but also because it accelerates social transformation.

(e) Educational facilities for the physically and mentally handicapped children should be expanded and attempt should be made to develop integrated programmmes enabling the handicapped children to study in regular schools.

For the cultivation of excellence, it is necessary that talent in diverse fields should be identified as early as possible and every stimulus and opportunity given for all its full development.

The school and the community should be brought close through suitable programmes of mutual service and support including participation in meaningful and challenging programmes of community service and national reconstruction should accordingly become an integral part of education. Emphasis in these programmes should be on self-help, character formation and on the development of sense of social commitment.

The immediate target before the country is that by 1975 we should enroll in schools 100 per cent of the children in the age group of 11-14. It requires

1. Universality of Provision
2. Universality of Enrolment
3. Universality of retention.

The All Educational Survey, 1958-59 has made a fair estimate stating that a total of 3,23,463 primary schools of which 1,50,215 would be independent schools, and 1,72,304 group schools and 944 peri-patetic-teacher schools.

The Debar Committee also estimated that out of every 100 children who enter class I only forty reach class IV and only twenty reach class VIII. Why is wastage proving to be such a baffling problem? There are economic, social and educational causes.

Provision of free mid-day meal is a necessary and admittedly successful incentive to draw and hold in the school children for their poorest and most backward areas. In the 3rd Plan, the provision of Rs. 3.82 crore has been made in the state plans on the number of children proposed to be covered is 119 lakhs.

The Government of India formulated National Policy for Children (1974) with an intention to serve as a 'pole star' to guide the official and non-official agencies alike in regard to the direction in which they should move in achieving full and integrated development of our children who constitute most valuable asset for posterity.

The following aspects were discussed by it :

(a) Preventive and promotive aspects of child health.

(b) Nutrition for infants and children in the pre-school age along with nutrition in nursing and expectant mothers.

(c) Maintenance, education and training of orphan and destitute children;

(d) Creches and other facilities for the care of children of working or ailing mothers.

Thereafter National Children's Board has been constituted and has been considerable expansion in the health, nutrition, education, and welfare services. Rise in the standard of living, wherever it occurred, has indirectly met children's basic needs to some extent. But all this once needs a focus and a forum for planning and review and proper co-ordiantion of the multiplicity of services to meet the needs of children.

Voluntary organizations engaged in the field of child welfare continued to have the opportunity to develop either on their own or with state assistance the field of education, health recreation and social welfare services.

To achieve the above aims, the state provided necessary legislative and administrative support.

The Govt. of India also called upon the citizens, state governments, local bodies, educational institutions and voluntary organizations to play their part in the overall effort to attain these objectives. Even then the percentage of girls in school enrolment in elementary stage was 37.4 by 1970-71.

Now there is a turn in the pattern of school education and at +2 stage. A pattern of education 10 + 2 had been introduced in several schools in the country. The NCERT had prepared a new curriculum and textbooks which came under heavy criticism due to various reasons. In the meanwhile there was a change of government at the center and the Janata Government with Morarji Desai came to power in 1977. A review committee popularly known as Ishwarbhai Patel committee was appointed by the union Minister of Education and Social welfare in his capacity of President of the NCERT. The Review Committee headed by Shri. Ishwarbai J. Patel (Vice-Chancellor, Gujarat University) had 30 members.

The aim of this curriculum area is to provide children with opportunities of participating in social and economic activities inside and outside the classroom, enabling them to understand scientific principles and processes involved in different types of work and in the setting in which they are found in the physical and social environment.

By 1980-81 the percentage of girls in school enrolment at the elementary stage was 38.6. The purpose of the common core programme will be to bring about attitudinal changes and to develop realness for work practice. Literacy in mother tongue, numeracy , technocracy, respect for national symbols, healthy attitudes, cleanliness and healthful living, taste for good and the beautiful surroundings, Co-operation and self–learning are its primary objectives.

In view of the fact that more than 80% of Primary Schools are in rural areas and it is strongly of the view that no rigid academic year should be prescribed. The school sessions should be scheduled according to local needs.

They were of the view that the number of pages in each textbook should be reduced to the minimum and that the language used should be understood by children of this age group.

In American Education the building of a good school community relationships depend in a large part on the Superintendents ability to discharge in their full scope the functions of planning, informing and coordinating. In India school administrative officers are the key persons upon whom the responsibility of a successful programme must fall.

It will also be desirable to frame laws, compelling industrial or mining organisatins and associated industries to establish and maintain elementary schools for the community in which they operate. For example, Article 67 – 71 of the Organic Law of 1942 in Mexico impose definite obligations upon employers. They are required to furnish complete and hygienic school quarters, adequately equipped with minimum necessities, such as libraries, text books and general school materials.

It may also be noted that the shift system is not a novel method, since it has been practised in a number of foreign countries, (Viz.) Germany, France, Portugal, the U.S.A. and Japan.

Even Denmark which is mainly an agricultural country like ours followed the same system. The children schools are part time schools. In rural schools, pupils of every class must be taught 18 hours every week, these 18 hours a week are worked out in different schools according to local circumstances. In Peoples China schools in rural areas are closely linked with the farming. The general principle is when you have more time, study more, and when you have less time, study less, when you are busiest, stop study for a while. The very fact that the system has played such an important role in the educational progress of a number of countries – clear indications of the practicability of its being introduced in this country too.

The National Policy on Education, 1968 marked a significant step in the history of education in post – Independent India. However, the general formulations incorporated in the 1968 policy, did not get translated into a detailed strategy of implementation, accompanied by the assignment of specific responsibilities and financial and organizational support. As a result, problems of Access, Quality, Quantity, Utility and Financial outlay, accumulated over the years, assumed serious proportions.

The Government of India in its broadcast to the nation on January 5, 1985, promised a new education policy that would equip the country both scientifically and economically to enter the 21st century. Thereafter a Status Report entitled 'Challenge of Education - A Policy Perspective' was issued by the Ministry on August 20, 1985.

By this time, the Government of India spent 2.70 per cent of total planned out lay on education. There were 5,28,872 primary schools with an enrolment of 87.4 per cent. Of them 40.3 per cent were girls. There were 1,00,39, 921 children from S.C. Community.

Thereafter came the prestigious trumpet call of the Government of India through National Policy on Education, 1986.

The document 'Challenge of Eduation-1985' was debated in the country at various conferences, seminars and study circles etc. It is of the great interest to note that the document was translated practically into all the regional languages. 5,80,0000 copies of the document in English, 2,40,000 in Hindi and 4,000 copies in Urdu were distributed by the Ministry inviting suggestions and comments from all the sections of the people. As a part of the nation - wide debate for the formation of the new policy on education, 12 National Seminars, 17 Sponsored Seminars were organized by the Ministry of Education and its national organizations. All the State Governments and Union Territories also organized Seminars, Workshops and Symposia. Thereafter the National Policy on Education was adopted by the Lok Sabha on May 8, 1986 and the Rajya Sabha on May 13,1986.

The policy said that National Perception – Education is essentially for all. This is fundamental to our - all - round development, material and spiritual.

The National System of Education implies that, up to a given level, all students, irrespective of caste, creed, location or sex, have access to education of comparable quality.

The New Education Policy will lay special emphasis on the removal of disparities and to equalize educational opportunity by attending to the specific needs of those who have been denied equality so far.

The central forms in the SCs educational development is their equivalisation with the non-SC population at all stages and levels of education, in all areas and in all the four-dimensions-rural male, rural female, urban male and urban female.

Programmme of Early Childhood Care and Education is child-oriented, freezed around play and the individuality of the child. A phased drive, symbolically called 'OPERATION BLACK BOARD' is undertaken with immediate effect to improve primary schools all over the country. De-Culturisation, De-Humanisation and alienation must be avoided at all costs.

The policy expected that it shall be ensured that all children who attain the age about 11 years 1990 will have 5 years of schooling, or its equivalent through the non-formal stream. Likewise by 1995 all children will be provided free and compulsory education upto 14 years of age.

Work experience, viewed as purposive and meaningful manual work, organized as on integral part of the learning process.

It started District Institute of Education and Training (DIETs) and also Institutes of Advanced Study in Education (IASEs), Colleges of Teacher Education (CTEs), in the entire nation wherein the former institutes to deal with Pre-service and In-service teachers of primary education and the latter with secondary education. It also stressed the need of Child Centered Education and Activity Based Teaching and Minimum Levels of Learning (MLLs).

MLLs are framed with the objectives of Achievability, Awareness, Evaluability and learning continuum by all the children irrespective of Caste, Colour, Creed and region from Kashmir to Kanyakumari.

As a part of achieving the objective, the Government of India has been furthering its endeavours keeping in view the goal of Universalisation of Elementary Education. After the declaration of the National Policy on Education, 1986, the Ministry of Human Resources Development, (formerly known as Ministry of Education), Government of India announced the Programme Of Action for its implementation. This was the first time in the History of Education Development in Independent India that such a follow up programme prepared. Twenty-three Task Forces were prepared and each was assigned a specific topic covered by the National Policy on Education, 1986 (NPE).

The Programme Of Action has the following subjects under 511 paragraphs.

- Early Child-hood Care and Education.
- Elementary Education, Non-Formal Education and Operation Black Board.
- Education on Women's Equality.
- Education of SCs,STs and others.
- Minorities Education.
- Education of the Handicapped.
- Content and Process of School Education.
- Evaluation Process and Examination Reform.
- Teachers and their Training.
- Management of Education.

The plight of educational opportunities to the masses were mirrored through Research during 1960s on progress and problems of primary education and highlighted the problems of non-enrolment and dropout. Poverty, engagement in paid and unpaid child labours, inaccessibility of schools, household responsibilities of girl children were sources of the prominent reasons. In response to these, a nation wide drive for providing sandwich forms of education to children in the age group of 9-14 year was launched during the 5th Five Year Plan (1974-79). Engaging educated unemployed youth of villages or slums to organise and conduct evening classes for non-enrolled children and drop outs and a token honorarium was the strategy herein. This is a strategy adopted by M.V. Parulekar as early as 1929.

The growing sensibility for providing meaningful educational programme to millions of drop outs, non school going children, and illiterate adults had made it to inevitable to search for alternatives in delivery mechanism.

Non–Formal Education had become an immediate alternative at this juncture for this age group. Nearly 5 Lakhs centers were in the country by 1993 with a view to safeguard the right of education for children. But the scheme gave a room for child labour and provided much scope for criticism and became a court case. Consequently the centers were run during the day time itself. Ultimately the scheme was abolished during 2001.

The educational scenario especially in the South Asian, the Subsaharan African countries, reflects a persistent concerned and a number of initiatives towards this goal. Realising and potential for an intervention to up grade quality, the international conference was supported and shared by the Commonwealth of learning, the Commonwealth Foundation and UNSESCO. The resolution about education for all in the Jamiten Conference and Daker International Conference have drawn attention to a large gap. The National Open School System (NOS) in collaboration with the Commonwealth of Learning (COL) led to the formation of Open School Education System.

It should be noted that, even in England, part time education in the age group of 6-10 was allowed till about 1900 and in the age group of 11-14, till 1918.

Through O.B.B., in Andhra Pradesh Teaching Learning Material was supplied to the schools in existence by 30.09.86. Salaries of newly appointed teachers under this scheme had been borne 100 percent by the Government of India.

The expenditure in the construction of additional classrooms was met upto 48 percent by Government of India, 40 percent Government of Andhra Pradesh, 12 percent Jawahar Rojgar Yojana. The total number of Mandal and Municipalities were 1104 + 85 = 1189. 20,286 Teacher posts were sanctioned to primary schools. 27, 000 school buildings were proposed while 23,979 were built. Teaching Learning Material was distributed to 43,275 Primary Schools and 306 Upper Primary Schools. 5,074 School Assistant posts were sanctioned to Upper Primary Schools.

Sri J.P. Naik has rightly opined (in his book 'Elementary Education in India A Promise to Keep') that development is not just factories, dams and factories. It is basically about the people. The human factor is of supreme value, literacy is an indispensable component of human resource development. The National Literacy Mission was considered as a Societal Mission which implied that there was a political will at all levels for the achievement of mission goals. It was launched in the month of May 1988 to impart Fundamental Literacy to eighty million illiterate persons in 15-35 years age group. 30 million by 1990 and additional 50 million by 1995. The focus of NLM was on rural areas, particularly women and persons belonging to SCs and STs.

The main foci of adult education should be thrice.

(i) Upgrading of vocational skills or on-the-job training.

(ii) Imparting the basic knowledge of science and technology in a simplified form with their direct implications of their health, family planning and other aspects of their life.

(iii) Citizenship a study of the cultural heritage of the country, history of freedom movement, national discussion (i.e.,) on poverty, unemployment, population growth, defence etc.

By 1990-91 the Government of India spent 1.78 percentage of Gross Development Production on elementary education. There were 5,60,395 Primary Schools, with 97.4 per cent of enrolment out of which 41.5 per cent were girls. There were 1,05, 794 children belonging to S.C Community. Thereafter the Government of India appointed Acharya Rama Murthy as Chairman of the Committee to review the National Policy on Education, 1986. The Committee submitted its report to the minister of state in the Ministry of Human Resources Development on December 26, 1990 and the same was tabled in the Parliament on January 9, 1991.

The review committee felt that in order to achieve equity and social justice and there- by remove elitist aberrations, education has been viewed in the overall context of social, economic, regional and gender based disparities. For example, any effort at vocationalising education will carry no meaning unless, concurrently, the government lay down an appropriate income and various policies. Likewise, national policies concerning removal of economic disparities such as for land reforms-employment, health and nutrition etc., have to be concurrently established/reviewed.

It also said that in order to achieve this objective, the existing government, local body and government aided schools have to be transformed through quality improvement into genuine neighbourhood schools. Private schools also should be similarly transformed in course of time by making them freely accessible.

It is the view of the committee that value education is to be construed as a continuous process which is to be sustained throughout the process of the growth of the individual from child-hood to adolescence, then for adult-hood and so on.

It further mentioned that the rural areas in general, and the tribal areas in particular,have suffered in terms of resources, personal and infrastructure facilities. This would mean concrete programmes being established on ground for the disadvantaged groups-SCs and STs, women, the educationally backward minorities and the handicapped with appropriate budgeting for the same.

Thereafter the Central Advisory Board of Education (CABE) in its meeting held on 8-9 March, 1991 examined the procedure to be adopted on consideration of the report of the National Policy On Education Review Committee (NPERC) and decided that a CABE Committee be constituted by the Chairman, viz., Union Minister of Human Resources Development, to consider the recommendations of the NPERC.

In pursuance of the above decision, the Chairman of the CABE appointed Sri Janardhana Reddy, Chief Minister and Minster of Education, A.P. as Chairman to review the implementation of the NPERC and other relevant developments since the policy was formulated and to recommend modifications to be made in NPERC. The Committee suggested as follows.

(i) A Standing CABE Committee On Education of STs and SCs and other Educationally Backward Sections should be Constituted, Educationists from these groups should have representation in that committee.

(ii) The Navodaya Vidyalayas should be set up in each district as originally envisaged. The scope of article 45 of the Constitution need not be enlarged.

(iii) ICDS and other CSS relating to ECCE should continue as Centrally Sponsored Schemes during the 8th five year plan.

(iv) Constitutional amendment is not so much needed as suggested by the NPERC as the manifestation of a National will to achieve Universalisation of Elementary Education. The Central and State Governments should bestow overriding priority to adult literacy and UEE and to provide programmes in these two areas total support, financial administrative and political-a support which is commensurate with the priority.

With the aim of exploring ideas for a new International thrust in basic education for all, UNICEF convened a consultation in February, 1988 of some two dozen people with major responsibilities of deep personal involvement in aspects of basic education on 6th February 1984. The heads of UNDP, UNESCO, UNICEF and World Bank jointly announced their support for a new International initiative for meeting basic learning needs and called for a World Conference on Education For All on 5-9 March, 1990 in Jometin, Thailand in which 155 countries participated.

Today nearly 4 of 5 children in the age group of 6-14 are in school. Two of Three persons are functionally literate. The exercise focusing on selected quantitative indicators of basic education was to specifically capture the progress made during the last decade of the twentieth century, euphemistically refused to as the Education for all decade following three global conferences on education for all held in Jomiten in 1990.

The international donor community at the Jomitien Conference, the country saw the emergence of a large multi-state programme for Education For All (EFA) under the banner of the District Primary Education Programme (DPEP). Alongside this, Rajasthan initiated a fairly large programme of EFA under the name of Lok Jumbish (L.J.)

In a historic judgement in July, 1992 the Supreme Court of India (1992) declared that education is a fundamental right and that “the state is under a Constitutional mandate to provide educational institutions at all levels for the benefit of citizens. The uproar against the judgement declaring the whole education, including higher professional education as a fundamental right, later required the Supreme Court to modify its judgement (1993) so as to confine the scope for elementary education every child/citizen of this country has a right to free education until he completes the age of 14 years.

The judgement also assures importance as we have also do not sincere to the UN/UNESO/ILO declaration as the human rights and the rights of the children, which India ratified. The judgement of the Supreme Court in the necessary background against which the efforts of the Union Government particularly in constituting a committee to consider the implications of the proposal to make elementary education a fundamental right under the Chairmanship of "Mahiram Saikia(Saikia Committee,1997) in subsequently proposed Bill for make education a fundamental right have to be seen.

The Saikia Committee has recommended amendment of the Constitution to make the right to free elementary education upto 14 years of age a fundamental right in the Constitution. Provision of free elementary education according to the committee includes exemption from tuition fee, provision of free text books for all primary school children and girls upto Upper Primary level, and provision of essential stationery to all children in primary classes while the committee recommended that the mid – day meal programme be continued, provision of other incentives such as free school uniform, cash incentives, scholarships etc., could be left to the discretion of the states, subject to economic capacities of priorities of the respective governments. It also suggested the State Government to make it compulsory by providing access of primary education to all children and the parents should send their children to schools treating it as a fundamental duty.

Accordingly the Parliament under 93rd amendment made education upto 14 years as a fundamental right of every citizen. Simultaneously, at an international level, basic education found a prime place in the development discourse as a component of the Human Development Index (HDI) brought out by the United National Development Programme (UNDP).

Providing elementary education for all, with an ever burgeoning population has not been an easy task. However an estimated 95 percent of the rural population living in 8,26,000 habitations has access to a Primary school within a radius of 1km and about 85 percent of the population has an Upper Primary School within a radius of 3 km.

Several states show a new enrolment ratio of more than 80 percent. Even traditionally under developed states such as Madhya Pradesh show a significantly high net-enrolment ratio of 79.2 yet some states such as Bihar, Jammu and Kashmir, Nagaland, Rajasthan, Uttar Pradesh, and West Bengal seem to face a serious problem demanding immediate attention.

Although female enrolment has shown a significant increase during the last few years, gender disparity does not seem to have reduced. In fact, not even 4 out of 10 girls in Uttar Pradesh belonging to the age group of 6-11 years are in Primary Schools.

There has been a significant decline in dropout rates between 1991 and 1999. This is particularly pronounced in the case of girls. Between 1991 and 1995 the dropout rate for girls declined from about 48 percent to 38 percent at primary stage. If the same trend continues, as estimates indicate, 7 out of 10 girls who joined primary school in 1992 are likely to remain in the system for at least five years.

According to the 1991 census, there are 11.28 million child workers (6.18 million boys and 5.10 million girls) in the age group 5-14. About 91 percent of these children are concentrated in rural areas.

The Ninth Five year plan has, under the respective plans for education and women and child development, addressed the issue of early childhood care and education more exhaustively than previous plans.

Pre- School Education, at the time of India's Independence in 1947, was primarily in the hands of a few voluntary organizations.

The first step taken in this direction by the Govt. of India was the setting up of a Central Social Welfare Board (CSWB) in 1953.

The CSWB sponsored a composite programme of Welfare Extension Projects with the creation of Women's Groups or Mahila Mandalies and Balawadis. The CSWB was also instrumental in setting up the Supplementary Nutrition Programme in 1970 and a Scheme for Crèches for Ailing and Working Mothers in 1974.

Through National Policy for Children in 1974 'Integrated Child Development Services (ICDS) was launched on an experimental basis in 1975, included Non-Formal Pre- School Education as a component, along with other components of health and nutrition, and had the enlarged scope of addressing the nutritional and health needs of 0-3 years olds and pregnant women, in academic with a life – cycle approach.

The nodal agency for coordination and monitoring of this scheme at the central level is the Department of Women and Child Development, Ministry of Human Resource Development and its counterpart departments at the State Level. Out of the 5,614 ICDS Projects sanctioned till 1996, 4200 became operational during the 8th plan.

It facilitates the realization of the goals of UEE by helping children develop necessary readiness for schooling in terms of getting them habituated to regularly attending a center-based programme away from home, and by developing in them certain pre-reading, pre-writing, and pre-number skills, concepts, and vocabulary which can help them negotiate the primary curricular better.

By 1990 there were 5,60,935 Primary Schools in the country. By 1990-91 there was a drop out rate of 41 per cent in Primary Schools. An estimated 95 per cent of the rural population in India living in 8,26,000 habitations has access to a Primary School within a radius of 1 kilometer.

The Gross Enrolment Ratio at the primary stage in India has exceeded 100 per cent. Despite all these achievements, a large number of children were still out of school and the goal of UEE continued to be elusive.

High drop out rate ranging upto 60 per cent, large number of out-of-school children (about 1/3rd) lack of access in 17 per cent (1.8 lakh) of habitations with 1 km radius and high wastage (33 per cent) taking 7.2 years for 5 years of primary schoolig were some of areas of concern.

Low levels of learning achievement, low participation of girls, SC, ST and other disadvantaged groups are certain issues. Issues relating to effectiveness and efficiency of primary education like poor functioning of schools, inadequate school infrastructure and facilities, high teacher absenteeism, large number of teacher vacancies, poor quality of education and inadequate funds.

National Policy on Education, 1986 is a landmark in the history of education and launched OBB in 1986 with focus on providing additional class rooms, teachers and a pack of Teaching Learning Material.

DIETs were established in 1988 under Centrally Sponsored Scheme to look after the teacher training. The Total Literacy Campaign was launched in 1988 to eradicate illiteracy. MLLs programme was started in 1991 to identify basic competencies in language, Mathematics and other subjects and to develop new text books.

Meanwhile, various states also initiated basic education projects around this time. The Andhra Pradesh Primary Education Programme (APPEP) with DFID assistance was the first of its kind. The Lok Jumbish project with Swedish International Development Agency (SIDA) assistance was initiated in Rajasthan while Bihar and U.P., also started similar basic education projects.

The Programme of Action 1992 provided fresh insights and directions for achieving UEE. It called for an integrated and decentralised approach to the development of Primary Education with focus on building capacities, particularly at district and sub-district levels. Imbibing the spirit of this policy initiative, emerged District Primary Education Programme (DPEP) in 1994.

Objectives of DPEP

- To provide all children with access to primary education (Classes I to V)
- Reduce primary drop out rates for all students less than 10 per cent.
- Reduce differences in enrolment, drop out rate and learning achievement among gender and social groups to less than 5 per cent.
- Raise the average achievement levels of students by at least 25 per cent in Language and Mathematics and at least 40 per cent achievement levels in other subjects.

- DPEP also seeks to strengthen the capacity of national, state and district institutions on organization, for planning, management and evaluation of primary education.

The programme has been covered in 219 (248 with bifurcated) districts of 18 states in three phases commencing from 1994 September to March, 2003 in the country. Each district is a unit and Rs. 40 crore is provided for implementation of the programme. Out of the total project cost, about 70 per cent of funds is spent on improving quality of education. Expenditure on civil works is limited to 24 per cent and management cost is 6 per cent. The government of India's share is resourced by the external funding. The total external assistance comes to Rs. 4,885 crore. Out of this Rs. 3,760 crore is soft loan from IDA and the remaining Rs. 1,125 crore is out right grant from European Countries, DFID, UNICEF, and Netherlands offers further external assistance about Rs.4000 crore for expansion of the programme including extension to Upper Primary classes.

The 52nd round of National Survey on School Organisation (NSSO) Report for 1995-96 indicates that 26.3 percent of children in the age group of 6 to 10 years never attended the school.

The DPEP from out of its operational strategies for a period of six years (1995-2000) are as follows.

Enrollement:

Phase – I			
In Formal Schools			1.3 million
Alternative Schools			0.63 million
Enrollement increase		1998-1999	8.9 million
		1999-2000	9.1 million
Alternative Schools/	:		
Education Guarantee	:	1998-1999	5.9 lakhs
Scheme centers increase	:	1999-2000	6.29 lakhs
Phase – II & III			
Enrollement including EGS /ALS		1998-1999	18.69million
		1999-2000	19.82million

Student Class room Ratio 41.8 to 39.7 percent, a decline.

The overall increase during this period is 24 percent with annual compound growth rate of 5.5 percent.

Gross Enrollement Ratio of phase – 1 is 101.7 percent for 1999-2000 if the enrollement in Alternative Schools is included.

These children mainly belong to the marginalised and difficult groups like working children, children engaged in household chores, migrating children, adolescent girls and children to whom access to education is restrained.

LEARNING

Phase-I

The Mid-Term Assessment Survey in 9 states (59 districts). The overall performance crossed the 60 percent of marks in 44 districts in Language and 51 districts in Mathematics of class 1. Of these a number of districts have crossed the 80 percent mark.

This data covered a sample of 80,906 students, 8,003 teachers and 2,781 schools spread over 56 districts of 8 DPEP states.

The Base line Assessment Survey (BAS) 1997. Comparative profile of students performance on BAS with that of the same test readministered in 2000 has shown substantial improvement both in Language and Mathematics.

Teachers

Pupil Teacher Ratio in Phase –I districts is about 38.

Pupil Teacher Ration in Phase-II and III districts is above 48.

More than 4,20,000 teachers were appointed in various regular, EGS and full time.

Alternative School Centers.

Equity

In 1995-96, 15 districts of Phase -I Index Gender Equity is greater than 95 percent, in 1999-2000 it has gone upto 29, with the remaining districts having Index Gender Equity between 85 to 95.

In 1998-99, in Phase – II there is a considerable improvement. The number of districts with IGE > 95 has increased from 31 in 1997-98 to 35, in 1998-99 and to 56 in 1999-2000. There are only 7 districts with IGE < 85.

The DPEP goal of reducing the difference in achievement between boys and girls in class 1 has been realised in 49 out of 56 districts in Language and in 42 out of 56 districts in Mathematics across 8 states.

In class 3, genderwise differences in achievement has been overcome in 11 out of 13 districts in Mathematics. Differences in achievement between boys and girls in class 4 are now have been squeezed to less than 5 percent in 41 out of 43 districts in Language and in 42 out of 43 districts in Mathematics.

Social Groups

ISE for SC is more than 100 in all Phase I districts. Of 72 districts in Phase II with SC population more than 5 percent, 7 districts of Karnataka had ISE SC <75.

Of 22 districts in Phase –I with ST population more than 5 percent, a number of districts with less than 75 percent ISE ST remain at the same level while the number of districts with ISE ST greater than 95 declined from 14 to 11. In Phase – II, there were 7 districts with ISE ST less than 75. The analysis for ISE is based only on formal school enrollment, whereas in many of these regions various forms of alternative schools or catering to the needs of the population especially in far-flung areas.

The report on Scholastic Attainment under MAS suggests that the difference in learning achievement in SC/ST children and others have been effectively reduced in many districts and across subjects.

Integrated Education for Disabled

This component made significant progress assistive devices and in strengthening resource support to children with special needs. DPEP has entered into an agreement with Artificial Limbs Manufacturing Corporation of India(ALIMCO) to conduct camps in project areas and provide aids and appliances. States have been asked to apply directly under Assistance to Disabled Persons for purchasing Aids and Appliances and Empowerment and also under IEDC scheme of MHRD, besides exploring convergence method.

To meet the shortage of qualified resource teachers, DPEP has entered into an agreement with the Rehabitation Council of India(RCI). RCI will conduct 45 day multi category foundation course to train teachers in DPEP in Special Education and teachers trained under the foundation course will be given provisional registration by RCI.

The current coverage is estimated to be about one percent. In other words in a period of 115 years, because of in appropriate strategies and perhaps inadequate awareness progress has been halting and grindingly slow.

As per the latest estimates, 2.64 lakh children with special needs have been identified in the project blocks, out of which 2.14 lakh (81 per cent) have been enrolled in schools.

In the process of imparting education to the disabled children it should be borne in mind that any philosophy or programme that aims to provide learning opportunities to these children does not depend on the characterstics of the child, but instead on the Vision, Commitment, and Creativity of Policy Makers, Administrators, Educators and above all, families.

Only by empowering its children by education, can India move towards economic independece and Psycho – social integration.

School Library Programme

In order to provide a litercy environment, to the children, the school library programme has been initiated in several states. This programme has been undertaken with the collaboration of National Book Trust.

Research Studies

About 500 Action Researches were completed so far in different states.

Community Participation

Community mobilisation and participation is an essential component of the programme, emphasising the decentralisation of the planning, management and implementation process.

So far, 2.04 lakhs Village Education Committees, 1.61 lakhs School Management Committees over 55,000 PTAs/MTAs/Mother Associations with assured representatives of SCs and STs have been established. Andhra Pradesh established 50,000 School Management Committees. Awareness Programmes were taken up by them(viz)

School Chalo (Uttar Pradesh), Barne Takora (Knocking the door compaign, Gujarat), Community Mobilisation – cum Data Capture Excersises like 'Ninad'(Orissa),Shiksha Darpan(Rajasthan) and Lok Sampark Abhiyan – II (Madhya Pradesh), Janma Bhoomi (Andhra Pradesh).

Community involvement in the form of contribution of resources in cash/kind by the village communities have been reported from various states, like AP Rs.1.5 crore, Maharashtra Rs. 7.5 crore, Gujarat land worth Rs.37.7 lakhs and Himachal Pradesh land for 700 schools. There is the increasing role of women from the deprived sections of the society on school related issues.

All the states however are unanimous on the resolve to maintain the core inventions, processes, systems and structures of DPEP like Block Resource Centers/Cluster Resource Centers/Village Education Committee, Teacher Training, Pedagogical processes, Alternative School/Non-Formal Education Centers and Community Based Activities.

Education Guarantee Scheme in Madhya Pradesh opens schools within 90days if an area without school within 1½ kms for at least 40 out of school children. The Village Panchayat maintains the same.

Back to School Campaign in Uttar Pradesh and Andhra Pradesh. Children are withdrawn from work and educated to the level comparing to their age.

Makhtabs and Madrasas

In Assam, Uttar Pradesh Muslim religious leaders or para teachers impart primary education especially to Muslim girls who do not come to formal schools after religious education.

Alternative Schools: In Madhya Pradesh under DPEP Alternative Schools are run with the help of Digantar an NGO, a four hour school based on free pace learning. There are no grades and the teacher is only a facilatator.

Multi Grade Schools in Kerala: These schools are opened in collaboration with Rishi Valley School Groups at certain habitations and villages which do not qualify for opening of new schools. It emphasises on group learning and use of Self - Learning Material. As in Tamilanadu, residential schools in Gujarat, seasonal hostels and vocational courses for children of migratory population during harvesting season are in force.

Sugar Schools in Maharashtra: These are for the children of families who migrate to the area of sugar factories during the season. These schools are close nearby to sugar fields or sugar factories. In some cases, children are accommodated in the nearby formal schools for about 6 to 7 months. Pedagogical Renovation and Quality Improvement, Text Books, Supplementary reading materiel, Pupil Evaluation , Teacher Empowerment (teacher training, copetensce building, attitudanal change, gender sensitive) are taken up here.

Decentralised Academic Support Institutions: Block Resource Centers/Cluster Resource Centers, SCERT, DIET,have been trained up at National, State level to extend academic support to the institutions. Teacher Grant of Rs.500, School Grant of Rs.2000 every year is being sanctioned for the purpose of strengthening the school teachers and schools.

Capacity building of Institution on Distance Mode: Distance Education Training Programmes are introduced. Teacher recruitment has been taken up every year and about 51 percent of teachers appointed are found to be women in DPEP states.

Early Childhood Education

DPEP finances expansion of ECE centers in village not eligible to be covered by the ICDS. To improve the quality of ECE, the programme also develops pre- school materials and impart training to field functionaries, ICDS Anganwadi and Balwadi workers. ECE is a vital component in the programme because it prepares children particularly, the first generation learners for primary school. Readiness has an impact on girls participation in primary education. Under this programme over 80,000 ECE centers has been opened besides strengthening over 35,000 Anganwadi centers.

The 12th Joint Review Mission reveals that so far 10,000 new schools are set up over 56,000 Alternative Schools in the country, increasing the enrolment by 2.55 lakh. Many of the Centres cater to a majority of SC and ST children. There has been significant effort to improving functions of Madrasas, particularly in Madhya Pradesh, U.P., Assam and Rajasthan.

Interventions in Maktabs and Madrasas are an important aspect for ensuring education of girls who have often been denied formal primary education due to social and religious factors.

In majority of cases, physical infrastructure is not suitable or adequate. Kerala, A.P., Rajasthan and West Bengal have made efforts for constructing semi-pucca buildings for Alternative School Centres with community participation, while Madhya Pradesh has accessed funds from the Tribal Development Department.

So far 35,000 school buildings, 39,000 Additional Classrooms, 15,000 R.C.Cs. were constructed. The IIT, Kharagpur Laboratory tests reveal that the structures constructed using these technologies are not only sound but also durable. They have also met with the community acceptance. The school designs are more child-friendly and barrier free, cost effective construction etc.

A study to access the drop out rate was carried out listing the Educational Management Information System data on enrolment and repeaters of 131 districts, for the year 1997-98 and 1999-2000. According to the study drop out rates are < 10 per cent in 24 districts, which includes all the 6 districts in Kerala.

In Uttar Pradesh 2,279 villages have achieved universal enrolment and 1774 villages are 'drop out free' in clusters covered by the Model Cluster Development Approach. Cohort studies have been conducted by Andhra Pradesh, Tamil Nadu and West Bengal and the same process has been initiated in Assam and Maharashtra.

The Government of India thought of providing educational facilities for the Urban areas through *Janshala with a slogan of Working Towards a Common Goal.*

Janshasala (Joint GOI-UN) Programme is a collaborative effort of Government of India and five UN agencies – UNDP, UNICEF, UNESCO, ILO and UNFPA-to provide prograqmme support to the ongoing efforts towards achieving UEE, Janshala, a community-based primary education programme, aims to make primary education more accessible and effective, especially for girls and children in deprived communities, marginalised groups, SC/ST/Minorities, working children and children with specific needs. A unique feature of Janshala is that it is a block-based programme with emphasis on community participation and decentralisation.

While UNDP, UNICEF and UNFPA together have committed a contribution of US $20 million for the programme, UNESCO and ILO have offered technical know-how. This is the first ever programme in the world where five UN agencies have collaborated and pooled resources to support an initiative in education.

The programme covers 139 Blocks, including 10 cities in 31 districts of nine states, i.e., Andhra Pradesh, Jharkhand, Karnataka, Madhya Pradesh, Chhattisgarh, Maharashtra, Orissa, Rajasthan and Uttar Pradesh with the approved outlay of Rs. 103.13 crores. Janshala Programme is to run for five years, from 1998 to 2002. The programme, at the state level, is being implemented through existing structures of educational administration.

Objectives of the Programme

1. To enhance and sustain community participation
2. To improve performance and teachers in the use of appropriate methods for multi-grade classrooms.
3. To enhance attendance and performance of school-age children, especially girls.

Approaches and Strategies of the Programme

1. Strengthen community-based mechanism for school management and support.
2. Develop government schools as empowered community schools.
3. Improve teaching methodology for multi-grade classrooms and develop empowerment package for teachers.
4. Apply an integrated social development approach to reach the difficult groups of children, especially girls.

Measurement of the children in their achievement levels is as follows as was evaluated by the SCERT in 50 schools in 4 development blocks (Mohanlalganj, BKT, Kakori and Chinhat) and one municipal ward (Hazratganj). The survey revealed the following facts:

- In Class II, the average level of learning for Language was 45 per cent and for Mathematics it was 52 per cent.
- In Class V, it was 41 per cent for Language and 34 per cent for Mathematics.

- In Class II, 13 per cent students were proficient in language, 19 per cent were moving towards proficiency and 18 per cent had achieved minimum level of learning (MLL). But 50.3 per cent of the students had not achieved MLL.
- In Class II, 22.6 per cent students were proficient in mathematics, 14.7 per cent were moving towards proficiency and 21 per cent had achieved MLL. But 41.7 per cent students had not achieved MLL.
- In Class V, only 0.6 per cent students were proficient in language, 8.5 per cent were moving towards proficiency and 42.4 per cent had achieved MLL. But 48.6 per cent students had not achieved it.
- In Class V, 0.7 per cent of students were proficient in Mathematics, 8.2 per cent were moving towards proficiency and 20.9 per cent had achieved MLL. But a high 70.3 per cent of the students had not achieved MLL.
- In 56 per cent of selected schools, the teacher-pupil ratio was 1:40.
- Category-wise, there was not much difference in students' achievement levels, though in Class V, scheduled caste students were better in Mathematics than students from other castes.

During the survey, it was realised that a majority of the children were reluctant to talk and even teachers were nervous. However, confidence grew and later both teachers and students started cooperating.

Teachers training had been taken up by the DIET faculty. Developed the Teaching Learning Material. Village Education Committees were formed and trained. MTAs/PTAs were formed and trained. Programmes like 'School chalo', 'Kalajathas', 'Summer Camps', 'Children's Fair', 'Shiksha Mitras', 'Computer Education', 'Training Camp for Disabled Children', 'Children's Own Library' and 'Educational Tours' are the major programmes envisaged in Janashala.

Mid-Day Meal Programme: In 1990-91 Seventeen State Governments were running the Mid-Day Meal Programme for primary school children of 6-11 age group with varying levels of coverage. Twelve states conducted the programme with their own resources.

Three states managed partly with their resources and with assistance from CARE. Andhra Pradesh and Rajasthan implemented the programme with CARE assistance and discontinued the scheme after CARE withdrew its support.

National Programme for Nutritional Support was introduced by the Government of India to Primary Education (NPNSPE) from 1995-96. NPNSPE envisaged a full coverage in a phased manner over a period of 3 years. The programme covered 2,499 blocks during 1995-96, 4,426 blocks during 1996-97 and 5,451 blocks during 1997-98. By December 31 1998, it covered 504 districts. It was expected to benefit 974.5 lakh students across 6.85 lakh schools.

The programme provides the states with the option of giving nutritional support in the form of any of the following alternatives

1. cooked meal (100 gms.) per day for 200 school days.
2. Pre-cooked meal or
3. 3 Kgs of wheat/rice per child per month per 10 months. Andhra Pradesh opted for 3 Kgs. of rice per child per month.

There was a limited variation in the attendance pattern of students during the pre-programme and post-programme period. The percentage of students with 80 per cent or more per cent of attendance rose from 59-64 between 1994-98. The proportion of boys having an attendance of 80 per cent or more was marginally higher as compared to girls. Caste wise, the attendance pattern of SC and OBC students was better than General and ST Category students.

Driven by the force of Article 45, Directive Principles of the state policy of the Constitution, the Education Commission/Committee Reports and Policy/Plan/Progamme documents have recommended several incentive schemes such as Mid-Day Meal, Free Text Books, Stationery, Free Uniform, Attendance Scholarships etc.towards the objective of UEE and UPE as a matter of priority.

Parents and school children expressed their preferences among the four major incentive schemes by placing them in the following order of priority:

Mid-Day Meal, Free Text Books, Stationery, Free Uniform, Attendance Scholarships.

Mid-Day Meal is the most popular incentive.

The Honourable Supreme Court of India, in W.P.No. 196/2001, dated 17-9-2001 directed the State Governments that hot cooked meal should be provided to all Primary School Classes children in Government, Government Assistant Primary Schools with a minimum of content of 300 calories and 8-12 gms. of Protein each working day of the school. (The cost is Rs. 1.25 per child per day besides rice/ wheat to the Implementing Agencies, Andhra Pradesh.)

The Sarva Shiksha Abhiyan is a historic stride towards achieving the long cherished goal of Universalisation of Elementary Education (UEE) through a time bound integrated approach, in partnership with States. SSA, which promises to change the face of the elementary education sector of the country, aims to provide useful and quality elementary education to all children in the 6 – 14 age group by 2010.

The SSA is an effort to recognize the need for improving the performance of the school system and to provide community owned quality elementary education in the mission mode. It also envisages bridging of gender and social gaps.

Objectives of Sarva Shiksha Abhiyan

- All children in school, Education Guarantee Centre, Alternate School, 'Back to School' camp by 2003.
- All children complete five years of primary schooling by 2007;
- All children complete eight years of schooling by 2010;
- Focus on elementary education of satisfactory quality with emphasis on education for life;
- Bridge all gender and social category gaps at primary stage by 2007 and at elementary education level by 2010;
- Universal retention by 2010.

During the meeting of Governing Council of SSA, February, 2005 it is revealed after four completed years of SSA (2000-04)inspite of SSA's mission mode programme there are only 47 children of the 100 enrolled in class I and enrolled in class VIII.

This is 52.7 per cent which, according to the Prime Minister is inacceptably high. The drop-out rate in classes I to V is 34 per cent while in classes I to VIII is 52.79. Amongst the girls the drop – out rate is 32.72 per cent while the same is in classes I to VIII is 53.45 per cent. Amongst the boys the drop – out rate is 38.85 percent while the same in classes I to VIII is 52.28 per cent.

The National Programme of Education for Girls at Elementary Level (NPEGEL)

The Govt. of India has approved a new programme called National Programme of Education for Girls at Elementary Level (NPEGEL) as an amendment to the scheme of Sarva Shiksha Abhiyan (SSA) for providing additional components for education of girls at elementary level.

The scheme could be applicable in a block where the level of rural female literary is less than the national average and the gender gap is above the national average. Mandals of districts which have at least 5% SC/ST population and SC/ST female literary rate below 10% shall also be taken up under this programme.

The target group is:

- Out of school girls
- Drop out girls
- Average girls, who have not completed elementary education
- Working girls.
- Girls from marginalized social groups.
- Girls with low attendance.
- Girls with low levels of achievement.

Development of material including teaching material, CDs, films and other material, helping in the review for development of textbooks, development of guidelines for incorporation of gender concerns, development compilation of supplementary reading material for girls including life skills, which would provide the support needed for girls education.

National Support group already headed under the Mahila Samakhya Programme at the Nation Level. Mahila Samakhya at State, District Gender unit and District Sub-District unit or Model Classes School in all selected district blocks be opened where the scheme is in operation.

At each model classes facilities will be used for learning through computers, film shows, reading material, self defence, life skills. riding bicycles, reading , games etc.

From 2004-05 the states prepared a sub plan for NPEGEL which have a part of SSA/DPEP and will be a district component of it.

LATEST TRENDS

Expenditure Trends

In DPEP–I, the cumulative expenditure upto August 2000 is Rs.647 crore, 73 percent of the approved project cost of Rs.882 crore. The cumulative expenditure in the European Countries assisted (Madhya Pradesh) upto 10th June, 2000 is Rs.420 crore, 84 percent of the approved cost of Rs.498 crore.

In DPEP- II , cumulative expenditure incurred upto August, 2000 is Rs.959 crore which is 41 percent of the approved budget cost. The cumulative expenditure incurred upto 30th June 2000 in respect of the DFID assisted project in Andhra Pradesh is 58 percent and in West Bengal about 36 percent.

In DPEP –III,(Bihar), the cumulative expenditure incurred upto August 2000 is about 16 percent of the EFC approved cost, while in Andhra Pradesh Eco – Restructuring Project (APERP) Education Component, it is Rs.250.72 crore which is about 44 percent of the approved cost of Rs.571.5 crore. In Rajasthan the cumulative expenditure upto 31st August, 2000 is only one percent and Uttar Pradesh DPEP-III is 2 percent of the EC approved project cost.

Mid-Day Meal

There was an allotment and expenditure of Rs. 1,675 crore during 2004-05. During 2005-06 the allotment is estimated to Rs. 3,010 crore.

The beneficiaries in the scheme are 11 crore children in the nation @ Re.1/- each child a day.

The ICDS has been extended to 1,88,168 Anganwadis.

There are 6,49,000 Angan Wadis in the country as the Government of India allocated Rs. 3,142 crore for them during 2005-06.

Child Labour

The Government of India, Ministry of Labour has been striving to remove the Child Labour through National Child Labour Programme (NCLP) during the X Five Year Plan (2002-07). The Government are going to release RS.1,25,000 to each society in the country to educate the masses on the issue of Child Labour. During IX Five Year Plan there is an allocation of Rs.249.60 crore while during X Five Year Plan the allocation will be Rs.602 crore towards the eradication of the Child Labour.

During the meeting of Governing Council of SSA, February, 2005 it is revealed after four completed years of SSA (2000-04)inspite of SSA's mission mode programme there are only 47 children of the 100 enrolled in class I and enrolled in class VIII.

This is 52.7 per cent which, according to the Prime Minister is inacceptably high. The drop-out rate in classes I to V is 34 per cent while in classes I to VIII is 52.79. Amongst the girls the drop – out rate is 32.72 percent while the same is in classes I to VIII is 53.45 percent. Amongst the boys the drop – out rate is 38.85 per cent while the same in classes I to VIII is 52.28 percent.

Expenditure of Government of India on Elementary Education upto 2001-02 on its GDP is 2.02 per cent.

Number of Recognised Educational Institutions during 2001-02 is 6,64,041.

Percentage of Primary Schools under different management during 2001-02 is

Government	47.75
Local Bodies	43.47
Total	90.92
Private Aided	3.07
Private Unaided	6.01

Enrolment by stages in Primary and Upper Primary Schools during 2001-02 is

(I-V) (VI-VIII) *(in Million)*

Boys	*Girls*	*Total*	*Boys*	*Girls*	*Total*
63.6	50.3	113.9	26.1	18.7	44.8
Scheduled Castes (In 000')					
12,251	9,253	21,504	4,551	2,945	7,496

Conclusion

The establishment of compulsory education is of considerable importance, and involves very complex measures. It calls for clear – sightedness, determination, prudence of great skill on the part of authorities. In a welfare country like India, it is of paramount importance to see that every citizen receives at least the basic quantum of primary education.

Ignorance not only prevents the Democratic ideal from being realized but also acts as a break on social growth and economic advancements. In fact it will not be wrong to say that through lack of elementary education, the full benefit of reforms in other spheres of life is not realised by the nation. It should also be appreciated that education and democracy should go together. It is in fact, futile to imagine a government resting upon popular suffrage to be successful unless those who elect for those who have to become the governess are purposely educated.

To be successful however, educational progress need, not only funds but substantial hard work, an ethical atmosphere, and cultivation of proper values of the entire academic community.

The most important aspect is the improvement of standards, the relating of education to local environment and particularly the introduction of work experience.

Even today there is much to do to fill in the gap of Social and Economic Inequality as thought of by J.P. Naik in the following lines:

"Education is a great levelling force. If elementary education is made universal, it will certainly help to reduce social and economic inequalities. But the very existence of these inequalities will hinder the provision of universal elementary education. The best results can, therefore, be obtained if there is a simultaneous attack on the reduction of social and economic inequalities".

"From the point of view of the Socio-Economic programme, it is necessary to adopt measures to cut down the consumption of the top 30 per cent of the people above the poverty line and especially to increase the consumption of the bottom 30 per cent. From this point of view, a programme of satisfying the minimum needs of the masses must become the 'core' sector in all our plans. It should include (1) the maintenance of a large public distribution system which will make the essential consumer goods available to all people at reasonable prices; (2) provision of employment to all so that every family has the wherewithal to buy the essential commodities; (3) liquidation of adult illiteracy and provision for non-formal education in the age group 15-25; (4) provision of cheap health services (with emphasis on programmes of drinking water supply and disposal of nightsoil); and (5) provision of housing plots with assistance to build cheap houses of their own. It is only such a plan that will help to improve the social and economic condition of the masses in the shortest time possible and will thereby accelerate the universalization of elementary education".

Let us remember the precious words of Gokhale in this context. The men and women who will be privileged to serve her by their successes will come later. We must be content to accept cheerfully the place that has been allotted to us in our onward march. We shall be entitled to feel that we have done our duty, and, where the call of duty is clear, it is better even to labour and fail than not to labour at all.

Let the schools have a question that what can we do within the available resources or with some feasible additions to them.

Let us dream of the schools to work as visioned by J.P.Naik.

(a) The school should be open for teachers on the prescribed day but the students should be required to attend a week later. In other words, in the first week of the opening of the school, the teachers should be on duty without being required to take classes.

(b) This period can then be conveniently devoted in continuous meetings and discussions and for preparing a detailed annual plan of work of the school in all its aspects: co-curricular, curricular, class plans, subject plans, and detailed plans for each progamme the school proposes to undertake.

(c) Similarly, at the end of the year there should be a week when teachers are on duty but the students have been let off. This week should be utilized for a careful evaluation of implementation of the annual plans.

If that process is taken care of, we will be in a position to uphold the vision of Education Committee 1964-66 which envisaged in its report.

"Qualitative improvement so that the standards achieved are adequate, keep continually rising and, at least in a few sectors, become internationally comparable."

REFERENCES

1. *India Education Report* – Prof. Govinda – NIEPA, New Delhi – 2002.
2. *EDU TRACKS– A Monthly Scanner of Trends in Eduation* – April, 2002. Neelkamal Publications, Hyderabad.
3. Working Towards a Common Goal – Janshala (GOI – UN) Programme, Department of Elementary Education & Literacy, Ministry of Human Resource Development, Government of India – New Delhi, (2002).
4. Teacher Education with special reference to AP – SCERT – 2001.
5. *DPEP Calling* – May-June, 2001.
6. *Sarva Siksha Abhiyan*, Ministry of Human Resource Development, Government of India – New Delhi (2000).
7. *DPEP Calling* – December, 2000.
8. *Universalisation of Elementary Education and Primary Education* – J.S. Rajput – 2000
9. *Landmarks in the History of Modern Indian Education* – J.C. Aggarwal – 1993.
10. *Pivotal Issues in Indian Education* – S.K. Kochhar – 1982.
11. *Elementary Education – A Promise to keep* – J.P. Naik – 1975
12. *History of Education in India (Modern Period)* – S.N. Mukerje – 1966.

13. *Education in India Today & Tomorrow* – S.N. Mukerje – 1964.
14. *Education and National Development* – Education Commission Dr. D.S. Kothari – 1964-66.

4

SECONDARY EDUCATION IN INDIA

Dr. K. Jayasree*

In our ancient tradition Education was regarded as the most important tool for self-realigation. So all progressive societies have committed themselves to the UEE with an explicit aim of providing "Quality Education for All". They have also recognised the significance of expansion of Secondary Education and simultaneously improving its quality. Secondary Education is the second level of schooling that falls between the Elementary-Primary level and higher educational/ College level.

In ancient India learning was considered as a means of Salvation/ Self-realigation. But British imposed English education focussing Western learning. Many Commissions have given their recommendations. After Independence also attempts were made for the quality improvement of Secondary Education but in Vain. Indian Education Commission has introduced '10+2+3' pattern in 1975. But critics considered the new patteern "A Fad, A Fraud and the Fallacy". National Policy on Education (NPE) was formulated which was evaluated further. To carry out the directions in the NPE, National Council for Education Research & Training (NCERT) prepared a model "National Curriculum" for S.E. Govt. has taken up many programmes at Central & State level. New innovative methods and techniques are being used. But much improvement was not seen. So it was suggested that atmosphere "free of fear" should be created. New techniques of teaching like CAM and ITM should be used. Teacher's own observance

* Faculty Member, St. Joseph's College of Education for Women, Guntur.

of basic values help children to internalise them. Girls' education has to be taken care of post elementary education should be job oriented. Women's associations help is also to be sought. The scheme of 'Computer Literacy and Studies' was introduced. But focussing life skills, accountability, maintaining dignity of students and emotional support for them should be the other goals of education. Balance between spiritual and technical productive based aspects is an urgent reform needed. It is in this context, paper probes into the present day challenges and opportunities for secondary education in India.

Introduction

Education has always been accorded an honoured place in Indian society. Education is not a simple unitary concept, that is it's not a concept like Gardening which refers to a particular activity.

'Savidyaya Vimuktaya' (Education is that which emancipates us). In our ancient tradition Education was regarded as the most important tool for self-realization.

Education is a process of human enlightenment and empowerment for the achievement of a better and higher quality of life. A sound and effective system of education results in the unfoldment of learners potentialities, enlargement of their competencies and transformation of their interests, attitudes, and values.

Recognizing such an enormous potential of education, all progressive societies have committed themselves to the universalisation of elementary education with an explicit aim of providing 'Quality Education for All'. They have also recognized the significance of expansion of secondary education, gradually reaching to a near universalization level and simultaneously improving its quality, effective empowerment of as many more learners as possible in order to achieve advancements in socio - economic and other domains of life. While higher education has also great potential in this respect, it can generally be made accessible to only a small section of the society. But school education can be provided in the present times to practically all members of the society and, therefore, its quality and efficiency assume special significance within the larger framework of personal, social and national development.

Meaning of Education

The Sanskrit word 'Vidya' is derived from its root "Vid" which means "to know". Education is the sum total of what is received through learning the knowledge, skills, ideals, values that are the out comes of learning as a process. It refers to the act of developing these in some one else or in one self. Education is also considered as the drawing out the best and making manifest what is latent in the child. In the later sense education is the moulding of the child after a preconceived model. This pattern varies with the socio - political - philosophical temper of the times and of the society . Hence

A.K.C. Ottaway Opined: "Education is an activity which goes on in society and its aims and methods depend on the nature of the society in which it takes place".

It follows from this that not only will educational systems and institutions be different but each society as will have its own ideal of men or cultural heroes for the young to emulate and the development personality will also vary from one culture to another. The ancient sages in India were all educational philosophers. In recent times this is fully illustrated in the case of Swami Dayananda, Swami Vivekananda, Sri Aurobindo, Sri Rabindranath Tagore, Dr. Radha Krishna, Mahatma Gandhi, J. Krishna Murthy etc.

Nomenclature of Secondary Education

Secondary Education is the second level of schooling that falls between the elementary - primary level and higher educational/college level. Before the introduction of 10+2+3 patterns of Education in India, there were several patterns of Secondary Education. The secondary stage consists of classes IX - X in 20 states/UTS. In other states/UTS, it consists of class VIII - X, senior secondary, intermediate stage consists of classes XI - XII in all states/UTS.

Education in Ancient and Mediaeval India

Education in India has undergone many vicissitudes before its political independence. Being a vast sub - content, there has been neither a national system of education for the whole country nor a common language as the medium of education. Religious philosophy has been a dominating factor in the field of education in ancient India. Learning was considered as a means of salvation or self realisation, mukti emancipation had been the highest end of life.

Brahmanical/Vedic Education

The Brahmanical education believed in mental discipline of its own kind. It involved control of mind in contrast to the training of mind as conceived by the westerns. The method of forming mind included recitation and meditation. The supreme methods were those of yoga and penance 'Chatur Vidha Purushardas' namely Dharma, Artha, Kama, and Moksha are the four ideals of life in ancient India. Education for the ancient Indians was both wordly and other wordly. The 'Guru' is the soul who quickens the process of self realization in his 'Shishya'.

Unfortunately this system of education received a big set back in the social changes that took place in the latter years. Vedic rituals and learning became more and more complex, caste system became more and more rigid, its operation restricted the educational opportunities. The rigidity, complexity, and exclusiveness of the Brahmanistic system led to a great revolt, which gave birth to two new religions namely Buddhism and Jainism.

Education Under Buddhism

Non-violence was the chief tenet of Buddhism. Education was very prosperous during the Buddhist period, which is rich in content and elaborate in system. It includes physical, moral, intellectual, and spiritual education. The education system aimed at the building up of character, the development of personality, and the preservation of the ancient culture of the motherland. The aim of education was to develop various aspects of life and also to ensure social service.

Education was imparted through monasteries, sangamitras. Even though the means of mass communication, media, transportation, Inventions, organisation and administration facilities of the modern times were lacking the Buddhist universities were an astounding phenomena at those times attracting the students from different parts of the world. The caste system did not influence the Buddhist educational centers. They were established to spread the gospel of Lord Buddha. The teachers were not Buahmins. Education was meant for all. The belief was that the mutual merit of man was not by birth or family status but by real merit.

Education Under Jainism

Vardhamana Mahaveera was the founder of the religion. Jain means a 'Conqueror' "Leader of school of thought". The nucleus of the sect had a strict monastic order which is eschewed ownership of everything mundane, even the garments. In A.D. The Digambaras develop into swetambaras, Wearing white dress liberation from the transmigaration of the soul was the chief tenet of Jainism.

Lord Mahavira made a very close study of social problems of his time and offered a number of solutions. His teachings, given about 2500 years ago are relevant today for the solution of many problems of man kind and for the promotion of world peace and international Brotherhood.

Education during the Mughal Period

Muslim systems of education had a theological basis. The philosophy of Islamic education had its roots in the 'Koran'. This is started in India in 7th & 8th centuries. There were two types of institutions, Elementary schools as private institutions are called as 'Muktabas' and High schools run in the mosque and at the residence of the teachers are called as 'Madrassahs' which are residential in nature and were meant only for boys. The methods of instruction were lecture after recitation, Imla (dictation), mutala, and muhasiba (assignment of a lesson), Tākror (repetition) etc. There was neither state control/state interference in the educational affairs with the exception of the rulers Shershah and Aurangajeb. Islamic education was primarily concerned with Muslims. Women's education was confined only to the upper strata and of higher order. There was no mass education it was extended to the Hindus too. It was sacred and democratic.

Education in the Pre-British Period

Before the advent of the British, there were indigenous schools for both the Hindus and Muslims doing immense service to the people. They were of two kinds. 1) Elementary schools 2) Schools of higher learning. Those who have aspired higher learning did not usually attend the Elementary schools but were educated at home only either by the parents or by the private tutors, engaged at home. Schools of higher learning are of two types again, one is patashalas of the Hindus and the Madrasah of the Muslims. The other Indigenous educational system of India had contributed the 'monitorial system' to England of which India can feel proud of. Even though this educational system had many favorable points to its credit, this system disappeared due to the indifference of the East India company and its policies. A new system of education (English education) imposed by the Britishers gained from grounds.

Education Under British Rule

Education in India under the British Government was first ignored then violently and successfully opposed, then organised on a system now universally admitted to be erroneous and finally placed on its present fooling. The Charter Act of 1813, made the company to accept the responsibility of educating the Indians, and allowed missionaries to spread western knowledge in India.

Education Under East India Company

The clause in the Charter Act 1813 is as follows: "To the effect, that after defraying civil and military expenses, a sum of not less than one lakh of rupees in each year shall be set apart and applied to the revival and improvement of literature and the encouragement of learned natives of India and for the introduction and promotion of a knowledge of the science among the inhabitants of the British territories in India". But this clause is vary vague with respect to how to spend this money. This led to many controversies. Hence the period between 1813 - 1835 is called as period of controversies. These controversies have been resolved partially by Maculays minutes in 1835 and laid the foundation of English education in India with focus on western learning. It says that "Create a class of people India in Blood and colour but English in taste and opinions in morals and in intellect". Lord Auckland's down ward filtration theory (1839) is also a failure. The wood's despatch (1854) is considered as an important land mark in the Indian educational history. It envisages many new schemes of education and was hence called as "The Magnacarta of Indian Education". Woods despatch (1854) says that education which is neglected is only company's responsibility which also encouraged grant-in-aid for the schools which follow Indegeneous system of education. The establishment of universities in the year 1857 had far reaching consequencies especially in the content, range, and scope of secondary education. The universities dominated secondary schools in every respect. Secondary education instead of being a self sufficient course preparing students to enter life after completing the course, became merely a step to wards the universities and university colleges with the result that schools could not function with an independent programme of their own.

Hunter's education commission report (1882) has advocated a policy of gradual withdrawal of the Government from direct enterprise leaving the secondary schools to private agencies with the exception of one in each district to be maintained by the government as a model school. Vocational and technical education for which diversified courses were recommended. A moral text book based on the fundamental principle of natural religion is recommended.

Curzonian Education Policy (1904) introduced improvement of schools and controlling private schools, introduced according of recognition to schools to send students for examination. As the result of the National Education Movement the modern Indian language came to be introduced as the media of instruction in schools. An atmosphere of nationalization and patriotic fervour came to prevail in all the national schools. The Education Commission of 1918 has reorganised Secondary Education by introducing intermediate course as the dividing line between Secondary Education and University Education. The Sargent Plan (1944) envisaged high school education for six years to select children between 11 and 17 and also recommended high schools were to be of two types - Academic and technical.

Education in Independent India

An opening balance on the eve of freedom is very disappointing. There were 5000 secondary schools with enrollment of 8,70,000 or 4% of the children of the 14-17 age group. The total expenditure on education was Rs. 57 crores or 0.5 percent of the total revenue of the government. Indian education had all along been like a Cindrella tied to the apron strings of the educational system of England.

Education was regarded as the potential instrument of social transformation and important means of development. So in a world of science and technology, it was education that would determine the levels of well being and prosperity of the people. The success in the grand enterprise of national reconstruction would largely depend on the quality of the young people.

During the pre-Independence period there was a unique expansion of secondary education, but it's quality was far from satisfactory. There was neither a planned development nor a deliberate attempt on the part of the British government for expanding secondary education. It was corollary to the mass awakening and public demand getting education. After Independence the face of expansion in secondary education was accelerated and various attempts were made for the quality improvement of secondary education in particular as imaginative well defined education policy is necessary.

Consequently a great priority was given to education and a large number of committees and commissions were appointed to inquire into various specific and general educational issues conforting the nation and suggested guidelines and recommendations for reformation and improvement. Importance of these are UEC, SEC, IEC, NPE etc., which reviewed various stages of education and suggested measures for structural and educational advancement. One after another, Five Year Plans were implemented since 1957 and considerable weightage was given on educational programmes both quantitative and qualitative. Education has been used as the main instrument of changes for the development of both physical and human resources. Emphasis has been laid on the strength of will, dedication and sacrifice for educational development and on social processes of education tousles tool, for realisation of national aspirations and for meeting national challenges.

The Secondary Education Commission recommended the new educational structure for secondary education after the 4 or 5 years of Primary or Junior Basic Education. So the secondary stage consists of class IX - X in 20 states/UTS. In other states/UTS it consists of classes XI - XII.

In order to meet the challenges, the Secondary Education Commission under the Chairmanship of Dr. A. Lakshmana Swami Mudaliar, V.C., Madras University was set up in 1952 and the commission submitted its report in 1953.

Development of democratic citizenship, vocational efficiency, personality and qualities of leadership are the 4 major aims recommended. It also recommended that multipurpose schools should be established to cater the individual differences of students to use and develop their natural aptitudes and inclinations in the special course of studies chosen by them. But the impact of the report on educational reforms in the country was negligible. In the independent India, inspite of a number of committees and commissions, satisfactory progress was not made. It was therefore felt that a comprehensive educational policy dealing with the aspects of education at all levels was needed. Accordingly the Government of India appointed the Education Commission in 1904 which is popularly known as Kothari Commission after its Chairman D.S. Kothari. It gave its recommendations in 1966. The following are considered to be significant.

(1) Significant role of education in national development and productivity; (2) Stress on science education; (3) Vocationalisation of Secondary Education; (4) 10 + 2 + 3 - uniform educational structure for the entire country; (5) Introduction of work experience as an integral part of school education; (6) Ten years of schooling of general education; (7) Specialisation or streaming in class XI and XII; (8) Increase in instructional days and minimising holidays; (9) Neighbourhood concept of schools; (11) Provision for adequate number of scholarships, establishment of book banks; (12) Identification of gifted students and special programmes for them; (13) Adequate residential facilities in schools; (14) More attention on the education of the backward classes; (15) Development plan for education in each district; (16) Two sets of curricula; (17) Prescriptions of three or four text books for each subject; (18) Importing of moral and religious education; (19) Guidance and counselling as an integral part of school programme; (20) Rich co-curricular programme; (21) Evaluation as a continuous process; (22) Creation of an Indian education services like IAS and other allied services; (23) Developing a wide range of correspondence courses; (24) Suitable pay scales for teachers; (25) Creation of Indian Education Services like IAS and other allied services; (26) Education acts to be passed by all states; (27) Three language formula.

Basing on the recommendations of Indian Education Commission the new pattern of education 10+2+3 was first introduced in 1975 in secondary schools affiliated to the Central Board of Secondary Education. Now almost all the states and UT have adopted the pattern.

New Pattern A Fad, A Fraud and the Fallacy

The new pattern is considered 'a fad' by its critics because it is based on the assumption that the compulsory teaching of mathematics and science upto class X will lead to the development of a scientific temper of mind of the students.

The critics call it a 'fraud' because its implementation has been only 'showy' and the authorities failed to provide necessary facilities. It is also pointed out by critics that it is a fallacy to assume that the addition of one year in schooling will lead to making students more mature and knolwedgeable. A review committee was appointed in 1977 under the Chairmanship of Ishwarbhai to review the syllabus and text books prepared by NCERT for the 10+2 patterns of education. The committee has introduced 'SUPW' instead of work experience, it also recommended broad syllabus frame and exclusion of subjects like economics, commerce and psychology in IX and X.

National Policy on Education

After 1947, for the first time a national policy on education was formulated in 1968. The policy guided the future development of education in India. The policy envisaged that the Government of India would also review, the progress made and recommended guidelines for future development. However, a review could not take place till 1985. After a country wide debate on the education reforms, made a new National Policy on Education was formulated and approved by the Parliament in May 1986 and a programme of action was chalked out.

The implementation of the NPE was evaluated by two committees namely Ramamurti Committee (1998) and Janardhan Reddy Committee (1992). These committees made some slight modifications in the NPE in 1992.

The main features of NPE (1992) with respect to secondary education are (1) National System of Education; (2) Navodaya

Vidyalayas; (3) Performance and Accountability; (3) Decentralization of the management of education; (4) Indian Education Service; (5) National testing service; (6) Raising resources. NPE 1986 has evirisaged that by 1995 all children will be provided free and compulsory education upto 14 years of age.

Revised NPE 1992 (para 5.12) has ensured that free and compulsory education of satisfactory quality is provided to all children upto 14 years of age before we enter the twenty-first century. A national mission will be launched for the achievement of this goal in respect to vocationalisation Review of the courses offered would be regularly undertaken. Government will also review its recruitment policy to encourage diversification at the secondary level.

The same suggestion is being stressed in NPE 1992 also by Ramamurti Review Committee (1990) on NPE. Rama Murti reviewed the NPE and submitted the report entitled "Towards An Enlightened and Human Society in 1991" (1) Development of a common school system; (2) Renewing disparities in education; (3) Right to education to be included in the fundamental rights; (4) Speedy promotion of women education; (5) Creation of work cultures reform in examination system; (6) Regional language as the medium of instruction; (7) Value education are some of the important features of the committee made with respect to secondary education.

CABE or Janardhana Reddy Committee on Policy (1992)

The Central Advisory Board of Education (CABE) was appointed in 1991 submitted its report in Jan 1992. (Revised NPG - 1992). The 10+2+3 structure has now been accepted in all parts of the country. Efforts will also be made to have +2 stage accepted of school education through out the country. The NPE (1992) gives more importance to dropouts, non formal education will be given importance and it shall ensured that free and compulsory education of satisfactory quality is provided to all children up to the age of 14 years before we enter the 21st century. A National Mission will be Launched for the achievement of this goal.

Curriculum and Syllabus

A UNESCO publication entitled "preparing text book manuscripts" (1970) has differentiated between the curriculum and syllabus. The curriculum sets out the subject to be studied, their order and sequence and so ensures some balance between humanities and science and consistency in the study of subjects has facilitating inter subject links. It follows that the curriculum determines the amount of school time allotted to each subject, the aim of teaching each subject, the place of the motor skills, which take time to acquire and possibly, the variations between rural and urban school teaching. The curriculum in the schools of developing countries is often directly related to the requirements for developments.

The syllabus determines the basic content of instructions in a given subject and the range of knowledge and skills which the pupils must acquire and establish in detail the themes and individual points to be studied in each school year. The syllabus is a refined detail of the curriculum at a particular stage of learning for a particular subject.

Curricular Patterns in Secondary Education

Educational system was geared to the needs of democracy, secularism and socialism. Attempts were made in the field of education to bridge the gulf between the objectives and realisation, to reflect the national needs and concern to serve rapid, economic development by increasing productivity to involve teachers and students in community activities, to promote social and national integration, to inculcate desirable, social, moral and spiritual values needed for a democratic and socialistic society. A high percentage of population belonging to SC, ST, BC are still socially underprevilaged or deprived among whom the number of dropouts, failures, and even unenrolled is too high. This is mainly due to their social, economic and psychological handicaps on the one hand and relevance, aversion and unsustainability of the educational system and academic programme on the other. Externally India is free but internally she is in chains. The chains are of many kinds and varieties - political, economical, social and psychological. Democratic spirit has yet to be infused into the mental makeup, habit formation and behaviour patterns. Our spiritual traditions should be reinforced with material culture of the west. We should take advatange of the Western advances in Science and technology and also of our own cultural and spiritual values. Man's knowledge and mastery of science and ideals of peace, nonviolence and compassion should go hand in hand. So science and Ahimas should join together in creative synthesis. Preparation of child for the democracy should be one of the important goal of education which is not only exacting but also challenging. Added to this education has to play a very significant role in promoting national and emotional integration and international understanding. The curricular aspects should reflect these issues and importance also should be given to cocurricular activities and crafts. So appropriate reforms may be introduced in the curriculum and new topics with all Indian importance and reference may be emphasized. Subjects like history, geography, social studies etc. were to be added to intensify national integration. After the recommendations made by many commissions keeing in view the above conditions existing and with a view to carry out the directives in the NPE, the NCERT, New Delhi, prepared a model National curriculum for Secondary Education (1988).

Curriculum Reconstruction in Secondary Education - A Brief History

1. The first major attempt was made by Gandhi (1937) who formulated Basic Education.
2. Diversified curriculum as suggested by SEC (1952-53)
3. A common curriculum for class I to X as suggested by IEC (1964-66)
4. 10 + 2 + 3 pattern was introduced in 1975.
5. Some changes in the curriculum as per the recommendation of Iswarabhai Patel Committee (1977).
6. Vocationalisation of education as suggested by Adiseshaiah Committee (1978).
7. National curriculum prepared by NCERT basing on the thrusts as contained NPE - 1986.
8. The CBSE, SBE modified the curriculum as per the recommendation of NPE.

Scheme of Studies Secondary Education - National Curriculum-1988.

National Curriculum for Elementary and Secondary Education (1988)

With a view to carryout the directives in the NPE. The National Council of Educational Research and Training (NCERT) New Delhi, prepared a model National Curriculum for Elementary and Secondary Education. The same was adopted by State Boards of Education and other agencies after making some modifications. The recommended schemes of studies for the Secondary Education is as follows.

	Subject	*Percentage of Time*
1.	Three languages	30
2.	Mathematics	13
3.	Science	13
4.	Social Science	13
5.	Work Experience	13
6.	Art Education	09
7.	Health and Physical Education	09
	Total	**100**

Curricular Reforms to be made

With the new challenges to be faced in the initial decades of the 21st century, which also marks the dawn of a third millennium, have profound implications, for the renewal of curricula, content and process of education. Curriculum and related aspects should be revamped and renewed urgently. It is time to initiate the process of having a fresh look on the curriculum in terms of context, approach and transaction. Mutual cooperation and collaboration between the school and the community is desirable for democracy and improvement of education. The school should be developed as the community centre or miniature community by making its programmes relevant to the life, needs and approaches of the people. Exchange programmes, talks by eminent people proficient in them, Parents Teachers associations, inviting parents to school functions, discussing about problems and progress of school and their children with them, sending detailed reports of the child to his parents are some of the innovations that can be made. Now-a-days SUPW has been introduced in most of the schools. Children are provided with opportunities of participating in social and economic activities in and outside the school enabling them to understand the scientific principles and processes involved in different types of work. The SUPW programme should involve cognitive conative, and affective knowledge and understanding as well as psychomotor skills of the students. Some activities related to health and hygiene, food, shelter, clothing, culture and recreation and community work and social service are to be taken up for SUPW programme. Students must realise that science must be harnessed for the welfare of mankind committed to high cultural and spiritual values. The essence of education should be "Asathoma Sadgamaya, Tamasoma jyothirgamaya, Mruthyorma Amurthangamaya". The following noble sentiments of best wishes for all the world expressed in vedic scriptures in the ancient life and culture have influenced its education as well through the ages. "Let all be happy and healthy Let all be courteous, gentle, and Let nobody feel the pinch of sorrow."

[Sarve Bhavanti Sukhani, Sarve Santumiramaya,

Sarve bhadrani pushayate, Makaschit dukhashaibhavat]

The curriculum should reflect these noble sentiments.

Methods and Techniques

Education functions as a stabilising force in a changing society. A society thus needs a stable set of values and unified purpose. Through utilisation of various methods and techniques education influences behaviour, forming habits and develops practices which are required of a good citizen. The Indian Society before independence was mostly traditional, and is suffering from casteism, communalism, and other social evils. The educational system was also mainly intended of producing educated persons 'Indians in blood and British in culture' in order to help maintain imperial administrative machinery. But now the Indian social order has to be modernised and science and technology have to be used for brining out propseity and happiness.

Philosophical Base for the Methods and Techniques to be used

Education is the quest for truth and non-violence. Mahatma Gandhi, one of the great teachers of human society (a profounder of non-violence) has rightly said that 'God is indefinable and his mysterious powers pervades everybody and everything in the universe.

God is life, light and truth. He is also an incarnation of the universal love and compassion. He has vividly said a proper and all round development of the mind can take place only when it proceeds pari-passu with the education of the physical and spiritual faculties of the child. Hence Gandhiji introduced 'craft' as the centre of the teaching learning process and tried to train the whole man - his body, mind and spirit. Dr. S.M. Patel observed that Gandhiji's philosophy of education is the naturalistic in its settings, idealistic in its aim, and pragmatism in its method and programme. Rabindranath Tagore, a world famous poet and an apostle of Satyam, Sivam and Sundaram tried to make educational experiments and innovations on the basis of intellectual, moral and spiritual values of the ancient India and worked for an understanding between eastern and western cultures. According to Tagore 'teaching while walking' is the best method of teaching. He was also an apostle of international brotherhood, modern humanism and national liberatarianism. Shri Aurobindo Ghosh is well known as a mystic or spiritual thinker, a patriot and a poet. Shir Aurobindo's educational philosophy is finding its fullest expression in the building of 'Auroville" called " a city of universal culture".

Know thy self (Tatwamisi), understanding the self (Atman) or knowing the inner aptitudes and aspirations of the child is the main task of the teacher. A good teacher is like light kindling other lights.

'Be fearless' is the sole message of Gita. Doing our duty as Dharma social welfare, Karmayoga (Communication of God through action) are the important principle teachings of Gita. Teacher has to use appropriate techniques so that pupils attain the ideal of self realised soul. The eight fold path of Buddha says that observance of purity is more than observance of rituals, non violence/noninjury are the main virtues of Jainism.

Swami Vivekanada has said the infinite knowledge of universe in the child's mind, the external world is only a suggestion, the ocassions which sets you to study his mind. He also said "We want education by which character is formed, strength of mind is increased, the intellect is expanded and by which one stands on one's own fact". The power of concentration is the only key to the treasure house of knowledge. Western science coupled with Vedanta - Brahma charya as the guiding motto and Shraddha in one's own self is the need of the hour.

Education of masses is also very important. They pay for our education, they build us temples but in return they get kicks. They are practically our slaves, if we want to regenerate India, we must work for the upliftment of these down trodden people. Our approaches should be of help to us in these contexts. There are various methods and approaches a teacher can follow like lecture method, lecture demonstration method, historical method, project, problem solving, laboratory heuritstic, Socratis, Questions and answer methods, and Inductive and deductive approaches etc. No method is superior. The teacher has to look for the context, content, and childs needs, capacities etc. More of activity centered methods have to be used. Sometimes the teacher may have to use interactive method through which she will be capable to give a scope for discussion among the children in order to develop not only social interaction but also better cognitive skills.

Inorder to make the child to learn in his own pace programmed learning which is a part of individualised instruction will be used, self learning modules, slide tape programmes and multimedia packages are some other means.

Programmes Undertaken by the Government

The All India Council of secondary education was established in 1955. The control of secondary school leaving examination was transferred to specially constituted boards of secondary education from universities. Extension services wings have been started in many secondary training colleges. The central board of secondary education was set for conducting a common all India higher secondary examination. Central schools were established. In order to improve science education, science club were established by AICSE and laboratory planning and developing science equipment were also established. In order to remove the defects, and maintain standards in text books, central bureau of text book research, was established in 1954. Central bureau of educational and vocational guidance was setup in 1954. On the recommendations of Education commission and in accordance with N. P. E., the CABE adopted an unanimous resolution in 1974 recommending the institution of 10+2+3 pattern of education all over India during the 5th plan during 1976–77. Vocationalization of education has become a state scheme. NCERT has started massive training programme for teachers and orientation to secondary education teachers. During Janata Government (1977) when national educational policy was implemented SUPW, social service and cocurricular activities have become part of curricular programme in secondary education. But there are still more reforms to be made.

Reforms to be Made

The threat of war, the nuclear bombs, the many tensions and conflicts that have brought about new crises are what is happening in the world. So a person has to be trained not only in technology but also how to meet these challenges adequately and completely. This should be the major function of education that is the function of school.

Everywhere in almost all the countries including India. There are technicians, scientists, educators, but who are unable to meet the enormously complex changes of life. So immediate action is necessary as the function of education is to bring about a mind that will not only act in the immediate but go beyond. In Krishna murthy schools learning implies the cultivation of the totality of the mind and the being of the child. It can happen only in an atmosphere that is "free of fear" thus enabling both teacher and students explore and question the world outside and within them selves. Nurturing the child's motivation to learn is to nurture the qualities like curiosity, freshness sense of wonder, and openness.

"You seek knowledge from books', what a shame ! you are an ocean of knowledge hidden in a dew drop" - the Sufi path of love,

For this the child should also develop deep inquiry and should also have a better understanding of concepts. The basic understanding of concept is essential for him to apply this knowledge in the situation he come across. At this juncture new techniques of teaching like concept attainment model (CAM) and inquiry training model (ITM) should be adopted. The CAM, enables the child distinguishes the positive examples for the concept from the negative and also identifies essential characteristics of the concept which definitely gives the child the "Basics of Thinking" and ITM teaches the child the inquiry process as it goes from facts to theories and develops process skills and also trains people to learn on their own. Learning is a joyful experience.

Taking cognizance of this, only committed professionals will adopt various methods of teaching taking into consideration how best to learn and bring about effective learning.

Teacher's Responsibility

Teacher is a second mother to the child. Apart from the curricular aspects the teacher should also take care of the child's other facets of development for an integrated personality development of the individual (child). For this the teacher evinces sincere concern and affection for the learner and is tolerant towards mistakes and mischiefs committed by them. The teachers have a very special role to play in motivating the deprived sections of the community to learn. This can only be done if teachers understand the community thoroughly and use various ways to mobilize it. Mobilised community can provide various resources to school personal as well as material to help the system. Therefore as a prerequisite, the teachers need to have deep concern and commitment towards the community which demands specific orientation. Basic values are to be inculcated in children by parents and elders at home and by teachers in schools. Teacher's own observance of basic values such as truth, beauty, goodness, honesty, love, punctuality, regularity, impartiality etc. will automatically help children accept and internalise them. Teachers have to undertake competency based teaching, develop remedial and enrichment programmes for respective groups, follows appropriate management techniques and set personal examples of value based behaviour. Teachers are expected to organise various types of activities and events in the school such as morning assembly, games, national events, annual programmes etc. to develop right attitudes and values. Schools are required to regularly arrange a variety of curricular and cocurricular activities including excursions, picnics, visits to museums, historical places, libraries and interactions with the individuals of outstanding creative attainments. Consequently every teacher needs to acquire excellence in performance outside the school inorder to effectively contribute to this sphere of activities through their vision, acumen and expertise in the changing times. Community can contribute continuously and significantly to the cause of quality schooling. Teachers too can contribute in constructive work undertaken by the community. Once the process begins in right earnest, the two way cooperation between the teachers and the community may go a long way in developing strong link between performance and competency in tune with the overall commitment of the teacher. The teacher should have the following competencies and commitments and performances for quality school education.

Competencies	*Commitments*	*Performances*
Contextual	to the learner	class room
Conceptual	to the society	school level
Content	to the profession	out of school
Transactional	to excellence	parents
Related to other	to basic values	community related
Educational activities		
Developing teaching learning material		
Evaluation		
Management		
Working with parents		
Working with community and other agencies		

Girls' Education in A.P.

It is estimated that around 16 million girls (58%) remain unenrolled (1997-98). Several factors seem to be suspending the education of girls. Girls are doubly affected by the absence of effective early childhood education programme as they are invariably burdened with the responsibility of taking care of younger siblings. Distance norms for opening middle schools, work against the interest of girls as often they are not allowed to go out of the village for schools. Further provision of basic infrastructure and women teachers in schools could considerably influence the situation through various EFA projects as indicated by recent efforts.

NGO's at Work

M. Venkatarangayya Foundation (MVF) of AP is doing pioneering work for imparting basic education for working children.

MVF emphasising the strengthening of Government schools, emerged not only as a basic programme of education but also an endeavour to bring about social change.

National plan of action for the SAARC Decade of the Girl child from 1991–2000

Rights can be declared and policies can be formulated to collect an liberal humanistic concern but unless the real life of the girl child in her family and community is torched by tangible efforts and actions, nothing can be achieved. Therefore a climate has to be created in which she can exercise her rights freely and fearlessly. One has to work for the transformation of those social and cultural values that shackle and constrict the girl child and mould her into stereotypical roles. For this, every forum and every platform should be used to create awareness and stimulate positive action. Along with this, effective implementation of the laws, for protecting her and provision of opportunities for her to benefit from them has to be insured.

Existing Problems

Secondary education is started as an urban middle class phenomenon and continues to be so even after fifty years of educational development in independent India. Rural female and urban poor form the bulk of the illiterate and out of school populations. Female literacy is negatively related with fertility rates, and shows a positive association with female age at marriage, life expectancy, participation in modern sectors of the economy and above all female enrollment. Rural urban and intergroup disparities were sharp.

Issues that Remain

Lack of provisions of post primary education for girls in remote rural areas and for disadvantaged groups, and not being able to give quality education, special focus on enrollment of SC, ST and OBC girls is also not being taken, absence of data in case of EBC, Education of out of school girls disability and therefore invisibility of children are some of the issues that remained.

Education being not free really, the minimal fees coupled with expenditure on books etc. being beyond the capacity of parents, a pervasive cynicism and frustration in the community is the major problem which has to be tackled immediately.

Improvement of quality of state and state aided schools, Curriculum reforms to make education more meaningful and relevant continued thrust on gender sensitive and gender inclusive curriculum and its transaction are needed.

Further gender inputs into pre and inservice education of teachers and teacher educators and text book writers and text book production boards is also needed.

Higher proportion of women teachers in rural areas is a must. Building up of inter sectorial convergence with respect to education, health, nutrition of children and adolescent girls. Building up of a functional relationship between the education department and panchayati raj institutions is also necessary. Lack of regular inflow of rural-urban statistics in girls education is another problem, so the following suggestions are made :

1. Alternate schools
2. Upgrading primary schools
3. Bus facility/motarable roads
4. Balika viday peths in every block (general education and vocational)
5. Problems of muslim girls taken care of
6. Vocational training for rural girls in health, employment needs to be installed. Transition rates for rural girls need improvement both at middle and secondary levels.
7. A national programme of strengthening science and maths teaching in all girls schools along with a scheme to meet shortage of science and maths teachers in girls schools needs to be installed.

For making girls education more popular school going should be made convenient and acceptable for girls. Special incentives should be given to women teachers, accommodation for lady teachers should be provided near the schools. A social climate should be created among the village community, family education should be made an internal part of secondary education Contents of education should emphasize the needs of women hood. The central and state governments should join hands and seek the cooperation of voluntary agencies. Part time education programmes are to be started. Post elementary education should be job oriented. Women's associations help also is to be sought.

Trends of A.P.

Andhrapradesh has been formed in 1956. The new syllabus was first started in 1959 - 60. When the introduction in course reached its 6th year (6th class) in 1964 - 65 the Government had appointed a high level committee consisting of eminent educationists and administrators along with the representative of UGC and the central ministry of education. The committee has recommended the 10+2+3 system of education. At the same time the government of India has appointed Kothari commission in 1964, which had similar structure to the entire nation. The recommendations of Kothari commission were approved and the government of India has issued a policy statement approving this structure as a national structure in 1968. Under these circumstances Government of AP has introduced the 10+2+3 pattern of structure in 1969 and had become the first state in the country to implement the educational structure.

According to the present structure, a student will have a minimum of 15 years of education to obtain a bachelor degree (general). In this system of school education the students takes two terminal examination and one main examination at 7th and other public examinations at the end of 10 years of schooling. There is another stream in this structure through which the student can divert from secondary school and take professional education, IIT and Junior Engineers schools etc. Intermediate is the basis to enter into the I degree courses. +2 or intermediate has been started from 1969. IEC recommended to transfer pre university to secondary schools by 75–76. But the state has preferred to establish Jr. colleges Educational development of AP did not get the advantage of an easy start of the patronage of feedal lords. After 1956 a systematic attempt has been made for universalisation of elementary education.

Early Christian Missionaries have made tremendous efforts in the direction. The policy perspectives, the curriculum, examination system and the strategies for curriculum transactions of the state level are largely determined by the directions given by NCERT, UGC and SCERT. The state government has established an autonomous body called the 'Telugu academy' for the preparation of Text books for all levels of education in Telugu, one of the most innovative educational programmes introduced by the Government was the scheme of residential schools. The main objective in introducing the scheme was to identify talented children of all classes in the age group of 9+ and then in creating an educational atmosphere by providing all facilities as a residential programme.

The scheme was considered to be forerunner for the Navodaya schools introduced in all parts of the country as a national programme in 1986. The Ashrama patasalas for socially disadvantaged groups is another innovative educational programme run by the department of social welfare and tribal welfare under the guidance of educational department. The examination results and the positions occupied by the students of these schools and colleges in Andhra Pradesh and else where speak about the achievements of the scheme.

The abolition of the detention system in school education in 1971 with two terminal examination, 7th and 10th standards is a successful reform introduced at the school stage.

Following are the other reforms made :

1. Free textbooks upto class V to all & for SC, BC, ST upto X class
2. Vocational education at secondary level
3. Operational Black Board
4. Midday meal
5. Integrated education for disabled as centrally sponsored scheme
6. A.V. Scheme
7. Open school system for children of 9 - 114 age group.

SCERT

State Council of Educational Research and Training is the organization at the State as NCERT (National Council for Research and Training) is the apex organisation at the National level which is designed to undertake research and training in Education at the school stage.

Functions

- Preparation of curriculum, syllabus. Instructional methods
- Development of quotation procedure and material

- Bridging gaps between method and techniques advocated in training and the actual classroom practices.
- Dissemination of knowledge to improved methods and techniques to be followed by educational institutions.
- Coordination with national and international organisations in academic programmes.
- Organisation of orientation programmes for the professional growth of teachers, teacher educators and superiors.
- Public action of journal, periodicals, books, etc.

Emerging Needs for Quality Education

- Establishing learning levels at the entry point of classes VIII, IX and X.
- Taking up remedial instructions identifying the hard sports.
- Improving educational level in a phased manner and raising the pass percentage in SSC upto 75% by 2005.
- Empowering training for improved performance
- Networking of resource institutions from SCERT to MRC level and
- Continuous resource support to teachers adopting, clientele based approach.
- Developing a strong base for recurrent in service training programmes by identifying among teachers and orienting them at state level by SCERT, IASE and CTE's.
- Organising training programmes for training handling maths, science, and English duly up dating the training package. 'GET SET' through CTE's and strong teachers organise need based training programme on "modular approach" through distance mode at every level so that clientele on large scale can be created.
- Disseminate latest trends on education through publications and distance mode by using state channels.
- Re-orient the vision and mission of resource institutions SCERT, IASES, CTE and CITEs to head toward knowledge based society.

- Upgrade the BEd curriculum. Make the BEd course for 2 years more M.Ed., colleges.
- A close and continuous dialogue with the attitude "Life long learner", rather "oracle of know all".

Curriculum Reforms made in Teacher Education

By having advanced methodology in MEd as a compulsory subject, Teachers in secondary schools can act help in guidance for continuing enrichment in the areas of methodology.

There must be a course in text book writing also at M.Ed., level. This can do more justice than others if they are given training and involved in text book, writing. Teachers in college of Education should have atleast 5 years of teaching experience in the schools without any break and two years of Headmaster ship. The experience helps professional advancement in the field of theory and practice of teacher education subject level professional associations to be started. A separate university of education is necessary to disseminate classroom research, official journal in education, apex body of education masters. Social changes are fairly rapid in the form of acceptance of new social values, developments of social needs and demands and so forth. They have educational implications. These developments and changes necessitate corresponding changes in educational objectives, Curriculum, methods and so on, and since preserves is just a stage, it can not serve the desired purpose. In service is capable of doing so. The scheme of computer literacy and studies 'CLASS' was introduced in the state during the year 1984-85 to provide students with broad understanding of computers and their use, to provide experienced hands in computers, to familiarise the students with the range of computer application in all walks of human activity and computer potential as computer information processor too, to computer and to develop competencies on using them

Vocationalisation of School Education

Vocational courses have been introduced in school education with a view to making school leaving pupils not only eligible for higher education but also to eqip them with skills required for gainful employment if need be.

1. Expose the students to vocational practice in the field relevant
2. Provide the students with essential information to familiarise them with the tools, materials and processes.
3. Need for skilled man power requirement.
4. Positive attitude for team work/self relevance and socially desirable values like dignity of labour, tolerance, cooperation etc.
5. Employment worthy, to take up self employment after the completion of apprentice training.

New ways of teaching like self study, discussion, independent thinking, project work, problem solving, using modern aids make class room interaction more interesting, challenging, rewarding and the students become active, use of guides, notes, dictation should be discouraged. Application type of questions to be asked. All the competencies required by the students should be evaluated. Devise strategies that will attract people who would be committed to education like:

1. Terms and conditions of service
2. Awards
3. Salaries
4. Sensitisation/Prevention of HIV/AIDS.

As per the statistical data for expenditure by level of education, the share of Secondary and Higher Secondary Education to total expenditure on all sectors was highest in 1999-2000 i.e. 4.97% and the lowest (4.09%) during 2001-2002.

There has been a considerable increase in the spread of educational institutions during the period 1950-51 and 2001-2002. During this period the number of Higher Secondary Schools are increased by 18 times.

Years	*High/Hr. Sec./Inter/Pre Jr. Colleges*
1950-51	7,416
1955-56	10,838
1960-61	17,329
1965-66	27,614
1970-71	37,051
1975-76	43,054
1980-81	51,573
1985-86	65,837
1990-91	79,796
1991-92	82,576
1992-93	84,608
1993-94	89,226
1994-95	94,946
1995-96	99,274
1996-97	1,03,241
1997-98	1,07,140
1998-99*	1,12,438
1999-2000*	1,16,820
2000-2001*	1,26,047
2001-2002*	1,33,492

High/Higher Secondary Schools

During 1973-74 to 2001-02, the maximum number of high/ higher secondary schools was under private management. The ratio of private managed to government managed varied between, 63: 37; 61: 39 in 1978- 79; 55: 45 in 1986-87; 53: 47 in 1993-94, 54: 46 in 1996-97 and 58: 42 in 2001-02.

However, a declining trend in the privately managed schools is observed while Government's share in the management of secondary and higher secondary schools increased to 38.96% in 1996-97 then slightly decreased to 36.16% in 2001-02. Further, the share of private aided high/higher secondary schools receiving annual grant from the government is declining while the percentage of private unaided schools is increasing.

Percentage of High/Higher Secondary Schools under different managements

Year	Govt.	Local *Body(LB)*	Govt. + LB	Private *Aided*	Private *Un-aided*
1973-74	26.54	10.85	37.39	57.02	5.59
1978-79	30.44	8.71	39.15	57.30	3.55
1986-87	37.49	7.73	45.22	44.79	9.99
1993-94	37.76	9.29	47.05	37.78	15.17
1996-97	38.96	6.74	45.70	36.20	18.10
2001-02*	36.16	6.29	42.45	33.99	23.56

Growth of Enrolment

The following table presents the growth of sex-wise school enrolment in different stages of school education from 1950-51 to 2001-2002. The total enrolment at the Secondary stages increases 20 times since 1950-51. The girls' enrolment is increased by 60 times during the same period in the above institutions.

Years	*Boys*	*Girls*	*Total*
1950-51	1.3	0.2	1.5
1955-56	2.2	0.4	2.6
1960-61	2.7	0.7	3.4
1965-66	4.4	1.3	5.7
1970-71	5.7	1.9	7.6
1975-76	6.5	2.4	8.9
1980-81	7.6	3.4	11.0
1985-86	11.5	5	16.5
1990-91	12.8	6.3	8.1
1991-92	13.5	6.9	20.4
1992-93	13.6	6.9	20.5
1993-94	13.2	7.5	20.7
1994-95	14.2	7.9	22.1
1995-96	14.6	8.3	22.9
1996-97	15.3	8.7	24.0
1997-98	16.1	9.3	25.4
1998-99*	17.3	10.5	27.8
1999-2000*	17.2	11.0	28.2
2000-2001*	16.9	10.7	27.6
2001-2002*	18.4	12.1	30.5

Girls Enrolment

The participation of girls at all stages of education has been increasing steadily through the years. Since 1950-51 girl's participation has increased many fold in Sec./Hr.Sec stages from 13.30% to 39.5%. However, the girl's participation is still below fifty per cent at all stages of education.

Years	*Sec./Hr. Sec./ Intermediate (IX - XII)*
1950-51	13.3
1955-56	15.4
1960-61	20.5
1965-66	22.0
1970-71	25.0
1975-76	26.9
1980-81	29.6
1985-86	30.3
1990-91	32.9
1991-92	33.8
1992-93	33.9
1993-94	34.3
1994-95	35.9
1995-96	36.1
1996-97	36.4
1997-98	36.6
1998-99*	37.8
1999-2000*	38.9
2000-2001*	38.6
2001-2002*	39.5

Scheduled Castes Enrolment

The total Scheduled Castes enrolment at the secondary/senior secondary (IX-XII) stages of school education from 1980-81 to 2001-2002 increased by 3.7 times. The Scheduled Caste girl's enrolment increased by 6.6 times during the same period in the above stages of school education. Sex wise details of enrolments for the year 2001-2002 are given in Table.

Enrolment of Scheduled Caste Students in Schools (in 000')

Years	*Boys*	*Girls*	*Total*
1980-81	906	246	1152
1981-82	973	273	1246
1982-83	1091	330	1421
1983-84	1395	382	1777
1984-85	1524	429	1953
1985-86	1378	432	1810
1986-87	1090	376	1466
1987-88	1521	507	2028
1988-89	1546	557	2103
1989-90	1701	630	2331
1990-91	1703	635	2338
1991-92	1878	703	2581
1992-93	1822	709	2531
1993-94	1981	827	2808
1994-95	1788	803	2591
1995-96	1854	887	2741
1996-97	1952	975	2927
1997-98	2026	1048	3074
1998-99*	2068	1149	3217
1999-2000*	2385	1399	3784
2000-2001*	2418	1994	3812
2001-2002*	2693	1622	4314

Strategies to be Taken

The first article of the World declaration on Education for all" adopted by the world conference on Education for all held in Jomtien in 1990 asserted that "Every person - child, youth, and adult shall be able to benefit from educational opportunities designed to meet their basic learning needs". Ten years after Jomtien, "The Dakar Framework for action" formulated six goals out of which the following there are applied to secondary education. (UNESCO, 2000, p.8)

1. To absorb primary school completers
2. Ensure gender parity in enrollment
3. Provide access for young people to appropriate learning and life skills. These are important for a child to pave way for him to a better adult life.

Global context sees peace and security threatened in many parts of the world from factors such as civil war, HIV/AIDS, poverty, wide spread degradation of renewable resources, illiteracy and attempts at cultural homogeneity. So education especially secondary education has a key role to play in making our world a better one. For all this skills are very important. Hence Dalor's report says that learning in schools need to focus not just in knowing but also doing, living together and being :

- Balance between vocational and secondary education
- Raise the awareness of importance of career guidance
- Increased flexibility and diversity in contents and processes
- Integrate technology and education
- Avoid over loading curriculum
- Standardized assessment system

are the important recommendations made for quality secondary education in the International Conference on Secondary education held between December 22 and 24, 2002 in Muscat. For successful implementation, a move from centralised to decentralised school and system management is necessary. Accountability in education is what is needed for evaluating the success of reform. The horrifying facts about violence be led to a serious consideration for which balancing between spiritual aspects and the technical productive based aspects is an urgent reform that has to be brought down. It is also crucial to maintain balance between what social institutions expect of students and how educators conduct teaching and listening in secondary schools. Maintaining the dignity of students should be the ultimate goal of education. Families should be emotionally suppórtive for their children.

The Redefining secondary education for 21st century says "After some successful examples of cooperative training, between industry and secondary schools, encouraging women and girls to join vocational training offering parallel, flexible nonformal schooling for those who are unable to join formal schools. Infromation, communication technologies also needed for the etied. More importance is to be given to discovery learning. There is an urgent need for secondary education goals to be linked more to sustainable development, citizenship and the world of work. Students are encouraged to be active in the teaching - learning process in all subject areas especially when students are introduced to information and communication technology. Initiating learning to live together is necessary by laying more emphasis on moral and human values and especially values of tolerance, dialogue and mutual listening. Human right clubs are to be established in secondary schools.

Schools should be gender friendly (i.e. such as building separate toilets for girls, issuing text books etc.) and affirmative actions such as helping poor girls financially, giving tutorial for academically weak girls and relaxing the selection criteria for entry into secondary schools should be promoted. Household chores should be shared among the siblings evenly. Government should also provide adequate infrastructure, housing for teachers, libraries/laboratories etc. provisions should be in such a manner that pupils go there not only to study but also to stay.

The allocation of students to different pathways depending on their state of readiness, their capabilities, their 'relaxations' and their desires as well as on the basis of reasonable ratios which take into consideration both individual choices and country's needs. So secondary education has to be redefined and structure the mind of the child and help him to locate/situate himself in an environment and gain control of his environment with respect to vocational education. More stress should be an vocational learning rather than just the notions of vocational education. Distinctions between blue collar (vocational education) and white collar (academic education) should not be valid and all doors should be open for competent learners through maximising flexibility.

Regarding commitment motivation there was a need for more comparative research related to social respect – what changes have there been in terms of financial incentives and social rewards, any 'increase' in social recognition and visibility through the media.

An experiment was made with an invention curricular in Malasia and found to be fruitful. According to this students are capable of creating artifacts that are beneficial and have commercial value. Importance has to be given to computer aided designs, self learning technical and living skills, students evaluating their own work because of which they will be tension free. Teachers also take interest in the students and helps at home also with their projects and motivate parents also to take interest.

Let the teachers and students have the vision of a quality classroom. By looking into the needs list of the academic and nonacademic goals made by the teachers, students and parents, teachers can elect leaders for each of the issues prioritized. Non academic activities include attendance, punctuality, discipline, cleanliness/hygeian, provision of clean drinking water, sanitation, maintenance of textbooks/note books, extra curricular activities etc.

Academic committees could be having leaders for each subject like maths, science, social studies, languages and encourage supervised study or peer teaching. The needs of the class are to be represented to the school development committee. This makes the child not only learning the life skills but also realising his rights and responsibilities which facilitates to meet the 7 R's of education namely Reading, Writing, Arithmetic, Rights, Responsibilities, Recreation and Relations. (social relations)

Conclusion

Population, pollution, poverty, peacelessness are the four important problems India is now facing. It was therefore concluded that unless illiteracy is eradicated not only mass poverty will be abolished but also democracy cannot be a success. "DAKAR World Education Forum" says that "No country can be expected to develop into a modern and open economy without having a certain proportion of its work force completing secondary education".

M. Ooreshosh says "Education is not acquiring a stock of ready made ideas, images, sentiments, beliefs etc. It is learning to look, to feel, to imagine, to believe, to understand, to choose and to wish. Young people are asked to hold them when they want to be held and leave them when they want to be left."

Whatever the reforms made and strategies developed, they have to be implemented whole heartedly. Added to this it is the mind of the person to be cultivated with good habits and initiation should come from him. Apart from the most excellent technological proficiencies, create the right climate and environment so that the child may develop fully as a complex human being.

This means giving the child the opportunity to flower in goodness so that he or she is rightly related to people, things and ideas to the whole of his life. So when the child leaves the school he is so well established in goodness both out wardly and inwardly.

We donot want bullets ruling the world but pigeons symbols of peace should rule the world. Arise, awake and strive for a peaceful world to create heaven on earth.

"Sarve Jana Sukhino Bhavanthu"

REFERENCES

1. Aggarwal, (2002), *Teacher and Education in a Developing Society*, Vikas Publishing House Pvt. Ltd., New Delhi.
2. Ahalya Chari (Chief Ed.), (2004), *Journal of Krishna Murthy School*, Krishna Murthy Foundation in India, Chennai.
3. Bruce Joycee, (1992), *Models of Teaching*.
4. Bhaskara Rao, D. (Ed) (2004), *Reforming Secondary Education*, Discovery Publishing House, New Delhi.
5. Department of Board of Studies, Ecology & Nuatural History, (1988), *Rishi Valley Experiment in Ecological Regeneration and Environmental Education - A Compitation*, Krishnamurthy Foundation, Nava Bharat Enterprises, Bangalore.
6. Govinda, R. (2002), *Indian Education Report NIEPA*, Oxford University Press, Delhi.
7. Jayasree, K. D. Bhaskara Rao, (1997), *Correlates of Socialization*, Discovery Publishing House, New Delhi.
8. Jayasree, K. D. Bhaskara Rao, (2004), *Methods of Teaching Science*, Discovery Publishing House, New Delhi.
9. Kochhar, S. K. (1990), *Methods and Techniques of Teaching*, Sterling Publishers Pvt. Ltd.
10. Kochar, S. K. (1982), *Pivotal Issues in Education*, Sterling Publications.
11. Murthy, S. K. (1982), *Contemporary Problems and Current Trends in Education*, Prakash Brother, Ludhiana.

12. Murthy, K.V.S.N., and Jayasree, (2004), *Bhoutikasastra Bodhana Paddatulu*, New Era Publications, Guntur.

13. Madras Mylapore Ladies Circle, (2004), *Quality Education*, Ladies Circle India, Kriticons Ltd., Chennai.

14. Mohanty, J. (1988), *Indian Education in the Emerging Society*, Sterling Publishers, Pvt., Ltd., Delhi.

15. National Council, (2002), *Hand Book on Paper Setting*, Secretary, NCERT, New Delhi.

16. Sree Rama Murthy, N., (2002), *Pradhamika Vidya*, Neel Kamal Publications Ltd., Hyderabad.

17. Subba Rao, K.P., et.al. (2004), *Pradhamika Vidya*, Sri Nagarjuna Publishers, Guntur.

18. Rama Krishna A. S., (2001), *Pradhamika Vidya*, New Era Publications, Guntur.

19. Rama Krishna A. S., (2004), *Patasala Nirvahana Vidya Vyavasthalu*, New Era Publications, Guntur.

20. Uma, D. and Sugandhi, (1986), *Inquiry Training Model-A Skill Based Approach*, Amit Udyog, Georgauu (E), Bombay

21. UNESCO, (2001), *The Invention Curriculum - A Malasian Experience*, International Bureau of Education, Switzerland.

5

NON-VIOLENCE
A TOOL FOR PROMOTING TOLERANCE IN SCHOOLS

A. Sriramakrishna*

The Gandhian principle of Non-violence as a tool to teachers to imbibe tolerance in Indian Schools at primary and secondary levels is presented. The methods to imbibe concepts of love, concern, compassion and goodwill to others along with freedom, justice Helmen Rights and conflict resolution as parts of big picture of non-violence that are needed to be adopted by the teachers are elaborated. The paper concludes with the string view that only Gandhian principles at early schooling will develop healthy, just and tolerant Society in future India.

Introduction

India has a long tradition of non-violence. Ancient Indian scriptures bear witness to the sublime message of non-violence and a long line of thinkers reinterpreted it to suit the social context from time to time. Notable among them have been Goutama Buddha, Mahavira, Nagasena, Ashvaghosha, Santideva, Aurobindo, Ramana Maharshi, Dayananda, Ramakrishna, Vivekananda and Mahatma* Gandhi. This line of ancient thinking is in consonance with the teachings of Jesus Christ and leaders of social thought like Ruskin, Tolstoy, Thoreau and Martin Lutherking.

* Reader, R.V.R.R. College of Education, Guntur.

So it is not entirely a new idea discovered and propagated by Mahatma Gandhi. We can find the origin of the concept of non-violence (Ahimsa) in the Upanishads termed as Vedanta which explain the metaphysical dimension of Yoga i.e., the seeming union of individual soul with the universal soul. The great Rishi Patanjali who formulated the Astanga Yoga (eight steps for emancipation) laid down Yama as the first step in which the individual aspirant has to observe the values of Ahimsa, truth, non-stealing, non-acquisitiveness etc.

The ancient Indian Rishis conceived of Ahimsa as a tenet of personal action and motivation. But it is Gandhi who made the principle of non-violence a popular method of social action. He, thus, attempted to apply the theory of Ahimsa enunciated by the ancient Indian teachers to the social and political plane.

The Concept of Non-violence-basic Principles

To understand the significance of non-violence it is necessary to acquaint oneself with the philosophy of Gandhi. Non-violence and Truth are the cornerstone of this philosophy. It will be helpful to reflect on what Gandhi meant by non-violence. The main principles:

1. Non-violence is not merely a negative attribute of abstention from injury to other living beings but is the positive virtue of love and compassion. Non-violence and love are one and the same. It connotes non-injury and passionless behaviour towards other human beings, animals and plant kingdom by not causing hurt or pain to them in thought, word and deed.
2. Non-violence is vitally integrated with truth which is viewed as God. It is the attribute of the soul, not of the body and therefore to be practiced by everybody in all the affairs of life. As non-violence and truth are intertwined it is practically impossible to disentangle and separate them. These two are both the means and the end.
3. the ultimate aim of non-violence is even to love the so called enemies or opponents. However, non-violence does not signify that man must not fight against the enemy and by enemy is meant the evil which men do not the human beings themselves. It is the acid test of non-violence that

in a non-violent conflict there is no rancour left behind and in the end the enemies are converted into friends.

4. A non-violent individual realizes that the same divine spark is present in every human being and will develop respect for all human beings and thus non-violence becomes a way of life – a way of life as the highest form of morality and spirituality.
5. Everything will be well with the man who follows the path of non-violence. The weapons at the disposal of the votary of non-violence are much more potent than those available to the votary of violence.
6. Non-violence must express itself through the acts of selfless service of the masses. Truth and non-violence demand that no human being may debar himself from serving any other human being, no matter how sinful he may be. A votary of non-violence cannot subscribe to the utilitarian formula (of the greatest good of the greatest number). He will strive for the greatest good of all and even die in the attempt to realize the ideal.
7. Non-violence is meant for brave never for the cowardly and abhors secrecy. It is fearlessness, Non-violence calls for the strength and courage of highest order to suffer consciously without retaliation to receive blows even for self-defence. It does not however mean meek submission to the will of the evil doer, but it means pitting of one's own soul against the will of the tyrant.
8. True non-violence means a complete freedom from ill-will, anger, envy, hatred, malice, lust, cupidity and uncharitableness. A non-violent individual replaces these negative qualities with love and compassion. In this effort he will not use physical force or retaliate violently but will employ peaceful non-violent non-cooperation as the technique for changing the status quo.
9. A votary of non-violence must cultivate the habit of unremitting toil, sleepless vigilance and ceaseless self-control. The richest grace of non-violence will descend easily upon one who follows hard discipline.

10. A non-violent individual while developing self-esteem will also recognize the dignity of other human beings. He does to other, what he expects them to do to him. He or she regards the whole world as one family. He will fear none nor will others fear him.

11. Non-violence is impossible without humility, self-examination and self-purification. It requires great patience and painstaking practice.

12. The science of non-violence can alone lead one to pure democracy. It respects the rights of others and at the same time their duties towards others. Through dialogue and consensus it strives to establish a non-violent global social order and to respect a variety of cultures. All society is held together by non-violence. Non-violence as boundless love crosses all boundaries and frontiers and envelops the whole world.

13. Non-violence is not merely a personal virtue. It is also a social virtue to be cultivated like other virtues.

14. Non-violence is the law of our species as violence is the law of the brute.

The aforesaid fourteen principles based on non-violence not only make the concept of non-violence clear but also provide situational and behavioural guidelines to test whether a particular or action is non-violent or not.

Main Principles of Gandhi's Concept of Tolerance

Tolerance implies abjuring the use of force and violence. It is associated with a package of human and social conditions the fulfillment of which is a pre-requisite for a culture of peace. Intolerance develops from a belief that one's own position is absolutely right as against the positions of others. It results in a feeling that one's belief system is superior to that of others. Instances of intolerance extend from simple lack of consideration for others to a cult like Apartheid in South Africa or Genocide of Jews in Germany during Nazi regime. Mahatma Gandhi was always ready to concede and accommodate the viewpoints of others on various matters though he had strong convictions. Gandhi's concept of tolerance embraces the following:

1. It is essentially based on appreciation for religious differences.
2. A tolerant person does not hesitate to adopt into his faith every acceptable feature of other faiths.
3. No religion is superior or inferior. Every religion is right from its own standpoint. Every religion contains certain features which may look odd to others. Hence, the necessity for tolerance.
4. True knowledge of religions breaks down the barriers between faith and faith. Cultivation of tolerance for other faiths will impart to us a true understanding of our own.
5. Tolerance does not mean indifference to one's own faith but a more intelligent and pure love for it.
6. Tolerance gives us spiritual insight which is as far from fanaticism as the north pole is from the South.
7. Tolerance consists in the realization that all principal faiths of the world are based on common fundamentals.
8. Tolerance is the only thing that will enable persons belonging to different religions to live as good neighbours and friends.

Basically Gandhi's reference to tolerance relates to the religious context but it has wider application to all other areas of human life-language, region, dress, food habits etc.

The Relevance of Gandhi's Concept of Non-Violence and Tolerance in Education Today

Today violent behavious is looming large and is on the increase day by day in all the countries but with a degree of variations, irrespective of social system, religion, philosophy and ideology. The two world wars and the growing threat of a third world war with weapons of mass destruction and annihilation, the continuing civil wars, the growing terrorism all over the world, the violent behaviour witnessed even in the classrooms, harassment of womanhood, suicides, homicides, rape, murder, crime, arson, loot, racial and communal riots all over the world manifest the height of violence and intolerance. Against this background Gandhian philosophy of non-violence which is essentially universal brotherhood and love is more relevant today than ever before.

While the present day curriculum does not adequately reflect the imperative need for non-violence, there is no denying the fact that the present day world requires the cultivation of qualities in the students committed to non-violence as a way of life for the simple reason that the alternative to it is disaster. Probably never in the history of the world the need was greater than at the present time for the inculcation of the virtues of non-violence. In the Indian school practice some stray lessons are found with the import of non-violence. Incidentally some episodes from the life of Mahatma Gandhi are narrated. But, they do not add up to much by way of conveying in effective way the message of non-violence with a view to influencing interpersonal behaviour. Before the message becomes the staple of the school routine teachers have to be prepared by exposing them to a planned programme of assiduous cultivation of non-violence.

The pedagogical programmes to promote gandhian principles of non-violence and tolerance at primary and secondary levels

The message and the practice of non-violence should cross the classroom threshold the primary and lower secondary. The transact this curriculum teachers have to adopt certain methods and strategies. Whenever questions of this land are discussed it is debated whether the material should be passed on to the clientele in the form of direct teaching or indirect assimilation as part and parcel of teaching various subject in the school curricula. It would appear that the latter method of conveying the message of non-violence is more advantageous and effective as direct teaching does not make a lasting impression. Non-violence as a message and habit should form an under current of the whole process of teaching and inter personal interaction in the school. It is commonly felt that non-violence cannot be internalized by mere cognitive learning. It has to be accompanied by attitudinal change through a series of planned programmes and activities.

Love, Concern, Compassion, and Goodwill for others: Non-violence can thrive better when there is perfect harmony between individuals and groups. Schools have to create the desired environment for the young ones to develop such harmony.

The concern and coring for others and the promotion of goodwill between individuals and committees can be realized by the student in following way. The teacher and the students may spotout a sick child or a child poorly clad or undernourished. This situation will enable the teacher to initiate a discussion in which the participating students show concern for the child who needs help. In this connection, the teacher will draw the attention of the class to the need to go for the help of the needy. He can cite examples of world leaders who have shown concern like Goutham Budha, Mahavira, Jesus Christ, Mahatma Gandhi, Martin Luthor King, Mother Terisa, Nelson Mandela and others. A detailed account of the concern shown by such great personalities can be given in a few minutes narration on their birthdays also. The techniques followed by them showing concern to the needy will be better appreciated by the children in this way.

Gandhi is very much influenced by some stories and lives of greatmen of the world which convey the message of non-violence and love. An episode from the life of Buddha wherein henurses and gives comfort to a wounded dove is the best example for teaching love and care. The entire life story of Buddha abounds in non-violence. He opposed animal sacrifice in the performance of Yagnas for propitiating Gods. The story of Sravankumar was another which deeply impressed Mahatma Gandhi. It is the story of a devoted son who carries his old parents and serves them with great care and love. From Indian mythology several stories can be cited from the lives of greatmen to underline the importance of non-violence. For example a story is told of a kite pursuing dove. The dove rests on the shoulder of emperor Sibi. The kite protests that it is denied the enjoyment of its prey. Sibi cuts a piece of flesh from his own thigh and offers it to the kite to save the life of the dove. This is the ultimate in compassion and sacrifice. Teacher may also narrate similar stories selected from other sources dealing with the same themes.

Students can also be asked to play the roles of various characters appearing in these stories, developing their own dialogue depending upon the class level.

The concern for all living beings can be developed among students by encouraging them to rear some pets like dogs, goats, birds, etc., Similarly students may be encouraged to plan saplings and rear them. They may also be encouraged to volunteer for service on the occasion of festivals, jataras and other occasions when large number of people congregate.

Visits to hospitals, orphanages, homes for the aged, mentally retarded and other social institutions will greatly help to show how the society is concerned about the needy. Concern for others and caring are an important part of non-violent attitude to life. Planned visits to these institutions will foster love and concern for others and appreciation of non-violence.

Audio-visual materials like films, videos, pictures can be shown while narrating the stories or lives of greatmen or explaining the works of the institutions mentioned above. A photo or a film on Gandhi caressing a leper in his Ashram or kissing a small kid may also be shown.

When this capsule is completed the students may come forward to form into a social service group or adopt scouting for their own class or institutions.

When concern shown for the needy neighbours goodwill is established between individuals and groups of individuals which will inturn promote the spirit of non-violence and strengthen social harmony.

Teacher may maintain anecdotal records of each student wherever he shows concern for the needy either in the school community or neighbouring community. No verbal tests will be helpful to evaluate the outcomes of these objectives, as the actual behaviour of the students in specific situations only can be assessed whenever occasion presents itself. Teacher need not bother about evaluation of all students at a given time immediately after the unit is completed. He may ask the students to narrate the related stories or the good deeds of greatmen or account of the school visits organized in relation to this unit.

Empathy

Since the same divine spark present in every living organism suffering of anyone has to be taken as one's own suffering. Such sense of equality of living beings has necessarily to be promoted through love to all living organisms, which is positive non-violence.

To enable the students to place themselves in the position of others by developing empathy and to work for welfare of the community during normal times and also in times of distress can be realized in the following way.

The class community may notice that a few students are not regular in attending the school. When the causes for their absenteeism are investigated into, many pitiable family situations preventing them from attending the school may be revealed. This is an occasion for the fortunate lot among the student community to place themselves in the position of the unfortunate children who are unable to attend the school due to adverse family circumstances. They may not afford the school dress, books, nutritious food, facilities to study at home, affection from the parents or guidance at home. Children of equal I.Q. placed in such divergent family situations are bound to show varying achievement. In order to correct such deprivation it is necessary for the affluent to share the difficulties of those less fortunate bretheren and also the community to uplift such deprived lot. For this purpose after discussion in the class on specific factors contributing to such a situation they may decide to raise donations from the community, contribute to the poor fund in the school, forgo lunches and contribute the money for their welfare, donate books, dress etc., and also associate themselves closely with such children both at the school and at home to encourage them to keep in step with the progress in the class. This discussion may be extended to the various welfare schemes launched by the state and Union Governments and social service organizations. When such discussion is organized students will naturally project themselves imaginatively their own consciousness into other beings; their work and art sharing joys and sorrows with them. Such empathy will enable one to identify oneself emotionally with others which is essentially for the development of the idea of feeling of oneness and solidarity of all living beings with love as its basis for promotion of non-violence and tolerance.

The teacher may also cite the work of social service organizations like sisters of charity, Ramakrishna Mission, Satya Sai Seva Samithi, Red Cross etc., who help people in distress like earthquakes, floods, tornado, forest fire, storm, tidal waves etc., Knowledge of these service oriented, philanthropic organizations will broaden the sympathies of school going children and help them develop an abiding interest and commitment for the service of the poor, week and the handicapped sections of the people.

Evaluation of these objectives are situational when students express readiness to go to the help of others in times of some difficulty to other members in school community or neighbourhood. Overall evaluation of all students need not be attempted. Only attitudinal changes are expected for such a discussion in relation to such objectives.

Freedom, Justice, Humanrights and Conflict Resolution

Conflicts arise out of struggle for power and advantage and in this process freedom, human rights and justice are transgressed.

To understand the nature, causes and sources of conflict and to explore, understand and use methods of conflict resolution at the local, national and global levels. To develop disposition to fight for justice, freedom and human rights when they are denied. To understand the relationship between struggle for power and violence and to find out ways and means of reasonable sharing of power for the welfare of the community. The following method can be adopted by the teacher to teach his students.

Students aspire for office to gain recognition and popularity in the management of student affairs. In this process there will be conflicts of personal interests and programmes. Such conflicts lead to violence on school and college campuses. Similarly conflicts arise in the state politics among leaders, sections and factions for sharing of power and advantage. In state polities stakes are very high. Political positions are very few and the aspirants are many.

Power is necessary for promoting social welfare. Keeping this in view the aspirants to positions should work in a cooperative manner sharing power with an attitude of give and take avoiding conflicts for the common good. This requires a close scrutiny of causes, generating conflict so that the same may be avoided.

In the struggle for power freedom of the opposite party is curbed and injustice done by violating human rights which are basic for equality, democracy and welfare. It is the duty of every enlightened citizen to organize civil disobedience or non-cooperation whenever freedom, human rights or justice are denied. Many incidents can be quoted from the life of Mahatma Gandhi when he fought for freedom, Justice and human rights. Mention may be particularly made of the philosophy of Satyagraha developed by Gandhi. Satyagraha (moral pressure) was a unique weapon invented and fashioned by Gandhi to protest against unjust order of things. He adopted Satyagraha during his stay and struggle in South Africa against racist oppression. Episodes like the following and the knowledge of a Satyagraha may be taught to students.

In response to a special situation faced by Indian settlers in South Africa Gandhi developed the technique of Satyagraha. Transwal Government promulgated an ordinance in 1906. Every Indian men and women or child of 8 years or upwards residing in transwal were to register his or her name with the registrar of Asiatics and take out certificate of registration. Indians who failed to apply for registration before a certain date ran the risk of losing residence in the transwal. Failure to apply for certificate was an offence in Law. Even a person walking on public thoroughfare could be required to produce his certificate. Police officers could enter private houses in order to inspect certificates. Gandhi organized the Indians and held a meeting in 1906 to protest against this unjust ordinance. The Indians, solemenly determined not to submit to the ordinance and suffer all the penalties attaching to such non-submission. The movement was given the name Satyagraha. It meant firmness in a good cause.

Several episodes of Satyagraha exercise like the champaran incident where the technique was practiced against Indigo planters who were taking advantage of the poor tenants in Bihar and the principles to be followed by Satyagrahi like the following can be taught to students.

6

TOWARDS IMPROVING QUALITY OF HIGHER EDUCATION

N.V.R. Jyoti Kumar*

India in the last five decades has developed a very large system of higher education. In spite of a quantitative expansion, only 6.7 per cent of the Indians in the age group of 17 to 23 is getting the benefit of higher education. In this paper, an attempt is made to highlight the need for improving the quality of higher education in India and to identify the dimensions that affect the quality of higher education.

In the backdrop of economic reforms and globalisation, it is felt that the Indian educated youth need to acquire relevant skills and competitive spirit in order to get better jobs in industrial sector. Globalisation has impacted every sector of our country including higher education. The present day students are highly mobile over national boundaries as more students prefer the foreign universities in search of quality education. Such a phenomenon will result in heavy drains on the foreign exchange reserves of the country. Many institutions of higher education across the globe are in the process of achieving excellence by developing international standards on the lines of ISO. The Indian institutions must conform to these standards to survive and thrive.

* Reader, Department of Business Management, Mizoram Central University, Aizwal - 796 012, Mizoram.

Introduction

India in the last five decades has developed a very large system of higher education. Since independence, the number of universities has grown from 18 to 256, colleges from 591 to about 10,000 and students from 0.2 million to seven million. In spite of such a quantitative expansion, only 6.7 per cent of the Indians in the age group of 17 to 23 is getting the benefit of higher education. Besides unequal opportunity of access, deteriorating relevance and quality of education and research, inadequate infrastructure, growing commercialization, relative decline in allocation of funds and mismanagement of educational institutions are some of the serious problems faced by higher education in our country. In this paper, an attempt is made to highlight the need for improving the quality of higher education in India and to identify the dimensions that affect the quality of higher education.

The phenomenon of unemployable graduates in India is attributable to the low quality of education and lack of relevance of the courses. Significant differences exist among the higher education institutions in terms of their administrative system, management practices, sources of finance, infrastructure facilities and quality of faculty. In the context of sweeping global changes and changing societal needs, the quality and relevance in higher education has to be raised to great extent. For example, India's share of publications in international journals has been less than five per cent. The number of international patents filed from India in recent years has been less than one per cent which means that we are not able to compete globally.

The national bodies like the UGC, the state governments and the universities generally apply the norms of 'minimum standards' of performance while permitting the new colleges or renewing the affiliation to the courses offered by such colleges. But an engineering college recognised by the AICTE cannot necessarily be taken as the one meeting even the minimum standards. As admitted by Dr. Hari Gautam, "Untaught students, non-teaching teachers and non-performing institutions are unfortunately not uncommon both in private and government sector... Work culture has been damaged beyond repair," S. Anandalakshmy, a well known educationist, said "

There are a few great institutions that offer quality education for students. But there are a large number of institutions, where lecturers intone an oft -repeated lecture, where readers do not read much that is relevant and where professors profess not knowledge, but merely superiority."

An eminent industrialist, Rahul Bajaj, in a convocation address observed, "It is the quality and level of education and training which will, in the coming decades separate successful countries and companies from those that will be left behind." Amartya Sen, the Nobel laureate, delivered a keynote address in the inaugural session of the South Asian Conference on Education held at New Delhi. He pointed out "University education in India is in a state of crisis. It is not a crisis of lack of resources. It is deterioration of quality... When it comes to higher education, there is no escape from seeking the highest quality we can get. Quality would vary from one university to another. However, the minimum level of quality should be ensured."

Such well known experts put forth many reasons for revamping the system of higher education on the issue of quality. In the backdrop of economic reforms and globalisation, it is felt that the Indian educated youth need to acquire relevant skills and competitive spirit in order to get better jobs in industrial sector. Globalisation has impacted every sector of our country including higher education. The present day students are highly mobile over national boundaries as more students prefer the foreign universities in search of quality education. Such a phenomenon will result in heavy drains on the foreign exchange reserves of the country. Many institutions of higher education across the globe are in the process of achieving excellence by developing international standards on the lines of ISO. The Indian institutions must conform to these standards to survive and thrive.

Dimensions of Quality

The quality of higher education depends on several factors. Bharat R. Sant identified the "core activities" that affect student development. They are: Quality of teaching, quality of examination process, quality of faculty development programmes and quality of courses.

Considering the student as a "customer", Ramachandra Aryasri in his study made an attempt to assess the level of the student delight in the environment of a technological university. He opined that several time-tested management concepts such as total quality management, business process re-engineering, academic audit, learning organisation, life-time learning, experiential learning, industry-institution interaction cannot be, any longer, confined to classroom discussions. No institution has got all the elements of perfection. But, the best practices which are adopted by premier institutions are not generally shared by others.

Since 1997, India Today has conducted an exclusive national survey every year to help students identify the centres of excellence in every major stream: Arts, science, commerce, medicine, law and engineering. In 2001 survey, the respondents were asked to distribute ten points across the seven parameters on a high-to-low importance basis: Reputation, curriculum, academic input, student care, admission procedure, infrastructure and job opportunities. In 2001 survey, quality of academic input was considered the most important factor followed by the reputation a college enjoys and then by curriculum, student care and infrastructure. In engineering, job opportunities assumed higher importance.

Dr. Ishikawa, a famous Japanese scientist, outlined the factors that affect student delight as: Academics, the environment in which the institution of higher education operates, administration, infrastructure, extra-curricular and examinations.

The present discussion is confined to three dimensions of quality, viz., teachers, administration and courses offered.

Teachers

The destiny of India is shaped in her classrooms. In olden days teachers were mainly responsible for passing on information from generation to generation. But, the big challenge in the twenty first century for teachers is to compete with the mass communication and also the internet. According to an estimate, the whole world's codified knowledge base (all documented information in library books and electronic files) doubled every 30 years in early 20th century. By the 1970s, the world's knowledge base doubled every 7 years. Information researchers predict that by the year 2010, the world's codified knowledge will double every 11 hours. Hence, the present day teacher has to prove to the world that nothing can replace him and nothing can substitute the face to face interaction in the classroom.

Although the pay scales of teachers have been increased significantly, they do not command much respect as in the past. In Andhra Pradesh, aided college teachers are very much involved in engaging private tuitions and they are responsible for setting up of residential colleges of their own. Such aided teachers often work against the interests of their parent colleges with a view to promote their commercial goals. There is a paucity of leadership on the administrative and political fronts to protect the interests of the underprivileged students who cannot afford to pursue self-financing courses.

The UGC, however, is aware of the crucial role teachers ought to play in the education sector. Their insistence on teachers passing the National Eligibility Test and their investment in Academic Staff Colleges could be considered indicators of such awareness. In order to improve the quality of teaching in the institutions of higher education, the following measures are suggested.

1. A mechanism for continuous evaluation of teachers by students.
2. Classroom visitations by subject experts.
3. Team teaching.
4. Active involvement of the teachers in the design of the courses.
5. Making the orientation and refresher courses more relevant and participative centered.
6. Changing the reward system so that effective teaching is adequately recognized; and
7. Stringent measures against those teachers who engage private tutions or who run private colleges.

Administration

Many aided and government colleges in the country, along with many state universities, suffer from chronic mismanagement. It is also proved many a time that the academic standards in aided and government colleges are low. Therefore, those students who are coming from economically and socially backward classes and who cannot afford to pay high fees in private colleges are the worst affected.

Over the years, the universities and government developed a myopic view of their roles in the filed of higher education. The universities need not be merely an affiliation granting bodies and the governments also need not be a mere funding agencies. Higher education institutions should prepare their mission statement keeping in view of the needs of the local and regional environment. The suitable strategies have to be evolved for the improvement of the performance of the institutions.

The UGC is contemplating to develop at least 20 universities of excellence which shall be able to provide the superior quality of education and research backed by special funding and greater autonomy. Universities should realise that autonomy and accountability are two sides of the same coin. Affiliated colleges account for about 85 per cent enrolment in higher education. A system has to be devised to encourage the colleges to make innovative changes and to experiment with new ideas. A fresh look need to be given to the scheme of giving autonomous status to colleges with a view to identify the major problems faced by such colleges.

Heads of the institutions, vice-chancellor in the case of universities and principal in the case of colleges, are the formal leaders. Nowadays, most of the principals are appointed solely on the basis of seniority and vice-chancellors are selected purely on the basis of political considerations. Such leaders generally do not possess the required visionary and managerial skills and they cannot serve as role models for fellow teachers. As rightly pointed out by Rahul Bajaj, "To realise our goals and aspirations, we need outstanding leadership in every field and at every level. Leadership means that there is no substitute for excellence, no tolerance of mediocrity and no compromise with integrity. Leadership is not just charisma, not public relations, not showmanship. Leadership is performance, consistent behaviour and trust-worthiness."

Courses

The higher education institutions in the twenty first century need to offer such courses which are in tune with the needs of the society and the expectations of the industry. The courses must be capable of meeting the challenges of social changes. The institutions need to design a variety of short duration courses keeping in view the specific requirements of underprivileged areas and groups. Vigorous efforts should be made to develop short-run vocational and technological courses. These courses must be aimed at the generation of employment. In recent years, it is observed that certain distance education institutions are providing flexibility is terms of choice of subjects in a given academic programme, and the time over which they may be pursued. The social science institutions have to prepare themselves to meet the challenges of knowledge driven information society. In case of professional courses like engineering and management, the partnership of the industry should be solicited in managing the affairs of the educational institution and in designing the curriculum. In fact, the philosophy of TQM is driven by the constant attainment of customer satisfaction through the continuous improvement of all organisaational processes. To achieve this, the higher education institutions should elicit the cooperation of all the stakeholders such as teachers, parents, students and alumni.

REFERENCES

1. Rahul Bajaj, *Outstanding Leadership*, convocation address at the 49th annual convocation of the SNDT Women's University, Mumbai.
2. S. Ignacimutha, S.J., *Quality, Relevance and Excellence in Higher Education*, convocation address delivered on 3rd March 2001 on the occasion of the convocation of IGNOU regional centre, Chennai.
3. Ramachandra Aryasri *Customer Delight in University Environment*, University News, April 2000, pp 3-13
4. Hari Gautam, *Sleeping Giants*, convocation address at the 18th convocation of Dayalbagh Educational Institute (Deemed University), Agra.
5. Bharat R. Sant, *Towards Achieving 'Excellence' in Higher Education*. University News, May 8, 2000. pp 3-7.
6. Raj Chengappa, *Top 10 Colleges of India*, India Today, May 21, 2001, pp 34-52.
7. NVR Jyoti Kumar, *Improving the Quality of Higher Education* (Telugu) an editorial page lead article, Vaartha, May 6, 2000.
8. NVR Jyoti Kumar, *Privatiasation of Higher Education* (Telugu) an editorial page lead article, Andhra Jyoti, October 17, 2000.

7

QUALITY CULTURE AND ACADEMIC GOVERNANCE

Dr. K. Chandrasekhara Rao*

The article presents a frame for academic governance in the light of the developments taking place in the international economic scenario, application of information technology tools in various sectors, and corporate governance as practised in the corporate sector. In the industrial set up, governance has been tuned towards adopting the new management systems such as ISO 9000 processes, Total Quality Management (TQM), and six sigma management systems. Product modernization and process modernization are increasingly taking to new pattern of corporate governance. Similar changes need to be brought about in academic governance of educational institutions by taking appropriate steps. A few steps suggested for reorienting academic governance are involvement of professionals and consultants to provide direction, and increase value addition to the decision making process, open house arrangement to make all the members of academic bodies accountable, and conducting of annual academic audit in every institution. It is suggested that the universities could adopt strategic business units, key successor factor, SWOT analysis, back office operations, etc.

* Head, Department of Commerce, Pondicherry University, Pondicherry.

Internationalization is the Reason for Quality Consciousness

Of late, the opening up of economies through Liberalization, Globalization measures and slowly but steadily adopting to WTO and GATT norms in every aspect of public system is the basic reason for quality consciousness during the recent past. In Industrial set up the Governance has been tuned towards adopting to new management system like ISO 9000 processes, TQM, six Sigma management systems. Product Modernization, Process Modernization are looking for adopting to better management practices, which are popularly called Corporate Governance in Industrial set up.

Public Systems Management through the principles of Koutilya's Arthasastra

If one draws from the givings of our ancient literature, Koutilya's Arthasastra clearly specifies the principles to be adopted in the management of any public system (even like Educational System) as follows:

1. Raksha – Protection of values, resources, culture, society.
2. Vridhi – Enhancement, value addition, growth profitability, social benefit.
3. Palana – Maintenance, smooth functioning of systems, fairness in dealings, broader social welfare oriented.
4. Yogashema – Safeguarding the health, equity, social benefit.

These principles become the Frame of Reference in the design of any Governance System. Against this background we have to explore into the better practices for Academic Governance.

WTO and Higher Education

Subsequent to GATT/WTO meeting at Doha it is abundantly clear that Education as a service is getting into the list of globally tradable products. Developing countries like India are expected to make their commitments in this regard. Few basic issues that are likely to change the present structure of Higher Education in the light of WTO could be as follows:

- Permission to Foreign Universities to open up their campuses in India.

- University Faculty positions are to be opened up to Global citizens (not to be reserved to only Indian Citizens/Indian Degree holders).
- Tenure appointments flexibility to shift to different Institutions/organizations.
- Indian Universities to get the MoU with foreign Universities to provide training to their students.

As we have seen in other fields, the WTO regulation are likely and slowly but surely will become reality in few years to come. The participants have no other go but to adopt to them.

IT Revolution and the Future Teacher

The application of IT in educational services has changed the structure of Teaching-Learning Process. Virtual Universities, cyber classrooms, online Lectures, Learning materials are becoming the reality. This is the challenge for Traditional Teacher, who is likely to be out of job if he fails to become flexible enough to specialize and mobile from one environment to another. The benefits likely to commensurate with the flow of Teaching Services globally. Effectiveness of TRIPS and TRIMS, Patent Rights makes one to be creative to continue in this field.

Corporate Governance—A Model for Academic Governance

The challenges of Globalization has been addressed by Corporate sector by adopting better management practices often called as 'Corporate Governance' Code. Hither to, closely held Board of Directors are now opened upto invite expertise from Executive Directors, Non-executive Directors from the fields of Economics, Academic and Finance. The cases of Dabur and Infosys are noteworthy. These boards are now made more accountable to stakeholders like owners (equity shareholders), customers, employees, suppliers, government through Annual General Body (AGM) meetings. Drawing the lessons from the experiences of Corporate Sector, educational institutions are also expected to strengthen their Governing Bodies with not merely academicians but also with professionals, consultants who can provide value addition to decision making process. These professionals should be able to provide direction to the growth of the Academic Governance.

Accountability of Academic Bodies—An Open House

Like in corporate sector the education system has its own stakeholders viz., students, teachers, employers of the young graduates, society and the government. In case of corporate sector, the effectiveness of polices taken up by the Board of Directors the end result of their decisions are evaluated and questioned in AGMs. Similarly there should be an Open House arrangement to make all the members of Academic bodies accountable to their decisions at periodic intervals. These open houses should be able to provide a platform not only to evaluate the past decisions but should be able to provide future direction periodically. While Board of Studies, Academic Councils be made accountable for Degree Programs, their suitability, Job potentiality, knowledge creation, value addition, contemporary ness and social relevance, the policies, programs, decision of Higher bodies be evaluated from the angle of their future consequences and strength to the survival of educational institution, image buildings etc.

ILLS IN HIGHER EDUCATION

Need for Academic Audit

In context of constructing a knowledge society the linkage between degrees and jobs/careers was been given a go-by. Every college/university is escaping from the responsibility of finding the salability of the subjects trained by them. Even the programs designed have become obsolete. Professional degrees like MBA, MCA have failed to incorporate the much needed practical internships before a graduate comes out of the campus. Today, we see the failure of business systems one after the other – Bank failures – Fialures of Mutual Funds – Crash of stock markets – Currency crises – purely because of lack of intlligence and skill needed to make the systems to work on efficient line. Educational institutions should take up responsibility for failures in systems which much depend upon the knowledge imparted in University system.

In the light of it, there is a need for annual Academic Audit in every institution. Like Financial Audit, the Academic Audit should explore into the value added nature of products designed in educational institutions. Why not universities close down generic degrees and go for application oriented programs? The schools of Management should for Job-order product design rather than producing and finding the lack of market for products. Lack of salability of 'subjects' may gradually lead to 'sickness' to the organization itself.

Administration Reforms are Urgently Needed

By following the practices adopted in successful business enterprises, universities can also think of concepts like Strategic Business Units (SBUs), Key Success Factor (KSF), SWOT Analysis, Back office operations etc. and try to adopt them. Suppose, if few schools/Directories are performing well, adoption of SBU concept will make the unit more accountable for results. The admissions, examinations may be given to Event Management Consultants. Hostel organization, campus maintenance, conveyance and Transport, Student support systems may be outsourced. Special Consultants may be appointed to assess Human Resource requirement in different disciplines before deciding on the Academic Programs.

8

CHALLENGES IN PROFESSIONAL EDUCATION IN EMERGING INDIA

Dr. C. Ramachandra Prabhu*

Since the dawn of education sector in India through all its ages, be it the ashrams of rishis, be it the Gurukulas of yester years, be it the world renowned universities of early India like Takshasila, Vikramashila and Nalanda, be it the Madrassahs of Muslim India, be it the colleges and Universities of British India or the institutions of learning of developing India in these five and half decades of independence, professional education is considered as "Education for wealth creation". In the present days of changing global scenario and particularly in the transition period of India from developing to developed nation by the year 2020, from that rugged stage professional education grows and matures into a grandeur beyond compare and with it also grows many novel challenges. The challenges like quality and quantity in curriculum, adoption and adherence of international standards to combat the spreading Foreign Universities, Creative Visualization, Inculcation of Moral and Ethical Values, Impact of Information technology, awareness in Environmental protection and laws, Human rights and above all the training for developing a well rounded personality of both teacher and the taught are explored in this paper along with other intricate and interlinked factors. The change in philosophy to be adopted by one billion of Indian people to collectively emerge as a super power is to shift from individual to group consciousness and this transformation should be echoed in

* Lecturer, Department of Physics, RVR & JC College of Engineering, Guntur.

the philosophy of our educational institutions. It is highlighted that embarking on an ambitious plan starts with articulation of success route until it becomes a routine with every individual involved in the process. In this light, the need for immediate implementation of pro-active planning in our Indian Professional Training Institutes is presented with emphasis on weighing intellectual abilities more than infrastructure.

Introduction

The dramatic changes in India in the past ten years are many folded. New economic reforms, adoption of right technologies in industry, green revolution, human rights protection, enforcement of environment protection laws, self sufficiency are to name a few. Many new ideas are finding place in almost all internal and external factors relating to growing India. So ideas, and born to them ideals, have echoed back and forth between two major classes prevailing, in India i.e. Rich and Poor. The rich and the poor of India are locked in a three legged race and simply cannot break free from each other and further the upward mobility of any of this class is also obstructed by strong and inflexible social structures. Gandhiji the founder father of the nation had foreseen this problem long back in his Sarvodaya movement (i.e. Welfare for all) and imbibed in us that "development means not just the advancement of the greatest number but it is a collective forward marching of both rich and poor. This total concept is dominant in India's Social philosophy down the age and has been articulated quite unambiguously, which is the greatest challenge going to be faced in professional education in the sense that the belief mechanism of future professionals of India has to be filled with this endurance.

Emerging India and Vision 2020

The emergence of India is a dream of our beloved President of India accepted by all Indians. The central factor identified for emergence of India by Dr.Kalam is knowledge. Knowledge has always been the prime mover of prosperity and power. The acquisition of knowledge has therefore been the thrust area throughout the world, and knowledge society can be the foundation for building a developed India (Abdul Kalam). In the words of Arun Shourie, India has to walk on many legs at the same time besides having focus as a national effort, scale and execution of the target by giving up the mentality that India is a country of shortages, deficits and smallness and by improving the pace and quality of execution of all the undertaken projects. His prescription for India to emerge as a super power (Arun Shourie) is to develop agriculture, manufacturing, services, information technology and education simultaneously without getting distracted by labels – he is for agriculture, she is for manufacturing and the like. Instead, the approach should be everybody is for the development of all fields. The former Union Minister Arun Nehru, feels that trade and economic matters have to dominate the political agenda for India to emerge with the end of cold war. He suggests that the global economy has to be dealt as an effective player, to create and distribute the wealth and to satisfy public demand for economic prosperity by a modified political decision making structure (Arun Nehru).

The dream of visionary President on emerging India was amalgamated in the form of a vision statement to stir the imagination and to motivate all segments of society to greater effort. It is an essential step in building a political consensus on a broad national development strategy, which encompasses interalia, the roles and responsibilities of different agents in economy, such as Central, State and local government, the private corporate sector, the small and tiny sector, people's organizations etc. The vision statement identified the potential risks and bottlenecks and their possible solutions in order to mobilize efforts in a focused manner such that it can operate at several levels of generality and specificity. The official document entitled "India: Vision 2020" was formulated by Planning commission by constituting a committee on Vision 2020 for India in June 2000 under the chairmanship of Dr.S.P.Gupta Member Planning Commission. This initiative brought together over 30 experts from different fields. Their deliberations, extending over a period of more than two years, has helped to throw up a range of interesting possibilities, critical issues and crucial decision points for government and private bodies for future action. The report of the committee examines many important issues, but the ones that stand out most powerfully are employment and education. In order to ensure access to food and other essentials of a healthy life for all citizens, India faces the challenge of generating 200 million new employment opportunities over the next two decades.

The report calls for rising employment generation to the top of the nation's development agenda and marshalling all available resources to create employment opportunities for all job seekers. It goes even further by identifying the sectors which offer the greatest potential for job creation as well as critical policy issues that need to be addressed in order to fully tap that potential. Education is the second main thrust area of this document. Greater coverage and better quality education at all levels from basic literacy to hi-tech science and technology is the essential prerequisite for raising agricultural productivity and industrial quality, spurring growth of India's budding IT and biotechnology sectors, stimulating growth of manufactured and service exports, improving health and nutrition, domestic stability and quality of governance. The report calls for concerted efforts to abolish illiteracy, achieve 100 percent enrolment at primary and secondary levels, and broaden access to higher education and vocational training through both traditional and non-traditional delivery systems. The document also examines issues related to population growth, food production, health, vulnerable sections of population transport, communication, energy, self-sufficiency, water conservation and air quality, trade investment, peace, security and governance. It gives projections of India in 2020 in business as usual and in the best case scenario in various important sectors and also identifies nodal points of Indian prosperity. Its central conclusion is that India has the opportunity to emerge as one of the world's leading economies over the next two decades, provided her citizens have self-confidence, the self reliance, the will and the determination to realize their individual and collective potentials (K.C. Pant).

The concept of emerging India and implementation of Vision 2020 was well supported by the report released by a leading investment firm of the world named Goldman Sachs. The main argument put forth by this report is that by the year 2050 the economies of Brazil, Russia, India and China collectively called as BRIC have a combined economic weighing outstripping that of G6 advanced nations which include the US, Japan, Germany, UK, France and Italy, in US dollar terms (Dominic Wilson and Roopa Purushothaman). Among the BRIC economies, India has the potential to grow into the world's third largest economy in less than 30 years from now after the US and China and by 2010, India's growth rate should exceed that of China. The report further forecasts that China will be the largest economy in 2050 at US$ 44.5 trillion followed by the US at $ 35.2 trillion and India at $ 27.8 trillion. The report also highlights that while growth in the G6, Brazil, Russia and China is expected to slow down significantly over the next 50 years, India's growth rate remains above 5% throughout that period. Further, India will be among the three largest economies of the world but with its per capita income will still be low, which phenomenon is expected to be true for all BRIC countries, except Russia. The report further states that individuals in Brazil, China and India will continue to be poorer on an average than those in G6 countries.

Challenges in Professional Education

Professional education means "that training imparted in an educational institute which makes the individual to get belief in certain doctrines and helps him to acquire knowledge in some branch, which can be used in his later life to publicly practice for earning a livelihood". Providing professional education is globally an onerous responsibility on the part of teachers because it calls for multi functions of teaching, training, invoking belief mechanism, drawing an ever disappearing thin line between technological advancement versus ethics and morality among the tender aged students with fragile personalities within the predefined frame work of professional education as "EDUCATION FOR WEALTH CREATION". Added to these responsibilities, the changing global scenario and particularly in this transition period of India from developing to developed nation by the year 2020, the new challenges that are tapping the intellectual doors of Indian professional teachers are the quality and quantity in curriculum. As rightly pointed by Inderesan, there are two models of advancement, the East Asian and the western. The East Asian model is based on high savings (hence, large investments) on quality education and borrowed technology. This model is liable to saturate and become unstable, because even if we make every one a Ph.D., there will not be any commensurate returns for the huge investment. The western model is based less on savings and capital formation and more on technology innovation. Unlike the returns from capital and education, which level off, technology innovation appears to have no bounds (Inderesan). The curriculum presently used in Indian professional education system is more classical or true replica of western system. The quantity and quality of curriculum should be made in tune with our aspirations of emerging as super power by 2020 and should contain more of the Indian context rather than craze for novelty.

The adoption and adherence of international standards to combat the spreading Foreign Universities in India is becoming mandatory. The standards in teaching, evaluation and certification should be checked comprehensively with knowledge gained by the candidate as the main criteria rather than anything else. The Indian tinge already incorporated in the quantity and quality of curriculum should not be sacrificed for the sake of International standardization. As the saying goes, if you build a better mousetrap, the whole world will beat its path to your door. That means, technology innovation will attract money. Creativity means to use one's intellect to produce novel and meaningful ideas. Imagination is the ability to create an idea or mental picture in one's mind. In creative visualization one has to use his imagination to create a clear image of something one wishes to manifest. Professional education should contain some training on creative visualization with step by step development of creativity coupled with imagination, methods for continuing to focus on a particular idea or picture regularly and giving it positive energy until it becomes an objective reality.

The Impact of Information technology should rightly be exploited by all the professional training institutes with appropriate design of their instruction by fostering mutual co-operation between information technologists and academicians reciprocally reinforcing each other on the deficiencies rather than quarrelling on the issue of who is superior to whom. The awareness in Environmental protection and laws should be made mandatory in the course work of every type of professional education as a clean and safer environment is the very basis of human existence on this planet. Every professional at one or other stage has to interact with fellow humanbeings and every professional act will reflect on some human element and in this light an abridged version of basic human rights should be taught in every professional course. The vision which the billion Indian people have adopted collectively has many intricate and interlinked factors other than the few mentioned, which challenge the very existence of tomorrow's professionals and hence a rigorous training is needed for developing a well rounded personality of both teacher and the taught.

Adoption of new philosophy and implementation of Pro-Active planning in institutes of learning

The change in philosophy to be adopted by one billion of Indian people to collectively emerge as a super power is to shift from individual to group consciousness and this transformation should be echoed in the philosophy of our professional educational institutions. It is needless to highlight that embarking on an ambitious plan starts with articulation of success route until it becomes a routine with every individual involved in the process. In this direction, the need for immediate implementation of pro-active planning in our Indian Professional Training Institutes with emphasis on weighing intellectual abilities more than infrastructure is the need of the hour. A special cell containing the experts in the institution with atleast two consulting experts involved in the vision 2020 should be initiated in every institute offering a professional course.

Freedom is the bottom line which should be reflected (1) in all our plans for growth (2) and while identifying and finding immediate solutions during growth period (3) and finally in making rules for staying stable and secured after the attainment of growth. Equality is one impossible thing which cannot be achieved among all the staff and students of our institutions because of our diversified backgrounds but if properly planned, we can achieve equity in implementation of the rules and regulations. Freedom and equity are two key factors which assure confidence in our professional teachers and they in turn can ignite a silence revolution in students with whom they interact and this finally lead to explosive results in achieving our collective target of becoming a developed nation.

To implement an ambitious vision plan which accommodates all the sentiments grown and nourished over the tough times of pre-independence and post-independent India becomes a perpetual walk on a razor's edge. Today's easy options could prove to be tomorrows regrets, and the temptation to cut corners for immediate benefits and the tendency to superficialise democracy be strongly debated and also has to be immediately curbed. The above two perspectives should be adopted on war footing as co-curricular activities in our institutions and all our professional teachers have to be first trained about the implementation of India Millennium Missions.

In order to chart a new course to navigate these existing and challenging times, we need to recognize the role which many key factors can play in pursuit of emerging India. The role of professional teacher in catching these enduring heights of emerging India in all its fineness and exploring the challenges and opportunities to embrace all the exuberance of developed nation by the year 2020 is like the honey bee extracting the nectar from flowers and depositing in the hearts of budding professionals of our mother India. As bulk producers of future citizens of India who may become planners, implementers or simply general public who has to be motivated, our professional teachers will play a major role in Emerging India.

REFERENCES

1. Abdul Kalam, A.P.J, 2003: *Igniting India's mind - The Week*, Dec. 28, Vol. 22 No.4, Malayala Manorama Publications, India, page-20.
2. Arun Shourie, 2003: *Dreaming a Big Dream - The Week*, Dec. 28, Vol. 22 No.4, Malayala Manorama Publications, India, page-64.
3. Arun Nehru, 2003: *More Pioneers, Please - The Week*, Dec. 28, Vol. 22 No.4, Malayala Manorama Publications, India, page-28.
4. Inderesan, P.V, 2003: *Aiming for the sky - The Week*, Dec. 28, Vol. 22 No.4, Malayala Manorama Publications, India, Page-48.
5. Pant, K.C, 2003: *India Vision 2020* - Academic Foundation Publication, New Delhi, India Page 11-12.
6. Dominic Wilson and Roopa Purushothaman, *2003: Dreaming with BRICs: The Path to 2050* - A report by Goldman Sachs, USA.

9

MANAGEMENT EDUCATION
REFLECTIONS ON THE NEEDS OF INDUSTRY

Y.V.S. Prasada Rao*

Despite the large scale growth of management education in India (the second largest industrial country in Asia only after Japan) still the requirements of industry are not properly met. Hence, the author feels that the need of the hour is to equip the incumbents with adequate skills and techniques by the educational institutions and uniforming the management education to produce good managers to the nation.

Today management education in India is really passing through transition stage. The significance of management education is evident from the development of advanced nations, where it is highly proliferated. Thus one can find positive correlation between economic development and popularity of management education. Professional management enables the optimum utilization scarcely available resources. This is very much relevant in the present era of globalization and liberalization. It is rightly pointed out by Eugene Stanley that the low level of management skills is one of the Chief obstacles to economic progress in underdeveloped countries. Hence, measures to increase the supply of the skills should be ranked high among the strategic factors for promoting sustained economic advancement.

* Lecturer, P.G. Dept. of Commerce & Management Studies, TJPS College, Guntur.

Introduction

As time passes the need for management education in a developing country like ours is accentuated with the growth of industry and service sectors which are becoming oriented towards professional management. This has created a growing demand for managers at various levels, of various types. The reality is not so. As notwithstanding the prejudice of family manager concerns towards professional management, it is opt to mention Peter Drucker who said that the ownership or absence of it, the main job of the manager is the same.

The multinational corporations which are recognized as models of good management are geared to achieve twin objectives at a stretch, namely maximization of profit and expansion of business. These organizations with tentacles across the world employed people of various nationalities and not just those who are dear or near to their owners. By means of progressive labour policies they have been able to derive maximum returns from the human input. They have been able to manage their operations efficiently through good systems of planning and control which have obviated the need for looking for one can shoulder the efficient managing of their subsidiaries and divisions.

Professional management is really modern management. Both private and public enterprises must shed their small business approach. The example of the multinationals evidences the fact that organizations can be trained and developed to meet the new challenges of development. Long ago it was widely believed that managers are born and not made.

Essentials Ignored

Ever since management education was first started in the country by the Indian Institute of Social Welfare and Business Management in 1954, it has grown up by leaps and bounds to match the whopping requirements of the industry and to provide employment to young professionals. Now there are as many 110 schools of management producing nearly 10,000 MBAs every year in India. In the rush to provide as many managers as possible, essential factors like personality, interpersonal relations, communication skills, identification of self with organization culture, etc. have been ignored.

Basically one must realize mere production of MBAs can not satisfy the managerial needs OF the industry. Industry does not accept what academic institutions produce. They must produce what industry requires. The incumbents must be good produce. They must produce what industry requires. The incumbents must be good practitioners of a bunch of managerial skills and techniques coupled with conceptual background. They must have necessary ingredients to cope up with the demands of the industry. A list of suggestive managerial ingredients is mentioned herewith.

(a) *Conceptual ingredients:* These include clarity of plethora of management principles and their application, which enable aspirants to have good perception of business problems and make them to arrive at optimal solutions.

(b) *Entrepreneural skills:* It means doing something on one's own which includes ability to initiate and bear risks, and organizing the activity in a systematic manner.

(c) *Communication aspects:* It includes ability to solve the problems and adoption of contemporary developments in the field of study.

(d) *Analytical & Intellectual Abilities:* In consists of logical thought, rationaizing the problems, assembling information into a new and meaningful pattern and situational decision making abilities.

(e) *Personality skills:* It contains self control and confidence, stamina and adaptability, communication skills and positive thinking and managing group processes.

Collective Decision Making Skills

(a) *Work Ethics:* Of course the most forgotten area in the field of management education is ethical standards. Ethics are as important as efficiency. Honesty, dependability, commitment and objective orientation need special emphasis.

Hence, the educational institutions can make adequate arrangements in their curricula to impart the qualities of a good manager to the incumbents. The management teaching techniques require a radical change. The western systems of thought had certain inherent defects which are now being reflected in the industrial organizations of the East. It is pointed by Richman that cultural differences affect the growth of managerial resources and the development of management as profession.

(b) *Collective Orientation:* Hence, collective orientation holds the key for our success and keeps us on fore front of economic development through increasing productivity. It is said about Japan that a major fact responsible for their progress is their ability to pull together and to work effectively in large organizations and groups leading to synergic efforts.

Enormous Variety—Need for Uniformity

There are a wide variety of graduation, Post-Graduation and diploma courses in response to the wave of popularity. The well accepted two-year post-graduate MBA does not necessarily ensure uniformely good quality. A host of universities across the length and breadth of the country starting from IIMs to privately managed commercial universities are offering the course. Some of these are identified with their reputation for 'easy-to-obtain' degrees. Besides, all of them are not able to maintain close touch and association with industry, which is so essential for a fruitful programme of this nature.

In addition to these, there are a variety of short-term programmes, workshops, seminars, symposia, etc. They are directed largely towards those already in management positions and only a few of them are meant for students. The diversity of these courses and programmes clearly indicates that there is lack of uniform conceptuality. No thought has been given to the fact that management is a specialization, as much as medicine is. Different curricula that look alike do not provide a clue on standards.

It is obvious that in many cases the planning of such courses is purely a business proportion to capitalize on the wave of popularity. Some of them certainly are the "fly-by-night" types and a large number of them draw those who are already working and need a diploma to secure promotion.

Industry requires not just managers, but quality managers. However, in the absence of any certainity about the ever-increasing number and variety of courses, it is not possible to identify those that are of adequate quality. The mushrooming of institutes and universities offering management programmes has created a glut, and no uniformity exists. Hence, there is need for standardization in this area, as in the courses for other professional education like medicine, law, engineering and accounting etc. A uniform examining body must be established. Levels need to be formed for degrees and diplomas. An all India level management institution is essential. It should standardize Management education in the area and identify the institutes and universities which offer adequate education. In this regard one can find the existence of AICTE but it is fulfilling only a part of above stated requirements. Hence, there is a dire need to create an autonomous body exclusively for management education which is truly professional to do the required tasks.

Then only the mushrooming of management education can be properly monitored to meet the growing requirements for professional managers. The future of industries, to some extent atleast, will be determined by the quality of managers. It is aptly observed by Haribson and Charles Myers that the high-talent of managerial resources decide a country's capacity to absorb capital and effectiveness of the material and manpower resources, and thus paves the path to national prosperity.

REFERENCES

1. Eugene Stanley, *The Future of Under Developed Countries*, Harper & Brothers, 1954.
2. Barry Richman, *Significance of Cultural Variables*, California Management Review.
3. K.Shamanna, *Professional Management in India*, Himalaya Publishing House, Bombay, 1985.
4. Haribson and Myers, *The Executive Overseas*, Syracuse University Press, Syracuse, 1956.
5. ILO Report on *Management Education in Developing Countries*, Management Development Branch, ILO, Geneva.
6. Patanjali Seth, *Ensuring Management Education is Standardized*, The Management Review, I/1983.

7. B.H.Lalvani, *The Future of Professional Management in India*, The Management Review, Vol.10, II/1983.

8. S.Pandey, *Managing Expectations: Issues and Challenges*, Indian Journal of Training and Development, New Delhi, May-June, 1992.

9. Dr.Stephanie Jones, *The Interactive MBA Revolution*, World Executive's Digest, Phillippines, Nov.,1993.

10. Brain O' Reilly, *Re-educating the MBA*, Business To-day, New Delhi, Feb – March, 1994.

SECTION–III
HEALTH SECTOR

10

HEALTHCARE IN INDIA
STRATEGIES FOR GLOBALIZATION

Dr. Talluru Sreenivas*, Dr. G. Prasad**

When we go through the Human Development Index of different countries we feel so sorry to see our country in 127th position. There were days when even the intellectuals in the country became pessimistic and felt that it would be impossible to bring back the past glory of India. Fortunately, since the nineties, there has been a change in the thinking of the great people in India and abroad (A.P.J. Abdul Kalam, Stephen P. Cohen) about the challenges that India can face and opportunities available for it to become one of the developed nations of the world. They say India's core strengths are derived from our resources – natural and human. It is here that we can foresee the health sector as wealth sector for India in future.

In this context, an attempt is made in this study to project health sector as wealth sector for India in the years to come. Analyzing the opportunities and challenges of International market, we can see India can build up world-class health facilities. In this connection, three strategies are worth mentioning…

- Building up of world-class health facilities and attracting patients from other countries on cost basis.

* Reader, Dept. of Management Sciences, R.V.R.& J.C. College of Engg., Guntur.s

** Professor, Dept. of Commerce & Business Adm., Acharya Nagarjuna University, Guntur.

- Supplying more dedicated doctors, nursing staff, and other paramedical staff to different countries, which are becoming sick due to the growth of aged population.
- Marketing of Indian Medicine (Ayurveda, Unani etc.,) abroad taking it as an opportunity and challenge.

At the end, a few suggestions are provided for the policy makers to implement these strategies to make India as a source of the world-class health facilities in all respects.

Introduction

India is a rich nation-culturally, emotionally and intellectually. When the rest of the world had not yet awakened to the light of learning, we were studying science. We had invented zero much before the others saw the dawn of civilization and invented steel[1] . Indians are known for their hospitality and warmth[2] . With their rich culture and deep-rooted values, Indians are able to take the lead in all things at global level. Indians are heading global corporations and top scientists in NASA are Indians. In this context the comments of distinguished educationalist Professor Rama Rao[3] are worth mentioning. "It is indisputable that the country has well established research facilities in the sciences with note worthy achievements. It is no exaggeration to state that there is no major Science Journal in thw world in which an Indian author does not figure, no major laboratory in which an Indian face is not seen, and no major conference without an Indian voice being heard." India is known for its rich contribution in the areas of cultural, social, spiritual values since times immemorial. Even today Indian contribution is acknowledged on the higher side in many economically developed and advanced countries. It is only in this country that some people even heckle and undermine the past glory and the contribution of the great scholars of this great country. The entire world is aware of the contribution of distinguished personalities in India like Chanakya, Charaka, Sushrutha, Patanjali, Agastya, Manu, the Buddha, Mahatma Gandhi.

Under foreign occupation, the country stagnated for centuries. The foreigners not only looted the material assets but also destroyed the social, cultural and religious systems. As such, even after 55 years of independence, the Indian economy is underdeveloped. Even today, a large percentage of people depend on Agriculture. Per capita income is low and capital per head is also very low[4]. Due to widespread poverty, most people have virtually no ability to save and whatever capital accumulation is done remains highly concentrated in the hands of a few people.

Demographically also, in one way India is backward, as both birth rate and death rate are high, life expectancy at birth is low and dietary deficiencies are common. Infant mortality among the poorest of the population is 2.5 times higher than that among the richest[5].

In addition to inadequate technological knowledge, the hold of blind traditions and customs is very strong owing to wide spread illiteracy, and these factors operate as a growth arresting factor[6]. In 2001 India's purchasing power parity estimate of GNP per capita was as low as $ 2840 as against $34320 of USA, $29640 of Norway, $53780 of Luxemburg, $27130 of Canada, and $ 251302 of Japan[7]. Though India is strong in tradition, it ranks as 127th in the Human Development Report preceded by Namibia and Morocco. Whatever may be the past, today India is famous for its Brainpower, Entrepreneurial genius, vibrant democratic polity and super power status in IT sector.

Unfortunately, since Independence, India and its polity could not use its potentialities. India's potentialities were never considered against those of the world. Till now leaders of the country have spent their time concentrating more on internal problems. For the first time, now, after the 90's there has been a change in the thinking of the great people in India and abroad (APJ Abdul Kalam[8], Stephen D.Cohen[9]) about the challenges that India can face and opportunities available for it to become one of the developed nations in the world[10]. They are of the view that India, despite her strengths, has not leveraged her full potentials to become a global player. It is the need of the hour to analyze how India can become a global power politically, socially, economically and technologically. It is our duty to know the impediments and find ways to overcome these obstacles. Though enumerating the challenges and understanding the opportunities, implementable strategies are to be identified in order to help India take her place among the comity of nations.

An attempt is made in this study to project health sector as wealth sector for India in the years to come. The authors have tried to probe into the potentialities of the country in the field of Medicine. Our country excelled in the area of Medicine for the last many centuries and it is only in the recent decades that India find itself unable to cope with the present developments in Medicine. Hence it is necessary to develop some suitable strategies for increasing its role in the international medical sector.

Analyzing the opportunities and challenges of International market, we can see that India can build up world-class health facilities. Three strategies are

- Building up of world-class health facilities and attracting patients from other countries on cost basis.
- Supplying more dedicated doctors, nursing staff, and other paramedical staff to different countries, which are becoming sick due to the growth of aged population.
- Marketing of Indian Medicine (Ayurveda, Unani etc.,) abroad taking it as an opportunity and challenge.

Before discussing these strategies, let us consider the present health sector environment in India.

Health Sector in India

India has an incomparably rich heritage in ancient systems of Medicine that make up a veritable treasure house of knowledge for both preventive and curative health care. These systems, through their safe, effective and inexpensive treatments, have the potential to make a significant contribution to the health care of the common people. Rigveda and Atharvaveda belonging to 500 BC (approx) contain many hymns on diseases and their cure with various plants and other materials. Around 1000 BC when Indian Systems of Medicine (ISM) were fully documented in Charaka Samhita and Sushruta Samhita. Thus, ISM is considered to be one of the oldest organized systems of medicine for positive health and cure of human sickness. The most important and massive ancient compilation of the school of medicine is known as Charaka Samhita. It contains several chapters dealing at length with internal medicine. About 600 drugs of plant, animal and mineral origin are described in it. So far so good. But traditional medicine was ignored when western medical knowledge and procedures were introduced into the country. At present, the achievement of Healthcare in India is very poor. It is a mixture of light and shade. There have been large gains in health status but these achievements present a rosy picture only when seen in isolation. If we compare them with the targets and goals that were put forth in various national health policies, we can visualize the real picture. This certainly dilutes the gains. Under these circumstances, the Indigenous systems of Medicine can be considered as more gainful through tapping the potential of this segment.

Health Statistics

India's health indicators are almost at the same level as the average of low-income economies. India compares unfavorably even with the low-income countries in terms of availability of health infrastructure and its utilization, as well as the overall disease burden[11] (Table 1). The number of physicians per 1000 population for the world is 1.5 and the figure for India is 1.0, which is at par with the average of the low-income countries. The number of Hospital beds per 1000 population for India is 0.7, which is much lower than the world average of 3.3 and the average of 1.5 in low-income countries. Per capita per year inpatient admission for India is 1.7% as compared to 9% for the world, as can be seen from the table 1.

Table 1: International comparison of Health Manpower, Hospital Beds, Inpatient Admissions and Out Patient visits per capita per year, 1998

Particulars	*Physicians per '000 population*	*Hospital Beds per '000 population*	*Inpatient Admissions per capita per year (%)*	*Outpatient visits per capita per year (%)*
Indian Public Sector	0.2	0.4	0.7	0.7
India (Total)	1.0	0.7	1.7	3.9
World	1.5	3.3	9.0	6.0
Low Income Countries	1.0	1.5	5.0	3.0
Middle Income Countries	1.8	4.3	10.0	5.0
High Income Countries	1.8	7.4	15.0	8.0

Source: India Health Report, 2003.

Table 2: Health Infrastructure of India and its States on 01.01.1996

Sl. No.	States	Rural			Urban			Total		
		Hospitals	Beds	Beds per lakh of population	Hospitals	Beds	Beds per lakh of population	Hospitals	Beds	Beds per lakh of population
1.	Andhra Pradesh	883	10117	20.81	2007	35715	199.67	2890	45832	68.91
2.	Assam	151	3949	19.82	117	8712	350.16	268	12661	56.49
3.	Bihar	100	3018	4.02	228	26072	229.65	328	29090	33.68
4.	Gujarat	179	5798	21.42	2349	57619	404.46	2528	63417	153.51
5.	Haryana	8	543	4.38	71	6637	163.67	79	7180	43.61
6.	Himachal Pradesh	19	549	11.63	38	4519	1006.46	57	5068	98.01
7.	Karnataka	25	3015	9.7	268	35434	254.77	293	38449	85.49
8.	Kerala	1443	44103	205.92	597	33096	430.94	2040	77199	265.3
9.	Madhya Pradesh	245	6128	12.05	118	11959	77.96	363	18087	27.41
10.	Maharashtra	469	10209	21.1	2646	68711	224.97	3115	78920	99.98
11.	Orissa	287	5115	18.65	143	97.69	230.67	430	14884	47.01
12.	Punjab	75	2330	16.31	145	12491	208.43	220	14821	73.07
13.	Rajasthan	14	1150	3.39	204	20037	199.04	218	21187	48.15
14.	Tamilnadu	89	4235	11.51	319	44545	233.49	408	48780	87.33
15.	Uttar Pradesh	83	2585	2.32	652	44693	161.9	735	47278	33.99
16.	West Bengal	112	6352	12.89	287	48878	261.27	399	55230	81.13
17.	India	4621	122453	18.5	10416	501366	232.36	15037	623819	73.71

Source: India Health Report, 2003.

The table 2 presents infrastructure in the health sector in India and its states in 1996. The table reveals that Madhya Pradesh has low number of beds per lakh of population where as Gujarat is enjoying the highest among the sister states.

It may be observed from Table 3 that there has been marked expansion in infrastructure for health sciences since 1951.

The table 4 provides information relating to the number of Doctors possessing recognized Medical Qualifications and registered with State Medical Councils for last 5 years.

Infrastructure available for Indian Systems of Medicine. There is a vast infrastructure of hospitals, dispensaries, teaching institutions and registered practitioners under different Indian systems of medicine, which can be observed from the table 5.

Table 3: Expansion of Health Services

Item	*1951*	*1961*	*1971*	*1981*	*1992*	*1996*	*1997*
Medical Colleges	28	60	98	111	146	165	165
Hospitals	2694	3094	3862	6804	13692	15097	NA
Dispensaries	6515	9406	12180	16751	27403	28225	NA
Community Health Centres	0	0	0	217	2186	2572	2628
Primary Health Centres	725	2565	5112	5740	20701	21917	22446
Sub-centres	–	–	28489	51405	131370	134931	136379
Hospital beds (all types)	117178	230000	348655	569495	834650	870161	NA
Doctors	61840	83756	151129	268712	395851	375291	484401
Nurses	16550	35584	80620	154280	385410	565696	NA

Source: Economic Survey 2000-01.

Table 4: No. of Registered Medical Practitioners from 1997-2001

S. No.	State Medical Councils	1997	1998	1999	2000	2001
01.	Andhra Pradesh	27052	27844	28510	29214	30687
02.	Assam	12936	13293	13763	14253	14586
03.	Bhopal	15794	16515	17271	18181	19021
04.	Bihar	30195	30720	31551	32226	33070
05.	Goa	1346	1569	1719	1916	2030
06.	Gujarat	28415	29492	30786	32177	33653
07.	Haryana	937	972	1018	1065	1146
08.	Hyderabad	13888	13888	13888	13888	13888
09.	Jammu & Kashmir	5674	5798	6151	6344	6875
10.	Karnataka	47706	50733	54012	57464	61163
11.	Travancore-Cochin	25644	26711	27908	29087	30173
12.	Maharastra	66477	70095	73708	77278	80764
13.	Orissa	12981	13343	13661	14009	14315
14.	Punjab	30047	30267	30832	31456	32155
15.	Rajasthan	17779	18504	19189	19744	20438
16.	Tamilnadu	57299	59305	61383	63434	65771
17.	Uttarpradesh	39319	39812	41711	42452	42452
18.	West Bengal	46591	47358	48377	49261	49941
19.	Delhi	16861	18567	20149	21698	22158
	Total	**496517**	**514786**	**535408**	**549474**	**545412**

Source: CMIE.

Table 5: Summary of Medical Care, Medical Manpower and Medical Educational Facilities available under Indian Systems of Medicine

Facilties	*Ayurveda*	*Unani*	*Siddha*	*Yoga*	*Naturopathy*	*Homoeopathy*	*Total*
Hospitals	2258	196	224	8	21	297	3004
Beds	40313	4872	1811	101	733	12836	60666
Dispensaries	14416	970	363	42	56	7155	23028
Registered Practitioners	367528	41221	12915	—	388	189361	611413
Undergraduate Colleges	196	40	2	—	—	149	387
Postgraduate Colleges	49	3	2	—	—	14	68

Source: India Health Report, 2003.

Table 6 shows the number of registered practitioners in Indian Systems of Medicine in different States. From the table, it can be seen that Siddha is very popular in Tamilnadu and in Andhra Pradesh there is great following for Naturopathy[12]. The number of patients taking Ayurveda treatment is very significant in Bihar whereas this number is very low in Assam. Maharastra is occupying first place in the case of Homeopathy whereas its following is very low in Assam.

Table 6: State-wise Number of Registered ISM and Homeopathic Practitioners as on 1st April, 1999

States	Ayurveda	Unani	Siddha	Naturopathy	Homoeopathy	Total
1	2	3	4	5	6	7
Andhra Pradesh	14,621	4614	–	298	8411	27,944
Assam	250	NA	–	–	464	714
Bihar	75,711	3250	–	–	25,669	104,630
Gujarat	16,223	234	–	–	3768	20,225
Haryana	18,553	1656	–	–	5664	25,873
Himachal Pradesh	6798	454	–	–	1076	8328
Karnataka	10,555	679	1	67	5871	17,173
Kerala	13,080	55	1345	–	7760	22,240

(Contd...)

1	2	3	4	5	6	7
Madhya Pradesh	47,130	427	–	2	6794	54,353
Maharashtra	46,519	2298	–	–	27,911	76,728
Orissa	3653	15	–	–	4733	8401
Punjab	19,924	5610	–	–	7256	32,790
Rajasthan	26,056	1849	–	–	3975	331,880
Tamilnadu	3366	916	11,569	21	16,060	31,932
Uttar Pradesh	55,921	11,963	–	–	24,711	92,595
West Bengal	2873	4927	–	–	36,107	43,907
India	367,528	41,221	12,915	388	189,361	611,413

Source: India Health Report, 2003.

The above statistics clearly reveal that India could build up strong health sector in all directions.

Strategies for Betterment of Indian Healthcare Industry

Once, we excelled in the area of Medicine, but since Independence, India has not been able to cope with the present developments. It is the need of the hour to bring out the hidden potentialities that are presented in different sectors. The authors are of in view that India has not leveraged her full potentials of health sector to become a global player. The following three strategies may help in this direction.

Strategy-1: Building up of World-class Health Facilities and Attract Patients from other Countries on Cost Basis

In the years since Independence, there has been significant gain in health status in India. The public and the private sector could build up world-class health facilities. Some of the hospitals in these two sectors are known internationally. The following are the centers of Excellence in Healthcare in India. (This is just listing and not a ranking. This list is not exhaustive. Due to place constraint we are not able to provide complete list of these hospitals.)

Table 7: Centres of Excellence in Healthcare–India

S. No.	*Name of the Hospital*	*Place*
1	*2*	*3*
	Cardiology and Cardiac Surgery	
01.	All India Institute of Medical Sciences	New Delhi
02.	Apollo Hospitals	Chennai
03.	BM Birla Heart Research Institute	Calcutta
04.	Escorts Heart Institute and Research Centre	Delhi
05.	Jayadeva Institute of Cardiology	Bangalore
06.	Krishna Heart Institute	Ahmedabad
07.	Madras Medical Mission	Chennai
08.	Manipal Heart Foundation	Bangalore
09.	Sri Chitra Thirunal Institute of Medical Sciences,	Thiruvananthapuram
	Cancer	
10.	Apollo Cancer Hospital	Chennai
11.	Aware Cancer Hospital	Hyderabad
12.	Dharmashila Cancer Institute	Delhi
13.	Inlaks and Budhrani Hospital	Pune
14.	Rajiv Gandhi Cancer Hospital	Delhi
15.	Tata Memorial Centre Ophthalmology	Mumbai
16.	Aravind Eye Hospital	Coimbatore
17.	Aravind Eye Hospital	Madurai
18.	Dr. R. Prasad Institute of Ophthalmic Sciences	Delhi
19.	LV Prasad Eye Hospital	Hyderabad
20.	Shankara Deva Nethralaya	Guwahati
21.	Shankara Nethralaya	Chennai
22.	Venu Eye Institute, Orthopaedics	Delhi
23.	Bombay Hospital	Mumbai
24.	HOSMAT	Bangalore
25.	Indian spinal Injuries Centre	Delhi
26.	Madras Institute for Orthopaedics and Trauma	Chennai
	Neurology, Neurosurgery & Behavioural Health	
27.	Indraprastha Apollo Hospital	Delhi
28.	Manipal Hospital	Bangalore
29.	NIMHANS	Bangalore

(Contd...)

1	2	3
30.	PD Hinduja National Hospital	Mumbai
31.	VIMHANS Multi Speciality Secondary and Tertiary Care	Delhi
32.	All India Institute of Medical Sciences	Delhi
33.	Amrita Institute of Medical Sciences	Kochin
34.	Apollo Hospitals	Chennai
35.	Bombay Hospital	Mumbai
36.	Christian Medical Centre and Hospital	Vellore
37.	Indraprastha Apollo Hospital	Delhi
38.	Post-Graduate Institute of Medical Sciences	Chandigarh
39.	Sri Satya Sai Institute	Puttaparthi

Source: The Economic Times Health Care 2001-2002.

The development of the corporate hospitals is the most important development in the private health sector in the 80's. The pioneer in the field was the Apollo Hospital in Chennai. This multi-crore rupee hospital with the latest diagnostic and therapeutic facilities was established with money raised from the share market. And it has set the trend for the others to follow. The Apollo Hospital was set up in 1983, and was followed by diagnostic centres of the United Group, Standard Medical Group, Surlax Diagnostic Ltd., etc. Within a period of just two years, between 1984 and 1986, Rs.200 crores was invested in these corporate ventures. In the words of Pratap C.Reddy "In the corporate sector we are able to establish hospitals with world-class facilities. To name some of them – Apollo Hospitals, Escorts Heart Institute, Nirmala Hrudayalaya, Medwin Hospitals etc. From the above examples, one can visualize the potential of Indian Medical professionals. In fact, it is the advancement in health care that has shown a big difference in 10 years. In 10 years India has demonstrated this by building nearly 1000 good hospitals of international standards in our country. I am sure India in the field of health care will be a Developed India. We can reach this in just 10 years".[13]

Indian hospitals are now excelling and providing World Class health services. What was viewed earlier as the preserve of the advanced countries in the West is now available quite easily in India. Of course, it costs money-Rs. 50,000 to 60,000 an hour to hire an aircraft – but aerial medivac (Medical Evacuation) is becoming increasingly possible across the country. In fact, atleast one or two medical evacuations by air happens every week in some parts of India. More and more hospitals and now even insurance companies are gearing up to handle medivac operations. A few days back when a tourist developed medical complications and fainted while on a holiday in Gulbarga recently, her parents in Austialia called up International SOS, an organization in New Delhi to airdash their daughter to Apollo Hospital in Hyderabad. A helicopter flew in from Bangalore and swftly moved her and in the process saved her life.[14]

The following Table gives the information relating to some important corporate hospitals established in India in the span of the last two decades. (Here also the list is not exhaustive and many hospitals, which came up recently, could not be added due to space problem.)

Table 8: Corporate Hospitals in India

Sl. No.	*Organisation Name*	*Place*
1	*2*	*3*
1.	Appolo Hospitals Ltd.	Chennai
2.	Apollo Indraprasta	New Delhi
3.	Escorts Heart Institute	New Delhi
4.	Gangaram Hospitals	New Delhi
5.	Batra Hospital	New Delhi
6.	United Diagnostrics International Ltd.	Mumbai
7.	Breach Candy Hospitals	Mumbai
8.	Hinduja Hospital	Mumbai
9.	Bombay Hospital	Mumbai
10.	Jaslok Hospital	Mumbai
11.	Cumballa Hill Hospitals	Mumbai
12.	Lilavathi Hospitals	Mumbai
13.	NM Wadia Hospital	Pune
14.	Ruby Hall Clinic	Pune
15.	Deccan Hospitals Ltd.	Hyderabad
16.	Madras Medical Mission	Chennai
17.	Wockhardt Heart Hospital	Chennai
18.	Manipal Heart Foundation	Manipal

(Contd...)

1	2	3
19.	Mallya Hospitals	Bangalore
20.	Jayadeva Institute of Cardiology	Bangalore
21.	BM Birla Heart Research Centre	Calcutta
22.	Seahorse Hospitals LTd.	Tiruchirapalli
23.	Tamilnadu Hospitals Ltd.	Madras
25.	Surlex Diagnostic Ltd.	Bombay
26.	Kovai Medical Centre & Hospitals Ltd.	Coimbatore
27.	A.D.S.Diagnostics Ltd.	New Delhi
28.	C.D.R.Healthcare Ltd.	Hyderabad
29.	Regency Hospitals Ltd.	Kanpur
30.	Noida Medicare Centre Ltd.	New Delhi
31.	Medwin Hospitals Ltd.	Hyderabad
32.	G.I.L.Hospitals Ltd.	Baroda
33.	Malar Hospitals Ltd.	Madras
34.	Sharma East India Hospitals and Medical Research Ltd.	Jaipur
35.	Devaki Hospitals Ltd.	Madras
36.	Secunderabad Healthcare Ltd.	Secunderabad
37.	Lokmanya Industries Ltd.	Bombay
38.	Ishwar Medical Services Ltd.	Thane
39.	Dolphin Medical Services Ltd.	Vijayawada
40.	Medinova Diagnostics Ltd.	Hyderabad
41.	Dr.Agrawal's Eye Hospitals Ltd.	Chennai
42.	ADS Diagnostic	Delhi
43.	Mayo	Baroda
44.	Peerless Hospitals	Calcutta
45.	Prema Hospitals	
46.	Regency Hospitals	Kanpur
47.	Sushrusha Citizen's Hospitals	Mumbai
48.	Drs Tribedi & Roy	Culcutta
49.	Dhanvanthrai Jeevan Rekha	Meerut
50.	United Diagnostics	Bhopal

Source: The Economic Times Health Care 2001-2002

Apollo is the only corporate with a chain of hospitals today. The exhaustive list of Apollo Hospitals engaged in tertiary, secondary and primary Health Care is given in the table 9. This speaks of the strength of the Corporate Hospitals in India and their ability to reach world-class standards.

Table 9: List of Apollo Hospitals engaged in Tertiary, Secondary and Primary Health of Indians

Sl. No.	*Name*	*Place*	*Classification*
	Owned Hospitals-Operational		
01.	Apollo Hospitals	Chennai	Super specialty
02.	Apollo Hospital	Hyderabad	Super specialty
03.	Apollo Specialty Hospital	Chennai	Cancer/Neuro/Ortho
04.	Apollo Cancer Hospital	Hyderabad	Cancer Specialty
05.	Apollo Hospitals	Madurai	Super specialty
06.	Apollo Heart and Kidney Hospital	Vizag	Cardiac
07.	Apollo Hospitals	Aragonda	Multi Specialty
08.	Apollo Hospitals	Chennai	Multi Specialty
09.	Al Khaleej Heart Scan center	Dubai	Diagnostic
10.	Apollo Emergency Medical Centre	Hyderabad	Multi Specialty
11.	Apollo Centre	Hyderabad	Diagnostic
12.	Indraprastha Apollo Hospitals	New Delhi	Super specialty
13.	Apollo (Secondary Care)	Hyderabad	Secondary Care
	Managed Hospitals-Operational		
14.	Abdur Razzaque Ansari Memorial	Ranchi	Super specialty
15.	Weavers Hospitals	Bihar	Tertiary
16.	Rajiv Gandhi Cancer Institute	New Delhi	Cancer Specialty
17.	Jahangir Hospital & Medical Centre	Pune	Multi specialty
18.	Central Travancore Specialists Hospitals Ltd.	Chengannur	Multi specialty
19.	Saumya Apollo Hospitals	Vijayawada	Super Specialty
20.	Lotus Apollo Hospitals	Erode	Multi specialty
21.	Jodhana Medical and Research Centre	Jodhpur	Multi specialty
22.	Niramay Hospital	Dabhol	Secondary care
23.	Kirms Apollo Hospitals	Nagpur	Multi specialty
24.	Amar Hospitals	Hyderabad	Multi specialty
25.	AMRI Apollo Hospitals	Calcutta	Multi specialty
26.	Venkatsai Hospitals	Ananthpur	Multi specialty
27.	NDMC Hospital	Bacheli	Multi specialty
28.	Florence Medical Centre	Siliguri	Multi specialty

Source: The Economic Times Health Care 2001-2002.

It is a well-known fact that our corporate hospitals are able to provide medical facilities at one-tenth the cost of a US hospital. Interesting thing is we are providing world-class quality at low cost. Technologically we are not lagging behind. In our hospitals, both in public and private sectors, rare equipment is made available.

We have demonstrated to the rest of the world that out here, we have not only brought in equivalent standards, but we are bringing them at lesser costs. Our heart surgery is not 30,000 to 60,000 dollars, it is 3000 to 5000 dollars. Bone marrow transplant abroad is 300 thousand dollars, we are doing it for 27,000 dollars. For a lever transplant in the US, it costs 500 thousand dollars and another 250 thousand dollars in the event of any complications. We are doing it regularly here for only Rs.19 lakhs and if it exceeds that, we bear the cost. One has to pay only for the material costs. This is the greatest satisfaction that we have today.[15] Our hospitals are known for their ambience. Our administrators are keen in selection of different items right from the location of the hospitals and professionally designed buildings to the solid infrastructure and high tech equipment. These hospitals have been equipped with latest diagnostic and electronic equipment such as Gama Camera in Radiology Department, CT/MR Stereotic System in Neurosurgery Department, Image Intesifier in Orthopaedic Department and so on. So, it is advisable to develop such corporate and public hospitals in all chief cities, attract foreigners and earn foreign exchange, which will have direct impact on the development of our economy. In fact, separate hospitals can be developed in order to meet the international standards, so that there will be a possibility of attracting patients from the most advanced countries. The present Health policy also emphasizes the need for providing health services on payment basis to customers seeking service from overseas[16]. There are instances where foreigners come to India in order to take indigenous medicine for arthritis from Kerala and for taking Fish Medicine in Andhra Pradesh, which helps in curing Asthma. Globalisation, in fact, is not to be considered as a threat, but is an excellent opportunity for the growth of the health sector. Taking this as an opportunity with all strengths in health sector we can play a dominant role in the international areana and the strategy here is 'World class facilities at low cost'.

Strategy-2: Supplying more dedicated doctors, nursing staff and other paramedical staff to different countries, which are becoming sick due to the growth of aged population

The healthcare industry is on the threshold of a major growth spiral, which shall assimilate all new technologies to provide cost effective healthcare. It is poised to become the biggest employer in all countries and shall not only employ the largest chunk of all available capital but also a large proportion of the skilled work force.[17]

The statistics of different countries based on population reveals interesting facts. There is significant increase in the population in different countries who are above 65 years and below 15 years, which can be seen from the table 10. There is significant increase in different countries, of the number of people above 65 years and below 15 years, as can be seen from Table 10.

Table 10: Population below 15 & above 65 Age Group-Countrywise

HDI Rank	*Name of the Country*	*Total Population (millions)*		*Population under age 15*		*Population aged 65 and above*	
		2001	*2015*	*2001*	*2015*	*2001*	*2015*
1	2	3	4	5	6	7	8
09	Japan	127.3	127.2	14.5	13.0	17.7	26.0
21	Italy	57.5	55.5	14.2	12.3	18.4	22.3
10	Switzerland	7.2	7.0	16.5	12.6	16.2	22.0
03	Sweden	8.9	9.0	18.1	15.7	17.4	21.4
24	Greece	10.9	10.9	14.9	13.2	17.8	20.9
18	Germany	82.3	82.5	15.4	13.2	16.7	20.8
06	Belgium	10.3	10.5	17.3	15.5	17.2	19.5
16	Austria	8.1	8.1	16.4	12.4	15.6	19.5
19	Spain	40.9	41.2	14.4	13.2	16.9	19.2
11	Denmark	5.3	5.4	18.4	16.3	15.0	19.2
17	France	59.6	62.8	18.7	17.8	16.1	18.5
01	Norway	4.5	4.7	19.8	16.6	15.3	18.0
23	Portugal	10.0	10.0	16.6	15.3	15.8	18.0
57	Bulgaria	8.0	7.2	15.3	12.6	16.3	18.0

(Contd...)

1	2	3	4	5	6	7	8
13	United Kingdom	58.9	61.3	18.9	15.9	15.9	17.8
05	Netherlands	16.0	16.8	18.4	16.4	13.7	17.4
38	Hungary	10.0	9.3	16.7	13.3	14.7	17.4
08	Canada	31.0	34.1	18.7	14.8	12.7	16.4
75	Ukraine	49.3	44.4	17.2	13.2	14.2	16.1
04	Australia	19.4	21.7	20.3	17.3	12.4	15.5
35	Poland	38.7	38.2	18.6	14.6	12.3	14.8
72	Romania	22.4	21.6	17.7	15.4	13.6	14.8
20	New Zealand	3.8	4.2	22.8	19.3	11.8	14.6
52	Cuba	11.2	11.5	20.8	16.3	9.9	14.4
63	Russian Federation	144.9	133.4	17.2	13.7	12.8	14.3
07	United States	288.2	329.7	21.7	20.3	12.3	14.2
26	Hong Kong, China	6.9	7.9	16.2	12.9	10.8	13.6
28	Singapore	4.1	4.7	21.5	12.9	7.4	13.1
34	Argentina	37.4	43.4	27.5	24.4	9.9	11.0
104	China	1285.2	1402.3	24.3	19.4	7.0	9.4
99	Sri Lanka	18.8	20.6	25.5	21.3	6.8	9.3
74	Thailand	61.6	69.6	25.9	22.0	5.6	8.1
65	Brazil	174.0	202.0	28.8	24.1	5.3	7.5
55	Mexico	100.5	119.6	33.3	26.4	4.9	6.8
96	Turkey	69.3	82.1	31.2	25.0	5.6	6.7
112	Indonesia	214.4	250.4	30.4	25.3	5.0	6.4
127	India	1033.4	1246.4	33.7	27.7	5.0	6.3
58	Malaysia	23.5	29.6	33.4	27.2	4.1	6.1
111	South Africa	44.4	44.3	33.6	29.2	3.8	6.0
120	Egypt	69.1	90.0	35.7	31.7	4.5	5.4
85	Philippines	77.2	96.3	37.1	29.9	3.6	4.9
106	Iran	67.2	81.4	33.9	26.8	4.5	4.9
144	Pakistan	146.3	204.5	41.8	38.1	3.7	4.0
139	Bangladesh	140.9	181.4	38.8	31.9	3.2	3.8

Source: Human Development Report, 2003.

The analysis of the table shows all the developed and rich countries in the world are going to have double digit population having the age group beyond 65. India will have only 6.3 of population beyond 65. It means many rich and developed economies are going to become sick and India is going to be a younger economy with more number of youth. The rich countries require more personal services, particularly health services and India in this area can excel and derive substantial benefits.

The aged in any country need medical facilities and personal attention. According to one study there is a shortage of around 1,26,000 nurses in the US, which may go up to 8,00,000 by 2020. For the last couple of years, there has been a steady flow of nurses out of India and into the UK and US.[18] Taking this as an opportunity, our Government can develop medical professionals by opening more Medical Colleges and Nursing Colleges, so that we can increase the supply of Doctors, Nursing staff and other paramedical personnel, who can be encouraged to go to different countries as well as different places in the country also. Healthcare is the largest industry in the world and it is the largest employment provider in the world. This is the largest industry with a business of $3.8 trillion. We need to develop this industry. Today we have only 4 million people working in the field of healthcare. There is a possibility that this figure could go up to 30 million, if enough networks are provided and enough doctors, nurses and technologists are trained.[19] While speaking on transforming India Prof C K Prahlad, the Management Guru, stated "Jaipur foot was developed indigenously for Indian conditions. These prosthetics, which are custom-fitted within four hours for people who have lost a leg below the knee, are of world-class standards and cost just $30 each. In the US, a similar prosthetic would cost $1,600. Who said cost arbitrage existed only in the IT and ITES sectors?"[20]

Further, the expansion of health care sector will boost medical equipment industry. According to one report the health sector, which is witnessing rapid expansion on gaining industry status and a search in medical insurance business, is likely to fuel the demand for medical equipment. Based on this premise, the equipment majors of the likes of Siemens, GE, and Kodak have started networking with health care companies which have drawn up ambitious expansion plans.[21]

Here there may be a question from the elite on the production and supply of numerous medical professionals. Further, their questions will dwell on quality, unemployment; fall in income to the doctors etc. These opinions are not correct. Because, for the last 50 years, seats in medical colleges were given on the basis of even on negative marks and the same people are working as doctors and they became popular doctors, serving the society without any problems. So, there is no meaning in discussing about quality. On the other hand, greater supply of doctors results in natural shift to rural areas to enable them to earn their livelihood. There is no meaning in trying to provide employment to all doctors who are produced. They should be left out to the market forces. Here our emphasis is on increase in supply, which can be taken as an advantage. They can be used in the Indian and International markets. In the next five years international market requires more medical professionals. Particularly countries in Europe and USA, Japan and other countries are going to face the problem of aged population and they require thousands of medical professionals. In this area, India is having strength as well as opportunity, compared to many other countries. According to the latest report, the Department of Health in England is looking for suitably qualified and trained doctors from India, in the field of Medicine, radiology, anesthesia and psychiatry to work as full time consultants in the UK. With around 3,200 doctors from the Indian sub-continent due to retire in Britain within next four years (according to British Medical Association figures) the British Health Department has advertised in India for consultant medical staff.[22]

Hence the strategy here is "Committed Indian Medical Professionals and Quality of personal service". What is needed is bringing down the regulatory mechanisms so that more and more participants in this field are encouraged. More and more healthcare providers, doctors, hospitals, nurses, and technologists will, thus, be developed.[23]

Strategy-3: Marketing of Indian Systems of Medicine abroad, taking it as an opportunity and challenge

India is well-known for its endless diversity of population, climate, topography, religious beliefs, languages and socio-economic and cultural settings, with rich heritage as well as in developing ancient systems of medicine. India makes up a veritable treasure- house of knowledge for both preventive and curative health care. Indian systems of medicine, through their safe, effective and inexpensive treatments, have the potential to make a significant contribution to the health care of the common people. But unfortunately their true potential is still largely unrealized in spite of the large infrastructure.

The term 'Indian systems of Medicine' comprises six different systems – Ayurveda, Siddha, Unani, Yoga, Naturopathy and Homeopathy. Though the term is generally used to cover these six systems, only 3 of them – Ayurveda, Siddha and Yoga - are indigenous systems. Unani is of Greek origin and came to India in medieval times. Naturopathy has some elements of non-Indian origin. Homeopathy, though German in origin, has a large Indian following. It is even considered to be one of the Indian systems of Medicine by many Indians. In terms of registered practitioners, Ayurveda is the leading system in Indian system of Medicine.

The Potential of Indian Systems of Medicine

With the advent of British rule, the indigenous systems lost official patronage and support. In the meantime, the elite shifted to modern medicine and consequently Indian systems of Medicine suffered a major setback[24]. Because of the above consequences, the modern medicine got huge investments in research and came out with new discoveries. There was a change of attitude after independence, but there was no follow up. Inadequate attention of policy makers and insufficient financial support made these initiatives largely ineffective. With its vast infrastructure and cultural acceptance, it is logical to expect Indian systems of Medicine to play a major role in Indian Health Care. Indian Systems of Medicine is suitable and plays dominant role while dealing with the expensive therapies especially to the unaffordable in a developing country like India. Now-a-days, there is burden of non-communicable diseases. Best strategy to deal with this situation is to emphasize on preventive health and healthy life styles. These are having greater values in Indian Systems of Medicine. Rich range of remedies in Indian Systems of Medicine provides for safer and more effective drugs to support the human battle against disease.

The authentication and impact of Indian Medicine was explained by Dr. APJ Abdul Kalam[25], the President of India, and his narration is worth mentioning here. We would like to narrate an incident here about who devoted health care and native herbal system that resulted in curing frostbite completely. DRDO has a laboratory in the upper hills of Himachal Pradesh called the Snow and Avalanche Study Establishment (SASE). This establishment has outstation observatories at altitudes of 15,000 and 19,000 ft. Recently, a team of scientists was moving from one station to another when they encountered a snow blizzard. Though most of the team members escaped unharmed, one of them got trapped in the snow. When he was rescued after two days, he had developed severe Grade IV frostbite in the feet and arms. The doctors at local hospital suggested to amputate the affected parts. Subsequently, the Delhi-based DRDO laboratory, Defence Institute of Physiology and Allied Sciences (DIPAS) was entrusted with the responsibility of providing healthcare through the use of an Indian herbal extract *Aloe Vera* along with allopathic treatment. DIPAS took it as a challenge and worked with the patient. The effort bore fruit and resulted in the complete recovery of the patient within 45 days of treatment, without any amputation. Faith in the Indian herbal system was restored! The experience brings out the tremendous potential of the Indian herbal system in combating various ailments, and also the patient-doctor relationship. We would like to suggest that doctors and medical specialists look at patients as integrated human beings or psycho-physiological entitites, and for whom the treatment has to be multifaceted. Certain diseases can be cured through the Indian system alone while others may require a combination of Indian and allopathic systems, with reference to the condition of the patient.

In fact, the Central Government is now focusing its attention on building up credibility for the alternative systems, by encouraging evidence-based research to determine their efficacy, safety and dosage and trying to encourage certification and quality-making of products to enable a wider popular acceptance of these systems of medicine[26]. The policy makers are concentrating on consolidation of documentary knowledge contained in these systems to protect against attack from foreign commercial entitiest[27]. The Government is also taking steps to market indigenous systems of Medicine in Foreign countries taking it as an opportunity. It is time traditional healers should think of using modern approaches to validate their products which will prove beneficial in approaching the groups of people who think adversely of traditional healers. Also this validation of biological action will prove immensely useful in marketing their products to a wider population.[28] Thus, the marketing of Indian Systems of Medicine with all its richness and lower cost may be the best strategy in the international market.

What the Government should do

To leverage full potentials that are available in health sector and to make the health sector as a global player, the Government of India may initiate the following measures.

1. Increase the expenditure on public health and education to minimum of 6 per cent as against <4 per cent at present.
2. Allow the private sector to establish world-class medical, Dental, Nursing, Physiotherapy and Indian systems of Medicine colleges along with centers of advanced Medical Technology by removing all the bureaucratic controls on their establishment.
3. Market Indian Systems of Medicine in the International Markets.
4. Link up of Hospitality and Health Industry.

REFERENCES

1. Chaudhuri Malay, Chaudhuri Arindam, *The Great Indian Dream*, MacMillan India Limited, New Delhi, 2003, p 1.
2. ibid.
3. Professor Rama Rao, *The role of Higher Education in Nation Building in India – My dream* – an Interactive lecture series-Agenda for the Nation, Excel Books, New Delhi, 2003.
4. *Human Development* Report, 2003.
5. *Planning Commission's Report of the Committee on India Vision 2020*, Economica India, 2003.
6. Abdul Kalam APJ, Rajan YS, *India 2020 – A vision for the new Millennium*, VIKING, Penguin Books India (Pvt) Limited, New Delhi, 1998.
7. *Human Development Report*, 2003 UNDP Publications, New Delhi.
8. Abdul Kalam APJ, op.cit.
9. Cohen Stephen D, *India*, 2000.
10. Abdul Kalam APJ, *Ignited Minds, Unleashing the power within India*, Viking Publishers, New Delhi.
11. *India Health Report*, 2003.
12. Ministry of Health Website.
13. Dr. Prathap C Reddy, *Health Care in India, India – My dream – An interactive lecture series – Agenda for the Nation*, Excel books, New Delhi, 2003.

14. Girish Rao, Economic Times, February 15, 2004.
15. Dr. Prathap C Reddy, op.cit., pp 134-35.
16. *National Health Policy*, 2003.
17. Abdul Kalam APJ with A Sivathanu Pillai, *Envisioning an Empowered Nation – Technology for Societal Transformation*, Tata Mc Graw-Hill, New Delhi, 2004, p. 109
18. *The Economic Times*, 26-01-2004.
19. Dr. Prathap C Reddy, op.cit,, p. 142.
20. *The Economic Times*, November 6, 2003, p. 5.
21. *The Economic Times*, January 31, 2004
22. *The Economic Times*, November 2, 2003, p. 14.
23. ibid., p. 144
24. *India Health Report*, 2003.
25. Abdul Kalam APJ, op.cit., p. 101.
26. *Indian Systems of Medicine*, Ministry of Health, Annual Report 2000-2001.
27. *The Hindu*, October 26, 2003, p. 11.
28. Abdul Kalam APJ, op.cit., p. 95

NOTE

- Recently the Council of Scientific Research and Central Council for Research in Ayurveda and Siddha released a CD on Ayurvedic Digital Library. The digital Library, which provides information about ayurvedic formulations in five languages – English, French, German, Spanish and Japanese - has been constructed as a follow-up to the controversy over the U.S. patent office granting a patent for use of turmeric for wound healing and also in the wake of repeated litigations on products such as basmati and neem. The project was implemented by the CSIR's National Institute of Science Communication and Information Resources and was co-sponsored by the Health and Science and Technology Ministries. The project is intended to cover about 35,000 formulations available in 14 classical texts of Ayurveda to convert the information into patent compatible format. The work has been initiated with a co-operative set-up of 30 Ayurveda experts, 5 Information Technology Experts and 2 patent examiners. The Digital Library will include all details in digital format about international patent classification, traditional research classification, Ayurveda terminology, concepts, definitions, classical formulations, doses, disease conditions and references to documents.

11

MARKETING OF INTEGRATED HEALTH CARE UNIT *A STUDY*

K.V.R. Prasad* and **M. Kishore Babu****

Good health and its natural corollary – defense against illness is fundamental and essential to every individual. The recurring refrain in any discussions of Indian health system is "finance", a refrain that grows more shrill and urgent because of policy failures and neglect of state at large. The crux of the problem is abysmally low public health expenditure around 0.9 percent of GDP, below the average of low income countries and even sub-African countries. Despite the increasing urgency of attention towards public health, the public health expenditure has been declining over the years. Indeed the Indian health system failed to develop a reliable mechanism to cater the poor and needy. It can be achieved by cross-subsidisation of financing activities, where different institutes are made active participants to finance select groups.

It is evident that very effective and time tested. Indian medicine systems i.e. Ayurvedic, Eunami, Naturopathy, Sidda etc. have lost official patronage with advent of British rule; colonial masters considered these systems are unscientific and unreliable. But India's rich heritage in ancient systems of medicine with its variable treasure house of knowledge can make a significant contribution to health

* PG Student, Appolo Hospital, Hyderabad.

** Lecturer, Dept. of Management Studies, Mahatma Gandhi College, Guntur-19.

care. Indian health systems are considered as complemented and Alternative systems of Medicine (CAM) can offer remedies in the treatment chronic ailments like digestive disorders, asthma, arthritis.

The present study explore the drawbacks of the conventional system and study the availability of infrastructure and human resources in various system of medicine. How all these systems and services can be effectively utilized through the concept of integration and attain a healthy community of people causing the progress of the nation.

Introduction

It is increasingly being recognized that health is an important contributor for productivity and economic growth of a country, but it is first and foremost and end in it self. Good health and its natural corollary – defense against illness is fundamental and essential to every individual. The recurring refrain in any discussions of Indian health system is "finance", a refrain that grows more shrill and urgent because of policy failures and neglect of state at large. The crux of the problem is abysmally low public health expenditure around 0.9 percent of GDP, below the average of low income countries and even sub-African countries. Despite the increasing urgency of attention towards public health, the public health expenditure has been declining over the years. Indeed the Indian health system failed to develop a reliable mechanism to cater the poor and needy. It can be achieved by cross-subsidisation of financing activities, where different institutes are made active participants to finance select groups.

A recent analysis of world bank (India – Raising the sights – better health systems for India's poor, May 2001) concludes that the hospitalised Indian spends more than half of his total annual income on buying health care, More than 40 percent of hospitalized people borrow money and sell his assets to cover expenses, yet no guarantee of cure from diseases.

It is evident that very effective and time tested. Indian medicine systems i.e. Ayurvedic, Eunami, Naturopathy, Sidda etc. have lost official patronage with advent of British rule; colonial masters considered these systems as unscientific and unreliable. But India's rich heritage in ancient systems of medicine with its variable treasure house of knowledge can make a significant contribution to health care. Indian health systems are considered as complemented and Alternative systems of Medicine (CAM) can offer remedies in the treatment chronic ailments like digestive disorders, asthma, arthritis.

In the changing demographic and epidemiological scenario, longevity has increased and people are more vulnerable to chromic ailments require long-term and expensive therapies which may not be affordable by an ordinary man. CAM can fill this critical gap and provide safe and cost effective treatment for many diseases. It is high time to look in to this matter to develop an integrated health care unit which combines modern Allopathy with complementary and alternative medicine system to offer comprehensive health care solutions to the patients and to society at large. With this researcher felt the need to probe into the depths of feasibility of integrated health care unit in Indian Scenario.

Present study: The present study titled "A Study of Establishing and Marketing of an Integrated Health Care Unit" is the explore the drawbacks of the conventional system and study the availability of infrastructure and human resources in various system of medicine. How all these systems and services can be effectively utilized through the concept of integration and attain a healthy community of people causing the progress of the nation. The functioning principles, strengths and weaknesses of all systems of medicine are been looked into keenly.

Objectives of Study

1. Integrating various therapeutic approaches for effective management of common ailments prevalent among the population.
2. Observing and studying perception of Doctors and customers towards different systems of medicine.
3. To study doctor's opinion towards integrated health unit.
4. Developing appropriate clinical governance protocols with proper referral and communication processes.
5. To study patient (customer) response towards introduction of IHU.
6. To develop cost effective Integrated Health care unit in primary health care for Rural as well as urban population.

Health Definition: The WHO defines health as a state of physical, mental and social well being, not merely an absence of diseases or infirmity.

Integrated Medicine: Integrated medicine is the methodology of integrating different systems of medicines. It is not the concept of a doctor in one system of medicine practicing all the other systems of medicines incorporating one or two therapies. For instance, yoga therapy and aromatherapy. "An integrated doctor is one who is an expert in one system and has enough knowledge of other systems of medicines and is open to accepting these systems".

Integrated medicine is a system in which main stream medical health care and Complementary therapies are integrated together within a practice, institution etc, each complementing the other.

Holistic Philosophy: The term 'holism' has its origin in the Greek worD ' holos' means 'whole'. Holism is the philosophy of life that relates to the whole rather than the parts. Physical, mental, vital, intellectual and spiritual – these are the five levels of being. For medicine to be holistic, it should be universally applicable, cover all aspects of health, on all the five level; more generally the mind, the body and the soul.

The fundamental principle underlying holistic treatment is that the natural defense and immune systems of an individual, when strengthened, has the potential to heal and prevent disease. The natural healing process is slow since the disease process is also slow. The holistic approach, nevertheless, combines the pick of the past, interlaced with the best of the present and prepares you for the future, giving you a comprehensive insight into the hitherto unknown areas of your system.

Alternative Medicine: These could include non-invasive, non-pharmaceutical techniques such as medical herbalism. Acupuncture, Homeopathy, Reiki, and many others. However alternative medicine can also refer to any experimental drug or non-drug techniques that is not currently accepted by 'conventional' medical practitioners.

Complementary Medicine: Refer to non-invasive and non-pharmaceutical techniques that complement 'conventional' medical treatment such as drugs and surgery.

Integrated Health Care: Integrated health care recognizes the effect of sociological, psychological, economic, ecological and even political influences on health.

There are presently more than 10 systems of medicine-Allopathy, Ayurveda, Homeopathy, Unani, Naturopathy, Siddha, Physiotherapy, Traditional Chinese medicine, Acupuncture, etc.

Taking into account one's body, mind, emotions, and spiritual life, Integrative health combines the best of modern scientific diagnosis and monitoring techniques with both ancient and innovative health promotion methods. These include natural and diet and herbal remedies, nutritional supplements, exercise, relaxation, psycho-spiritual counseling, meditation, breathing exercises and other self-regulatory practices.

Allopathy: Allopathy is the conventional form of medicine using pharmaceuticals and invasive techniques for diagnosis and treatment. Allopathy has evolved over the years with the various discoveries and inventions made in the field of science. A patient is physically examined, then diagnostic tests are conducted and after the confirmation of disease the therapy is instituted. There are several disciplines in Allopathy: General medicine, General surgery, Obstetrics & Gynecology, Pediatrics, Orthopedics, Neurology and Cardiology, etc.

Ayurveda: Ayurveda means the "science of life" in Sanskrit. It is one of oldest and the best documented among the ancient systems of medicine. From the Charaka Samhita (600 B.C) and the Susruta samhita (500 B.C).

Homeopathy: The term homeopathy comes from the Greek word ' homios' means like and 'pathos' means suffering. Homeopathy works by looking at the symptoms, will take into account the individual's mental, physical, emotional and spiritual health before deciding the treatment. Homeopathy is based on the principles that 'like cures like'.

Naturopathy: Naturopathy is based on the fundamental principles of Ayurveda. The basic tenet of Naturopathy is to live according to the laws of nature: disease occurs due to the accumulation of toxins in the body, and to cure the ailment, the body is purified with the use of natural methods, dietary regulations and exercise.

Unani: The Unani system originated in the fourth and fifth century BC in Greece under the patronage of Hippocrates (460BC-377BC) and Galen. The system is based on the humoural theory that good health depends on the balance of the four humours: blood, phlegm, yellow bile, and black bile.

Physiotherapy: Physiotherapy is health care profession, which involves assessment, treatment, prevention, both in health and in disease, right from a neonate to an aged individual.

Acupuncture: Acupuncture is an ancient Chinese method of treating ailments. The word acupuncture is made of two parts- 'acus', which means a needle and 'puncture'. This method provides relief from illness by needle puncture of specific points on the body. The stimulation of these points by needles leads to a balance of energy forces and this is responsible for cure of diseases caused by imbalance of body energy.

Siddha: Siddha means a "master" thus the name denoted the mastery of such practices. The most famous of the siddha was Nagarjuna, whose rasatantra forms the basis of this system. The distinctive features of Siddha are its reliance on minerals and metallic compounds, and its emphasis on rejuvenation therapies.

Yoga: Yoga is not really a system of medicine. Its objectives are self-realization and spiritual union with the all-pervasive divine cosmic power. But certain intermediary practices and yogic attitudes have proved beneficial for reducing stress, preventing many lifestyle-related diseases, and promoting general health and well-being.

Research Methodolgy

Research Design: Research design is descriptive, cross-sectional, in nature. The design is intended to draw opinions of Doctors and patients on I.H.U. inception in large scale.

Data Collection: Primary data is collected through survey method using 'questionnaire' as the tool.

Structured – non – disguised questionnaire: The researcher pre-tested the questionnaire with a sample of 50-custoemrs and 20-Doctors and as the result was positive the main study. The rest of study was taken up.

Scaling techniques: Researcher has used 'Nominal scale' as it is very useful in preliminary or exploratory work, and is sufficient to know the broad dimensions of a certain phenomenon.

Sampling design: The researcher has divided the sample into two strata Customers and Doctors, based on the non-probability 'Convenience sampling' method. This type of sampling is also called 'accidental sampling' as the respondents in the sample are included merely on account of their being available on the spot where the survey is in progress.

Sample Size: The total sample selected for this study is 200 customers and 70 doctors.

Limitations

- Due to time constraint and resource limitations, the sample size had to be kept small in comparison to the population.
- As study was restricted to Hyderabad only. The view of the rural population was not collected.

Need for IHU (Integrated Health Unit) Opinions of Doctors

1. Among 70 doctors taken for study, 88 percent of respondents opined that Allopathic medicine alone may not offer comprehensive diagnosis and treatment for all diseases and require the support of other systems.
2. Allopathy is given top rank because of its effectiveness in diagnostic capabilities, the latest technology availability and skilled surgeons. Homeopathy is given 2nd rank by majority of respondents and Ayurveda is ranked third – followed by physiotherapy and Naturopathy in next slots.
3. Among conventional systems of medicines 51 percent of doctors stated that Allopathy is highly reliable than others.
4. 71 percent of doctors felt conventional and Alternative systems of medicine (CAM) are reliable. 89% of respondents said it is cost effective and will not cause any side effects.
5. 80 percent of doctors agreed that integrated systems of medicine is order of the day. 17 percent of doctors disagreed to integrate two or more systems of medicine.

At the same many allopathic doctors cautioned that simultaneous use of medication may lead to drug interactions and adverse reactions.

6. In response to need for making all medicine systems available under one roof, 94 percent of respondents have strongly supported said it may help the patients in many ways.
7. 50 percent of doctors opined that they were unable to treat adequately with single system of medicine. But 50 percent of doctors are loyal to their practicing medicine and want to continue with the same practice.
8. It is observed by doctors that patients have tried with other systems for same decease before approaching them. 83 percent of doctors have witnessed this situations. This may conclude that patients are trying different health systems with growing consciousness. Doctors are willing to reciprocate by referring to those systems that have proven method of treatment for certain conditions.
9. 91 percent of doctors felt, it is important to discuss the process of treatment with the patients and also other system possibilities.
10. 97 percent of doctors opined patient centred approach is better in treating the patient to enhance doctor – patient relationship.
11. 94 percent of doctors stated that they interact with other systems of medicine directly or indirectly through publications. It is clear indication that doctors do tend to know other systems without preconceived notions which help in cross-pathy referrals.
12. 91 percent of respondents are aware of integrated medicine and 94 percent of agreed to associate with an integrated health unit established under good administration.
13. Latest technology would definitely be of use for providing better and cost effective health care but with doctor touch opined by majority of doctors is 80 percent.

14. Integrated health unit concept is welcomed by majority and their expectations are as follows. Cost effective service, specialist care with patient centered approach, must be able to cater to the large population, and good interaction and co-ordination among doctors may be enhanced.

Patient's Response for Need for IHU

1. Total sample of 200 respondents have opined differently towards efficacy of Allopathic medicine. 30 percent of respondents have opined Allopathic medicine offers comprehensive health solutions; 24 percent said it will not offer solutions; 36 percent said only in few conditions, and 10 percent of respondents do not have knowledge in this regard.
2. 98.5% of respondents have experienced allopathic system in some way or other. 43.5 percent of respondents have experienced Homeopathy along with other systems, 36 percent of respondents have experienced Ayurveda. 33 percent have utilised physiotherapy services for their Musculo skeletal related ailments and 13 percent used naturopathy.
3. During the course of treatment 71 percent of people have shifted from one system of medicine to another system, this concludes that one system alone cannot satisfy the patients to their satisfaction. The reasons for change of medicine system include no satisfactory relief, side effects, doctor's advices etc.
4. 50 percent of respondents could able to arrive at a solution, after changing from the treatment to another. 30 % of respondents could get partial relief.
5. Complementary and Alternative systems of Medicine (CAM) is advocated during chronic pains and skin problems in 40 percent and 33 percent of respondent cases respectively.
6. 51 percent of people spent more than 2000 often on allopathic system, 17 percent of respondents spent 1000-2000 and 15 percent of respondents spent 500 – 1000 towards treatment expenditure.

7. Majority of the respondents ranked Allopathy as more reliable and effective than other systems. At the same time majority of respondents stated that CAM is cost effective, has no side effects and even easy to follow the doctor's advises.
8. It is found that 46 percent of respondents were advised to go for preventive health care by the doctor and rest of respondents were not advised with any preventive health care treatment.
9. It is strongly opined by 83 percent of respondents opined that Doctor should inform about better alternative system of medicine according to diagnosis.
10. 80 percent of patients have appreciated the concept of Integrated health unit where Allopathy and CAM can be offered under one roof and supported the contribution of latest technology i.e. Telemedicine, Teledoc and online treatment as value addition to cause of treatment.
11. Admiringly 70 percent of respondents are aware of integrated medicine. It is a good sign that people are conscious of latest developments.
12. The respondents hold varied expectations towards IHU include IHU should have coordinated approach by all medicine practitioners, should offer comprehensive treatment with patient centered approach, concept should be disseminated at all levels; should be accessible, affordable and reliable.

Integrated Health Care Unit-model

The most important aspect of the Integrated Health Care Unit is the integration of the Allopathi stream of modern medicine with that of the Complementary and Alternative Medicine. This integration comes from proper programming and communication of all systems of medicine.

Once the Integrated health care unit is established and fully developed it is extremely rewarding and lucrative.

Until recently, Allopathic Medicine had failed to recognize the healing benefits of Complementary and Alternative medicine in the treatment of chronic health problems. With the arrival of this latest trend, the two fields have converged and thereby creating the upcoming treatment modality 'the integrated medicine'.

The Integrated Health Care Unit is a hospital which primarily aims at providing outpatient service to the general population using both the Modern medicine as well as the complementary and alternative medicine in providing better health care.

Approaches to Integrate the Operation

One of the methodologies is to create a 'panel of experts', to include both doctors and practitioners. The diagnosis of the patient is discussed with the panel to create a comprehensive treatment program for healing the patient with the Allopathic medicine as well as the Complementary and Alternative Medicine.

The second method is to have each patient undergo a thorough consultation with the primary doctor of the faculty of medicine of his choice. This doctor investigates the patient thoroughly and establishes the root cause of the disease or the problem. The doctor then takes the opinion of the doctors of the faculties of medicine and makes referrals/treatment accordingly.

The doctors need to have a full understanding of a patient's health history and current medications that the patients are undergoing, so as to avoid/performing contra-indicated services or using contra-indicated products.

The treatment information should be explained to the patients fully and all their doubts should be cleared so that patient compliance is better during the treatment. The recording of all types of treatments should be made is one single case-record so that all other doctors treating the same patient can have an idea as to what kind of treatment is being followed.

Important Functioning Principles

- The word 'integration' describes an attitude not a discipline. And it is an attitude that can be shared and enjoyed by orthodox medical doctors as well as by those who practise alternative medicine.

- IHU doctors will use the best diagnostic techniques available. They will use high-technology equipment if it will help in the better diagnosis of the patient's condition. They will use drugs when drugs offer the best hope; they will use acupuncture if that offers that best solution; they will use homeopathy, surgery or osteopathy. They are truly eclectic in their endeavours. Most important of all they will give precedence to the patient's own natural healing powers.
- It is important that the practitioner sees his patient as a whole human being, that he knows the limitations of the type of medicine he himself practises, that he is prepared to refer his patients practitioners in other disciplines and, most important of all, that he is prepared to allow his patients to share the responsibility of their own treatment.
- IHU doctor tells you about the many possibilities available, rather than assume there's only one right way. He offers you his recommendations but respects and support your choices should the two of you differ. He has an open mind, and with his knowledge of the different systems of medicine modalities and therapies he can direct you towards the right treatment.

Planning and Designing of the Integrated Health Care Unit

The layouts given are specifically designed for an urban center. The layouts are so planned that the lower floors contain the consultation rooms, middle floors contain the investigations and pharmacy and the upper floors contain the therapeutic areas.

The core areas of activity of the Integrated Health Care Unit are

1. Treatment (Out Patients)
2. Diagnosis
3. Counseling
4. Dispensing medications through the Pharmacy

The consultation rooms in the ground floor are divided for each system of medicine i.e. Allopathy, Ayurveda, Homeopathy, Naturopathy, Unani, etc. The consultation rooms of the upper floor are to be allotted to the Nutritionist/Dietician, Psychologist, Administrator, etc. The physiotherapist's room is attached to the physiotherapy treatment area.

On the second floor all the diagnostics as well as the physiotherapy treatment zone is allotted. The diagnostics include X-ray room, Ultra-sound room, a laboratory area where all the basic and essential tests are done. The ECG can be done with a portable machine in the ground floor itself.

On the third floor the treatment area is set up. There are 4 massage rooms on this floor two each for Naturopathy and Ayurveda. There are attached baths for each of the massage rooms. There is a Jacuzzi and steam room where 4-6 people can have steam at a time. There is also a mud therapy room.

A small cafeteria is also provided in this floor at the waiting area where fast foods and fresh fruit juices are serve to the customers.

Process Flow of the Patients at IHCU

Packages: Packages can be designed to cater to the requirements of the various segments of population. Some of the packages that can be implemented in an Integrated Health Care Unit are enlisted as below:

1. *Preventive/Diagnostic Wellness Check up*
   - Health Cheq
   - Pregnancy care (Antenatal care)
   - Cardiac Risk Scan
   - Stress Check
   - Obesity Check
   - Executive Health Scan
   - Child Health Cheq
2. *Therapeutic Packages*
   - Asthma Rx
   - Hypetension Rx
   - Diabetes Rx

- Paralysis Rx
- Menopause Management
- Post-Natal Management
- Stress Rx
- Obesity Rx

3. *Rehabilitative Packages*
   - Geriatric Care
   - Cardiac Rehab
   - Cancer Rehab
   - Pulmonary Rehab
   - Neuro Rehab
   - Life Style Management
4. *Rejuvenation Packages*
   - Annual
   - Half Yearly
   - Monthly
   - Weekend
5. *Master Health Check Up*
   - Doctor Consultation
   - Lifestyle Scan
   - Diet Counseling
   - Investigations Like:
     1. Urine
     2. Stool Test
     3. Serum Urea & Serum Creatinine
     4. Lipid Profile
     5. Heamogram
     6. Hbs Ag
     7. X – ray chest

8. ECG
9. Blood Grouping & Typing and HIV testing
10. GTT

Hiring and Staffing Policies

Staffing is an essential and vital element of a successful operation of the Integrated health care unit.

Care should be taken so that Cross-pathy practice is not being done which is in the better interest of the doctors themselves.

As the retention of good doctors is a very tough job, the management of the hospital should see that the doctors are satisfied with their job profile and also there should be ongoing educational programmes and training sessions so that the professional competency is maintained with the ever changing lines of treatment.

Marketing Strategy for the Integrated Health Care Unit: Marketing of any new concept has lots of challenges in it. Marketing of a service always depends on the positioning, quality, efficiency and the pricing. The whole marketing strategy should be based on this need and availability gap.

Some of the Marketing Strategies for the Integrated Health Care Unit are as follows:

1. *Medical Tourism:* Medical Tourism is the highly happening concept now globally. People from different countries are coming to India for various treatments.
2. *Brochures:* These are one of the important methods of advertising of the Integrated Health Care Unit. A beautiful and colorful brochure containing the write up about the Hospitals as well as the Integrated Medicine should be distributed to the Doctor community as well as the select population.
3. *Hoardings and Billboards:* Very well designed Billboards should be kept at very strategic place like areas where there are many hospitals/clinics are located.
4. *Advertisements in the Mass Media:* Newspapers: There should be advertisements in the newspapers in the local news sections.

- *News Reports:* The management should also take care that regular news reports are coming out in the newspapers about the various activities that are being carried in the I.H.U.
- *News Letters:* The doctors should be encouraged to give articles relating to their practicing medicine for publication in the newspapers, as this will have a very good impact on the general population and this incures no cost like in the News reports.
- *Local Cable Network:* Advertisements should also be put in the local cable networks, as this will cater to the target population at a very low price.
- *Flyers:* This is also one of the cost effective means of advertisement where the flyers are put inside the newspaper and distributed to all homes.

5. *Health Awareness Programs:* The Integrated Health Care Unit should conduct health awareness programs for various groups of population like:
   - Residential Complexes
   - Corporates
   - Multinational Companies
   - Schools and Colleges
6. *Tie-ups with Corporates:* The marketing personnel should visit all the corporates and make them aware of the facilities that are offered in the Integrated Health Care Unit and arrange for the tie-up.
7. *Tele-Marketing:* Tele marketing practices can be adopted.
8. *E-Marketing:* A web site with all the information should be started.
9. *Celebrity Endorsements:* The celebrity endorsement may yield better mileage to promotion.
10. *Seminars/Conferences:* The center should take every opportunity to conduct or take part in the seminars/ conferences which will give a wide awareness in the peer group. This with help in getting more referrals.

11. *Kiosks:* Setting up of demonstration windows/kiosks/touch screens in important public places/offices.

Rural Reach Model of the Integrated Health Care Unit:

The rural reach model of the Integrated Health care unit works with minimal investment in the technology part. The principle works in the following way:

1. The health worker is allotted a certain number of villages based on the number of people he can take care.
2. The health worker goes to the villages and meets the patients in those villages.
3. Then he collects the information on a 'cell phone' regarding the diseases from the patients and sends them to the information technology department of the Integrated Health Care Unit.
4. I.T. department then processes the information and gives a hard copy of the patient's condition to the doctors concerned.
5. The doctors then go through the details and request from the health workers regarding any other clarification required.
6. Then the doctors gives the appropriate treatment for the concerned patient.
7. The information in sent to the health worker through email or SMS by the information Technology department.
8. The health worker dispenses the medicine from the kit he is carrying with him.
9. The health worker regularly checks the condition of the patient and sends the information to the concerned doctors.
10. If there is no Improvement in the condition of the patient then the patient is sent to the Hospital for further treatment by the concerned doctor.
11. A nominal amount is changed for the entire duration of the treatment and collected in installments by the health worker.

Marketing

- Community awareness meetings with the help of gram panchayats, schools, self help groups, yuvak sanghs.
- Participation in melas and organizing health camps.
- Training workshops for CAM doctors in rural areas.
- Use of media like Radio.
- Process Flow of the Rural Model.

Conclusions and Recommendations

The need analysis study gives us the conclusion that an 'Integrative Health Care Unit's is highly accepted by doctors and the people equally. Accordingly we designed a model, which can be used as follows:

- The model is universal and can be implemented by a corporate group either as a single unit restricted to limited space in a building or can be spread out as a vast resort.
- It can be attached with an existing Hospital, building its image of being holistic.
- The government can utilize the rural model to provide health for all in rural areas, meeting the state's responsibility of fulfilling the fundamental right to health of every citizen. By doing this it can encourage the CAM system practitioners and support further research.
- Private – public partnership can be formed to use the existing infrastructure of the government facilities and the management skills of the private.
- Individual entrepreneurial practitioners can combine with other system doctors and upgrade their existing clinics into integrated centers providing holistic, multi system treatment.
- Every thing said thus integrated health care unit utilizes optimally all the infrastructure and human resources available in all systems of medicine without bias, and provides cost effective health care with wide array of choices to the people. IHU is the solution for achieving "health for all".

12

MARKETING OF HOSPITAL SERVICES IN INDIA

Dr. Talluru Sreenivas* and **Professor G. Prasad****

The main purpose of the paper is to study the growth and state of the art of the hospital industry in India with a particular focus on the role of service marketing in strengthening the effectiveness of hospital as a part of service sector. It is needless to say how important the sector has been in the national economy in terms of its contribution to the GDP. Nearly 50% of the GDP is now accounted for by the service sector. Though Service sector has gaining prominence in terms of its dominant role at the national level as an important contributor to the GDP, much thought has not yet been given by the academics in terms of introducing the latest management techniques, most importantly marketing strategies, towards improving the effectiveness and efficiency of the hospital system in providing service.

It is gratifying to note that there has been a phenomenal growth in hospital services in India, in terms of increase in the number of hospitals, doctors, nursing, paramedical staff. Recognising the importance of hospital service, as an economic service, even the corporate sector has started entering into hospital segment, investing huge amount of money and in conformity in the mindset of the private enterprise, it has become vital to think in terms of effective utilization

* Reader, Dept. of Management Sciences, RVR & JC College of Engineering, Guntur.

** Department of Commerce & Business Administration, Acharya Nagarjuna University, Nagarjuna Nagar, Guntur.

of this resource, with a view to provide better service to the clientele and to make a reasonable rate of return on the investment for the stake holders. In this context the service marketing gains importance in supplying the relevant tools to strengthen the internal, interactive and external marketing such as Total Quality Management (TQM), Business Process Reengineering(BPR), Bench Marking, Empowerment, Motivation and suitable promotional activities which go a long way in improving the overall effectiveness of the hospital industry. Accordingly, an attempt has been made in this paper to discuss these ideas at the conceptual level and relate them specifically to the hospital sector.

Introduction

A service is any act or performance that one party can offer to another that is essentially intangible and does not result in the ownership of anything. Its production may or may not be tied to a physical product. Earlier, the perception of service was confined to work with only service motto, but now-a-days the services have been commercialised and professionalised. It is due to the emergence of a materialistic age in which the financial health of an organisation or the economic status of an individual are found to be important parameters to evaluate excellence. The developed countries have been successful in tapping the potentialities of the service sector by setting a new paradigm and now the developing countries are following suit. The banking services to meet financial requirements, the education services for qualitative improvements in the system of education, the hospital services to make available to the society the good health care facilities etc. call for a high degree of managerial proficiency which is possible when managerial abilities increase in the service sector.

With a shift from rationalistic approach to a holistic approach, management thoughts have changed substantially. It has enlarged functional responsibility of the manager in managing goods or services. This approach is essential for the organisations to make decisions in the best interests of the society. One step ahead is the customers' or users' satisfaction in which the organisations are expected to serve the interests of all living beings. The above facts prompt the idea that it is essential to align services with the principles of marketing. The marketing strategies with proper innovation may have far reaching impact in finding the priorities for managerial decisions with regard to the services to be offered. This makes available to the society the world class services, in accordance with the changing needs. It can be said that service sector is gaining prominent role at the national level as an important contributor to the GDP. No other service is of greater consequence to the society than the medical service made avail to the public, the management of which is not so far on scientific lines either in public or private sectors. Much thought has not, yet, been given by the academics and administrators to introducing the latest management techniques, most importantly marketing strategies, towards improving the effectiveness and efficiency of the hospital service organisation, the most important of health care services. This paper proposes to study the growth of the hospital industry in India and the role of Marketing with particular focus on the hospitals. It also proposes to introduce the concepts which strengthen the internal, interactive and external marketing in hospital sector.

Conceptual Exposition of Services

It is necessary to define the term service and to examine whether a hospital can be categorised as a service organisation. The increasing interest in the service sector has been accompanied by considerable disagreement as to what constitutes a service. Many authors have sought to develop definitive descriptions of a service. Yet no adequate and acceptable definition has emerged. According to U.S. Government's standard industrial classification, "establishments primarily engaged in providing a wide variety of services for individuals, business and government establishments, hotels and other lodging places, establishments providing personal, business, repair and amusement services, educational institutions, membership organisations and other miscellaneous services are included."

According to Yakeshel and others, services can also be defined as action(s) of organisation(s) that maintain and improve the *well-being* and functioning of people. Here the authors have emphasised the well-being of people. It may be on a commercial or voluntary basis. The peculiarity in service industry is that the raw material is a human being with specific attributes and output also is a human being processed or changed in a predetermined manner but with a qualitative improvement in well-being or functioning. Services have a number of unique characteristics that make them so different from products. Services call for separate attention in respect of delivery system, organisation and other areas of management. Some of the most commonly accepted characteristics are intangibility, inseparability, heterogeneity, perishability, ownership and simultaneity. In the light of the above definitions, one can try to see if the hospital services quality for all characteristics of services described.

The overall process which is involved in hospital business is service. There is nothing which is tangible. It is perishable also. Organisations engaged in hospital business provide a wide variety of services like providing accommodation like hotels, complete nursing care, and provide equipment for diagnosing ailments, arrange transportation in the form of ambulances, catering services to the patients and attendants. The hospitals provide services to different sections of the people, free services to the people who are below poverty line and to some others as a policy.

Business of hospitals also could be called a service. According to Sir Beveridge, services refer to social efforts including government to fight against five giant evils such as want, disease, ignorance, squalour and illness in the society. Here too, one finds that hospital services also fight against these evils. The main objective of hospital is to provide diagnostic and curative services for specific ailments, and removing ignorance about diseases and squalour.

Even Prof. A.V.S. Rao's definition is relevant to the hospital organisation. The gist of Prof. Rao's definition is that the services are provided free of charge or commercially. This aspect is self-explanatory and needs no elaboration. Whatever be the mode, patients are getting immediate care through one of the ways. According to the definition given by Yakeshel Hasenfield and others, one can notice that efforts of hospitals are directed towards maintaining and improving the well-being of the persons who come to the hospital for any reason. While talking about services, Yakeshel has touched upon that of input and output. But unlike manufacturing organisations where input is in the form of raw materials, here both input and output are human beings. The difference is only the changed condition of the individual after availing of some services. Thus, hospitals fall very well within the limits of the definition of the term 'service'.

Increasing Importance of Marketing of Services

There is phenomenal growth of services-marketing both in developed and developing countries. One important reason for this growth is rapid industrialisation which helps in increasing per capita income. The corporate sector plays a key role in engaging services of different consultants like legal advisers, auditors, accountants, tax experts etc. In agrarian economy also this specialisation plays a significant role. The westernisation of culture, liberal cultural exchange policy of the government, increased communication facilities, knowledge transfers, increase in the population levels, and sophistication in the market, have necessitated the development of service sector. Professional bodies have been rendering education in different areas of management which has given enough scope for the development of service sector. Most countries of the world are showing interest in utilising this sector of the economy. The instrumentality of this sector in the sphere of socioeconomic transformation cannot be underestimated. The service sector creates and expands job opportunities. It is significant to mention that in USA, more than 85% of the jobs are created from the service sector. This confirms the growing influence of this sector. More specifically, in developing countries like India, the service sector can contribute much in strengthen-ing the economy and motivate organisations to enter service sector.

Development of service sector minimises excessive dependence on technological advancement. The service sector provides an opportunity to make an optimal utilisation of untapped and valuable resources. The services sector in the Indian economy accounted for 28 percent of the GDP at constant prices in 1960-61. This share increased to 31 percent in 1970-71, 37 percent in 1980-81 and more than 40 percent in 1990-91. In India, during 1990s the development rate is 25% where as it was only 15% in India's Gross National Product in 1950-51. It is important to mention that such a positive trend is found in all developing countries. From the above discussion, one can say that there is remarkable growth of service sector both in developed and developing countries and, thereby, an increasing necessity to manage this sector on scientific Management principles.

Changing Concept of Hospital

In this section an attempt has been made to observe the changes in outlook of the hospital Management. The word hospital is derived from the Latin word 'hospitum' which means a place where guests are received. Hitherto, the concept of hospital is that it is a diagnostic and treatment centre, incidentally providing boarding, lodging, medical care and continuous nursing care for cure of disease, illness or injury. The concept of hospital today is different from that of the past. Earlier, a hospital was regarded as a curative organisation and performed traditional custodian functions. But now it has undergone many radical changes and it is being recognised as a social institution, in addition to being a curative one. A hospital develops its own individual character by providing services to the society at large. Now-a-days, hospitals are considered as a patient-focussed centres instead of provider-focussed centres.

Up to 1950s Indian economy was agricultural. Subsequently, the circumstances have changed and the country launched upon the industrial phase, leading to manufacturing economy. Now we are moving to service economy where customers are more critical and keen towards quality services and demand higher standards. In this era, importance is being given for relations along with physical facilities. The patient is the focal point and the hospital has to strive for maximum patient satisfaction and has to provide patient oriented service. But traditional and rigid hospitals failed to respond effectively to the problems arising out of changing needs. At present public hospitals are run by a Superintendent, who is the senior- most physician, with a small number of administrative staff. A good doctor may not be a good administrator. He himself is a doctor and has to attend to many administrative matters. Time has changed and specialisation has become the order of the day. In the changed circumstances, the public, today, are showing greater interest in corporate hospitals which provide sophisticated service and diagnostic facilities under one roof. Moreover, these hospitals concentrate on patient-focussed care with quality assurance.

Growth of Hospitals

Here is a brief survey of the growth and development of hospitals from ancient times to modern times in India.

Hospitals in Ancient Times : Medical treatment was identified as a part of religious service in 4000 B.C. During pre-Christian era, hospitals were established in Greece, Egypt and India. In 1134 B.C. Greek temples, served as rest places for patients who were under observation. Greek medicine reached its zenith during the golden age of Greece. The first hospitals possessing modern features were found in ancient Egypt and India. Between 273 and 232 B.C. Indian Hindu physicians initiated surgery, built Cikistalayas. They were noted for their cleanliness.

Hospitals in the Middle ages: This era stressed on humanitarianism. These hospitals were built adjacent to churches so that the priests could care for the patients. By 500 A.D. almost every city in old Roman empire had church related hospitals. Scientific medicine was rediscovered. During 14th century, medicine was increasingly separated from religion. During 16th and 17th centuries, European religious brotherhood established hospitals in the western world. In this era, there was remarkable growth in voluntary sector. In a developed country like America, for instance, the first hospital constructed for sick and injured was Pennsylvania hospital, founded in Philadelphia in 1751. The second voluntary hospital was constructed in 1773 followed by Massachusetts general hospital in 1861 and New Heaven Hospital in 1862. It has been estimated that by 1840, there were about 50 permanent hospitals in the United States, most of which were voluntary organisations.

Hospitals in 19th Century: In 19th century, the functions of hospitals underwent radical change. Emphasis was laid on medical, surgical and nursing care. Hospitals continued to offer free services for the indigent and began to establish differential pricing policies based on economic capabilities. This was a period of evolution of modern nursing practice. Nursing care was significantly influenced by the theories and principles of Florence Nightingale.

Development of Hospitals in 20th Century: The 20th century is a period during which hospitals have been called upon to provide an increasing number of services to the patients, resources for the education of physicians, nurses and other members of the health team and facilities for medical research. American Hospital Association emerged in 1907 to provide leadership in the field of hospital administration. The gradual shift from symptom-centred medicine to people-centred medicine is given in the following chart.

Development of Medical Science up to the year 2000
From the empirical era to the era of political health science

	Empirical Era	*Basic Science Era*	*Clinical Science Era*	*Public Health Science Era*	*Political Health Science Era*
1850+	1850+	1900+	1950+	1975+	2000+
Purpose & Philosophy	Symptom-centered, Diagnosis and treatment of symptoms	Bacteria-or disease- centered Diagnosis and treatment of disease	Patient-centered Diagnosis and treatment of the individual	Community-centered Diagnosis and treatment of the community	People-centered Diagnosis and treatment of total body.
Education	Lectures, Authoritarian instruction	Laboratory instruction	Clinical instruction besides teaching	Clinical public health instruction, community side teaching	Social experience, learning social and economic understanding, Managerial, Political Psychology and process, country health programming
Research	Historical	Basic laboratory, development of new tools	Clinical, Development of clinical techniques	Community Development and criteria planning techniques	Social, economic indices for health development, subject indices for quality of life, intersectional activity process, networking process
Behavioral Science	Unknown	Not needed. Individual activity	Ancillary social sciences-An adjunct to medicine speciality, group activity.	Integrated social sciences, sophisticated skills equal with public health science, inter-disciplinary team activity	Inter-related, social, health, economic and political sciences, intersectoral team activity.

Source: WHO: World Health, July 1974, p. 14, cited in Goel S.L., Public Health Administration, Sterling Publishers Pvt.Ltd., New Delhi, 1984, p. 43.

Growth of Hospitals in India

In India, the history of medicine and surgery dates back to the earliest of the ages. But hospitals as institutions to which a sick person could be brought for treatment were of much later origin. The Ayurvedic system of medicine was developed in India after the Aryan invasion of the Indus Valley. In those days religion, art and medicine were combined. In sixth century B.C., during the time of the Buddha there were a number of hospitals to look after the crippled and the poor. King Ashoka was responsible for building outstanding hospitals and for the spread of social medicine. The Upakalpa Niyam Adhyayam gives specifications for hospital buildings, rooms and wards. The decline of Indian Medicine started with the invasion of foreigners in 10th century A.D. During Muslim rule, physicians trained in Unani system of medicine. The first hospital in India was probably built in Goa, and the one in Madras in 1664. The establishment of a hospital in Mumbai was in 1676. The earliest hospital in Calcutta was built during 1707-08 and in Delhi in 1874.

During 17th century, the European doctors employed by the East India Company played an important role in introduction of modern medicine in India in its present form. At that time, Sir Thomas Roe introduced modern medicine in the court of Jahangir, the Moghul Emperor. During 18th century, Western medicine was introduced to serve their armed forces. In this century, the people realised the value of medical practitioners and hospitals. In the 19th century, modern medicine took a firm root. Allopathic Medicine became dominant. In 1835, in India there were 1250 hospitals and dispensaries, which served 6% of total population.

In late 1907, teams were sent by world council of churches to survey Christian Medical work in India. By 1920, foundation was laid for contemporary hospital system. By 1960, health institutions like other industrial organisations became more complex. A survey of hospitals by Dr.McGibony and Christian Medical Commission, 1968, pointed out that large sums of money were invested in buildings, equipments and for training and not in managerial aspects.

Present Status of Hospitals in India

It is gratifying to note that there has been phenomenal growth in hospital services in India in terms of number of hospitals, both public & private, doctors, nursing and paramedical staff. In the last few decades, even middle class urban patients have come to rely heavily on private providers for both ambulatory care and inpatient services. There has been a steady growth of private hospitals since 1970s both in terms of institutions and bed strength. Before the '70s the private bed strength was less than that of the public sector across the states. During the '90s, in Andhra Pradesh, the bed strength in the private sector was higher than that of the public sector. In 1974, the total number of hospitals in Government Sector was 2832 and only 644 in private sector, at the ratio of 81.4% : 18.6%, whereas in 1980, the total number of hospitals in the public sector came to 3735 (64.7%) and there are 2031 hospitals (35.3%) in the private sector. In 1991, the position of hospitals in Andhra Pradesh is 4379 (40.2%) in the public sector and 6522 (59.8%) in private sector. This trend clearly shows the development of private sector.

In India, there are more than 4400 hospitals with 4,11,868 beds under Government control. The hospitals that are managed by other non-governmental agencies number 6,763 hospitals with a bed strength of 2,30,235. The total number of hospitals comes to more than 11,000 with a bed capacity of 6,42,103. The analysis shows that population served comes to 76,082 per hospital and 1324 people per bed. In the past four decades, there have been rapid changes in social, political and economic fields in India. Commendable progress has been made in the medical field, as in other fields during this period. According to Health information of India (1992), India has 128 Medical Colleges with 11,174 hospitals and 6,42,103 beds admitting a million patients, and giving treatment to an unestimated number of outpatients. These hospitals can be further categorised as rural and urban. India has more than 3,568 rural hospitals with bed capacity of 1,26,474 and 7,606 hospitals in urban areas having 5,15,729 beds.

As per the doctor-population ratio statistics in the developing countries, India is having one doctor for every 387 people. China is having one doctor for 1034 people. There has been a steady growth of hospitals per one lakh population from 1950s to 1990s. In 1950, there were 7 hospitals per every ten lakh population. In 1980, hospitals were increased to 10 per ten lakh population. During 1990s it came to 13 per every ten lakh population. Bed ratio per one lakh population in 1950s was 32 and it is 83 during 1980s and it rose upto 97 in 1990s, as can be observed from Table No.1.

Table 1: Number of Medical Practitioners, Hospitals, Beds and Number of All Types of Beds Alongwith Ratios

Year	*Medical Practitioners registered*	*Practitioners for one lakh population*	*No. of hospitals*	*Hospitals per ten lakh population*	*No. of beds*	*Bed ratio per one lakh population*	*No.of beds (all types)*	*Bed ratio per one lakh population*
1951	61800	17	2694	07	–	–	117178	32
1961	83700	21	3054	07	–	–	230000	57
1971	151100	27	3862	07	–	–	348655	64
1981	268700	39	6804	10	476226	68	569395	83
1982	271500	38	6897	10	486805	68	583773	82
1983	284200	39	7189	10	500628	69	599074	82
1984	296500	40	7369	10	514989	69	627120	86
1985	308200	41	7474	10	535735	71	656850	88
1986	320304	41	8067	10	555264	72	694121	91
1987	331886	42	9803	12	585889	74	706471	91
1988	355695	44	10840	13	598059	74	751091	95
1989	368651	46	11079	13	602490	74	794712	97
1990	381978	46	11571	13	629453	75	806409	97
1992	410875	48	13692	16	696203	70	834650	97

Source: Health Information of India, 1994, Central Bureau of Health Intelligence, Ministry of Health & Family Welfare, New Delhi.

There has been phenomenal growth in infrastructure for health sciences since 1951, as can be observed from Table No.2. Apart from this, Central Government emphasises greatly on control and eradication of communicable and non-communicable diseases like Malaria, AIDS, Cancer etc. Various programmes to this effect are being implemented with assistance from the World Bank.

Table 2: Expansion of Health Services

Item	*1951*	*1961*	*1971*	*1981*	*1992*	*1996*	*1997*
Medical Colleges	28	60	98	111	146	165	165
Hospitals	2694	3094	3862	6804	13692	15097	NA
Dispensaries	6515	9406	12180	16751	27403	28225	NA
Community Health Centres	0	0	0	217	2186	2572	2628
Primary Health Centres	725	2565	5112	5740	20701	21917	22446
Sub-centres	–	–	28489	51405	131370	134931	136379
Hospital beds (all types)	117178	230000	348655	569495	834650	870161	NA
Doctors	61840	83756	151129	268712	395851	375291	484401
Nurses	16550	35584	80620	154280	385410	565696	NA

Source: Ministry of Health and Family Welfare cited in Economic Survey, 1998-99.

Apart from Allopathy there exist alternative systems of medicine which are very prominent in India. They are Ayurveda, Unani, Siddha, Naturopathy, Yoga and Homeopathy. In India in 1991, there were 2054 Ayurveda hospitals, 170 Unani hospitals, 108 Siddha Hospitals, 18 Naturopathy and 275 Homeopathy hospitals, as can be observed from Table No. 3.

Table 3: Number of Hospitals under Indian System of Medicine & Homopathy by Management Status as on 01.04.1991

Management	*No. of Hospitals*					
	Ayurveda	*Unani*	*Sidda*	*Naturopathy*	*Yoga*	*Homeopathy*
State Govt./U.T.	1896	147	106	7	3	146
Local bodies	77	1	-	-	-	-
Others	62	13	-	7	3	124
Central Govt.	19	9	2	4	1	5
Total	**2054**	**170**	**108**	**18**	**7**	**275**

Source: Health Information of India, 1993, Central Bureau of Health Intelligence, Government of India.

Hospital Marketing—A Need

Human resources are most precious endowment in a country. The success of a plan of the National Economy rests on the health and well being of its human resources apart from educational skills. This focuses attention on the health services. The development of health care facilities is influenced not only by the opening of hospitals but more so by their management. In the recent past, corporate sector entered health care sector and opened hospitals with super specialisation. This makes it necessary to apply the principles of Marketing to public and private hospitals for their successful functioning. The application of marketing strategies is considered essential as it makes possible a fine fusion between the user's and provider's interests. The users expect world-class services and the providers naturally want a reasonable return. The concept of marketing hitherto used in commerce only, has brought about dynamic changes in the health-care delivery system.

Many of the corporate hospitals over the last one decade have developed a marketing culture in their set up which has enabled them to scale new heights in their ventures. In advanced countries, the marketing has taken deep roots whereas in the developing countries the need is being felt just now. Marketing hospital services is the least understood one and is felt as being not very urgent by many health professionals today. Many of us still prefer to be victims of established rules, ethical codes, social constraints and spiritual laws. There is an inbuilt tendency to think that services will be sold out automatically, built-in wards in a hospital will overflow if a doctor has a degree and money will flow if an equipment is bought. Administrators are keeping other issues aside as secondary and focussing their attention on upgrading their infrastructure. But unfortunately, marketing, which is very essential fcr survival of any hospital, is being almost ignored. Technological sophistication has raised the cost of services. Inflationary pressure, over-population and illiteracy have complicated the task. All these things necessitate application of marketing principles in the hospital services, as the following points make clear.

1. Through application of marketing principles in a hospital, one can optimise the cost of services. It is particularly important in the developing countries like India where the users are unable to bear the burden of costly medical

services. Marketing principles would minimise the cost of services by expanding the scale of operation.

2. Application of marketing principles helps in increasing health consciousness. Particularly in developing countries, the general masses are found disinterested in maintaining the defined norms of physical fitness. This is due to illiteracy and partially due to living habits of the families.
3. Marketing principles bring about behavioural changes in providers that satisfy the users of the hospital services. It suggests a holistic approach towards the user.
4. Another strong justification for applying the marketing principles in the hospital services is related to the financial soundness of hospitals. It provides avenues for generating internal resources.
5. The significance of marketing in hospital services is supported by the fact that potential users are facing problem of communication gap. The users of rural or suburban areas fail to get the latest information regarding the hospital programmes. Promotion strategies like advertisement and publicity will increase the number and the revenue, consequently.

In the Indian environment, almost all hospitals with rare exceptions, are mismanaged. To be more specific, Government hospitals are now found on the point of collapse. There is every necessity to bring fundamental reforms in managing these outfits. No doubt there are number of alternatives before us but the best possible cannot be determined, unless we assign due weightage to the marketing principles.

Marketing Strategies for Hospital Industry

Until recently, service firms lagged behind manufacturing firms in using marketing strategies. Many service businesses at that time were small and did not use formal management or marketing techniques. Professionals also believed that there was no need to use formal marketing techniques. Furthermore, service businesses were more difficult to manage using a traditional marketing approach. In a product business, the product is standardised and sits on a shelf, waiting for a customer to reach for it, pay and leave. In a service business, there are more elements. In a hospital, when a patient or his relatives comes to the hospital for treatment, he observes the number of patients waiting for service by the doctor or other related supporting services. The patient and his well-wishers see the physical environment consisting of building, interior, equipment and furniture. The patient also examines the behaviour of the person to be contacted, and front office personnel. Bitner proposed that ambient factors like temperature, lighting, layout etc. and signage like pictures, signboards, posters, audio system, communication patterns affect the attitude of the customers as well as the employees toward the service, pleasure or arousal.

It is said that a hospital with better layout and better signage result in greater pleasure but not arousal towards using the services again or for recommending to others. Thus service outcome is influenced by a host of complex elements. Gronroos specified that services marketing requires external marketing, internal marketing and interactive marketing. This model can be used in Hospital Industry successfully. The following diagram shows Gronroos model as applied to hospital service.

Figure-1 : Three types of marketing in hospital industry

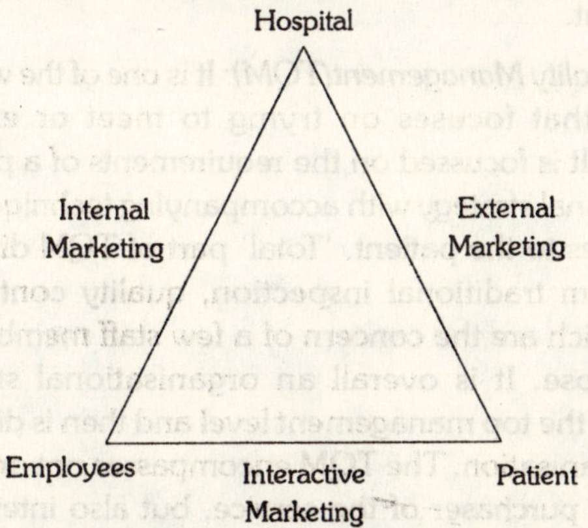

External marketing describes the normal work done by the hospital to prepare, price, distribute and promote different services to the customers. Internal marketing describes the work done by the hospital organisation to train and motivate its employees to serve customers well. On the other hand, interactive marketing describes the employee skill in serving the patient. The patient judges the service not only by its technical quality but also by its functional quality. Professionals must provide high touch as well as high tech.

Purchase of hospital services is usually an outcome of previous experience passed on to the user by the word of mouth more than out of advertisement. They rely heavily on price, abilities of personnel and physical cues such as branding to judge the service quality. Patients are highly loyal to the service provider when satisfied.

The following are some of the strategies to strengthen internal, interactive and external marketing in a hospital industry.

Strategies to Strengthen the Internal Marketing

Hospitals, the public service institutions, have to apply strategies to strengthen internal marketing for its success. Strengthening of Internal marketing is one of the important aspect because nursing care, the clinical skills of the medical staff and the attitudes of the paramedical and other supporting employees are pivotal for successful running of a hospital. Some of the aspects that can be taken into account while strengthening the internal marketing are Total Quality Management, Business Process Re-engineering, Bench Marking, Empowerment.

Total Quality Management(TQM): It is one of the widely accepted approaches that focuses on trying to meet or exceed patient expectations. It is focussed on the requirements of a patient. TQM is an organisational strategy with accompanying techniques that deliver quality services to the patient. 'Total' part of TQM differentiates the approach from traditional inspection, quality control, or quality assurance which are the concern of a few staff members designated for the purpose. It is overall an organisational strategy that is formulated at the top management level and then is diffused through the entire organisation. The TQM encompasses not only the external end user and purchaser of the service, but also internal customers and outside suppliers and support personnel. That "the customer is always right" is an important slogan of the TQM. Team work and co-operation are more important than individual action. Every one will be involved in quality effort. Here the quality is defined by the customer, not by the organisation or the Manager. Thus TQM is a people-oriented approach. Though originally TQM concept is an industry-oriented, gradually it is realised that it can be applied with benefit even in service organisations, especially in hospitals. Due to high costs of medical care, increasing sophistication in diagnosis, recent trends in treatment of diseases, decrease in resources and increased competition, many hospitals are under pressure to cut down their costs while improving the quality of care.

The quality in medical care refers to the degree of excellence of the care extended to the entire satisfaction of the patient, while meeting or even exceeding the accepted standard with improved efficiency related to technological advancement. Quality care is not a temporary effort but it aims at continuous improvement in the patient-care, teaching and research to make the hospital a centre of excellence in the health care system. For effective and efficient implementation of TQM programme, preparing staff in all categories to involve in quality effort is a basic prerequisite. As a next step, there should be adequate hospital information system to ensure reliable feedback. Another prerequisite is standardisation of procedures and identification of areas where changes are needed to plan for improvement. Some approaches to arrive at quality in the process of a hospital activities follow hereunder:

1. Standards are to be laid down for the services of various departments. Vertical divisions between various hierarchies of staff are to be replaced with horizontal integration to develop strong lateral relationship between these groups. An evaluation system is to be developed to measure the performance of individuals to strike a balance between quality and resources.
2. Efficiency of the repeated process in hospitals can be improved by employing optimization techniques i.e. work study, Programme Evaluation Review Technique (PERT), queuing theory etc. Here, the focus is on reducing the variability of the process so as to standardise and to make the organisation stable.
3. In order to improve the quality of medical services, medical audit is to be initiated. It helps in strengthening hospital

procedures by exposing the bottlenecks in diagnostic and supportive services of the hospital. It acts as a stimulus to practise scientific medicine. It helps in preventing the irreparable mistakes in dealing with life of the patient. It helps in maximising the resources with the final aim of providing better quality patient care at minimum cost. Medical audit gives an account of medical care rendered in terms of lives saved, avoidable and unavoidable deaths, diseases arrested, patients restored etc.

4. In order to enhance the morale of the employees in providing quality medical care to patients, the quality circles are to be created. A quality circle is a voluntary association of workers engaged in similar work with an orientation of human relations. These circles help in developing and utilising the human resources effectively through constant interaction. It helps in improving the quality of the services and reduces the cost of production considerably.

5. Purchase of useful equipment, identifying good specifications, performance review of similar equipment in the market, sound warranty and service contract terms will give long and trouble-free service of the equipment and ensures total quality.

6. The patient satisfaction is of paramount importance in a hospital. Ultimately the patient judges the quality of hospital services and hence it is the responsibility of the top management to reidentify the expectations of their patients and translate them into operational requirements to achieve acceptance.

7. As a part of quality assurance programme hospitals have to identify the deviations from normal cases and group certain diseases, basing on discharge summaries. This process is known as identification of diagnostically related groups which in turn helps in arriving at total quality.

8. The workers have to be recognised and rewarded with suitable incentives to keep them motivated for on going quality management performance.

Business Process Re-engineering (BPR): Hospitals can use Business Process Re-engineering as a way to respond to environmental pressures to increase productivity and to cut costs. It is a problem solving approach. It emphasises on the fundamental rethinking and radial redesign of business processes to achieve dramatic improvements in critical, contemporary measures of performance, such as cost, quality, service and speed. BPR involves a total redesign of operations by analysing jobs and critical questioning like 'How can this work be done most efficiently?' Rather than modifying current work procedures, the re-engineering process begins with a clean slate and plans the job from the beginning to the end. BPR starts with top management's rethinking of the basic mission of the organisation. This provides direction for the re-engineering effort. As a next step top management will play an active role in leading the process and thus ensuring overall cooperation from the personnel. Then operations will be designed from the outside by first finding out what the customer wants. Finally it involves top-down and bottom-up initiative.

Bench Marking: Besides the popular BPR technique, now the concept of Bench Marking is receiving attention. Bench Marking is the process of comparing work and service methods against the best practices and outcomes for the purpose of identifying changes that will result in higher quality output. Bench Marking incorporates the use of human resources techniques such as goal setting to set targets that are identified, pursued, and then used as a basis for future action. The Bench Marking process involves looking both inside and outside the organisation for ways of improving operations. It helps in creating a need for change by showing the organisation how procedures and work assignments should be altered and resources reallocated. It helps organisations to improve their total quality in service organisations, particularly in the hospital sector. Bench Marking is essential for setting standards that are acceptable to the user.

Empowerment: It is a people oriented approach. Empowerment is the authority to make decisions within one's assigned duties without getting approval from anyone else. Two characteristics make the concept of empowerment unique. One is that the personnel are encouraged to use their initiative and the second is that employees are given just authority and resources, so that they are able to make a decision and ensure that it is implemented. Participation, innovation, access to information, and accountability are the basic conditions necessary for empowerment to become operational and a part of organisational culture. Empowerment assumes that employees are willing to improve their daily work process and are competent enough. Participation is one of the basic prerequisite for empowerment. Empowerment encourages innovation because employees have the authority to try out new ideas and make decisions that result in new ways of doing things. In order to enhance the willing co-operation of the employees they are exposed to free access to information. As a result of this accessibility, work teams are able to manage and control operations more effectively. Although employees are empowered to make decisions, they are also held accountable for results. However, this is not intended to punish the personnel or to generate short term results. The intention is to ensure that the empowered employees give of their best to achieve the set goals.

Strategies to Strengthen the Interactive Marketing

Like many other services, hospital services too require personal interaction between patients and the employees. These interactions strongly influence the patients' perception of service quality. The stay of a patient and his attendants in a hospital is greatly influenced by the friendliness, knowledgeability and helpfulness of the hospital staff including the staff of the front office, reception services, house-keeping etc. Therefore, the management faces a tremendous challenge in selecting and training all of these people to do their jobs well, and, perhaps even more important, in motivating them to make an extra effort to serve the patients.

For this reason, Human Resource Management policies and practices are considered to be of particular strategic importance for delivering high quality services. Another adoptable strategy is establishing a patient-oriented culture throughout the hospital (TQM) and empowering employees to provide quality service. Job redesigning, providing a system to recognise and reward outstanding achievement and motivating the employees to reach higher goals, are some of the adoptable strategies to strengthen interactive marketing.

Strategies to Strengthen the External Marketing

Product, place, price and promotion are the important aspects to be covered in external marketing. By using the information taken from research and analysis phase one has to decide what the product should be. The main products of hospitals are medical services. The nature of the hospital, the changes in environmental conditions, technology and global competition govern the product mix of a hospital. After developing the initial product description, one has to identify the positioning strategy. It is describing the product in terms of each target group of patients. Sometimes the product will be the same but the way it is positioned may be different. It is essential that the decision-makers give weightage to the factors influencing the medical care, medical education, training and research facilities. While formulating product mix one has to give importance to the task of satisfying the users. The marketing strategies should satisfy the users with the help of refined services. As explained earlier, while formulating product mix one has to consider the environmental factors, the doctors, paramedical staff and other supporting staff.

Location of a hospital is another crucial decision to be taken by the administrator. It should have neat and clean surroundings. In addition, it is also important that the policy-makers should make all possible efforts for the beautification of the surroundings and premises. While selecting a suitable site for the location of the hospital, the management should be careful to the availability of infrastructural facilities like transportation, communication, electricity etc. The place should improve the quality of services. The financial involvement on the beautification of premises and surroundings is nominal but its impact on the hospital output is of high magnitude. The hospital authorities have to give due weightage to disposal of wastages, as this plays vital role in maintaining cleanliness in the premises. The pricing decision should be market-driven. The hospital must first determine its own costs for delivering services. This market-driven pricing should be compared with the competitors pricing structure. Research helps in determining the pricing sensitivity. The hospital must aim at pricing the services in tune with the paying capacity of the population. If the strategy is welfare oriented, the task of satisfying the users is also simple. But satisfaction too depends on sophistication and sophistication in turn depends on pricing. Hence, pricing should be fixed on sound lines basing on socio-economic factors of the target group.

The last step in creating the marketing mix is developing promotional strategies. In addition to the positioning strategies developed for each target group, specific promotional strategies also should be developed. The main purpose of promotional strategy is to convince the target group and compete with similar institutions. Promotion can be both personal and impersonal. Personal promotion can be person to person where as impersonal promotion can be through advertising, publicity and sales promotion. Advertising is important to contract avenues for a multiplication in the number of users of the services. In promotional activities, there is great need for creativity, sensitivity and accessibility. It is also important that, through promotional strategies the general masses should get information regarding the treatment facilities which are available in the hospital. Another promotional strategy is providing health care packages for a fixed price to fast-growing health conscious customers. Still another strategy is achieved through regular means, which includes word of mouth publicity. Hospitals can adopt insurance tie-ups with insurance companies. Yet another strategy is to publish magazines, which give information about various services. Hospitals can arrange frequent public lectures, seminars and workshops to spread awareness about health care. As a promotional strategy hospitals can adopt master check-up at reasonable prices. The prices should depend on economic levels of the population and should attract the general masses.

Conclusion

It is needless to say how important the service sector has become in the national economy in the terms of its contribution to the GDP. Though the service sector is gaining prominence in terms of its dominant role at the national level as an important contributor to the GDP, much thought has not yet been given by the academics in terms of introducing latest management techniques, more importantly marketing strategies, towards improving the effectiveness and efficiency of the hospital system, in providing service. Marketing of hospital services is needed to educate large numbers of people. There is a need for marketing the hospital services in order to provide the right kind of information and education and to cure the ailments of the patients in the best possible manner.

An attempt is made in this paper to study the state of the art and growth of the hospital industry in India and to develop a model to market hospital services. This paper has tried to discuss relevant tools which are helpful in strengthening the internal, interactive and external marketing such as Total Quality Management (TQM), Business Process Re-engineering (BPR), Bench Marking, Empowerment, Motivation and suitable promotional activities at the conceptual level and also has tried to relate them specifically to the hospital sector. It is hoped that these concepts could go a long way in improving the overall effectiveness of the hospital industry. Good Marketing Programmes will build up more awareness among the public, create loyalty, and establish a kind of tie-up with potential customers. Thus it may be concluded that application of marketing principles in the Indian hospitals cannot be ignored or delayed any longer.

REFERENCES

1. Sasser W.E., Orson R.P., Wycoff D.D., *Management of Service operations*, Boston, Allyn & Bacon Inc. 1978, p.2.
2. Hasen Field, Y.Ritchard AE, *Human Resources Management*, The University of Michigan Press, 1974.
3. Sir William Beverdge, *Report on Social Insurance and Allied Services*, London, HMSO, 1942,p.24.
4. Rao AVS, *Service Sector Management in India*, Hyderabad, Allied Publishers Private Ltd.,1988.
5. Bhatt Sanjeev, *Marketing of Services, The Economic Times*, April 28th 1988.
6. Jha SM, *Services Marketing*, Himalaya Publishing House, New Delhi, 1997,p.15.
7. Mary Risley, *House of Healing*, Garden City, New York, Double Day, 1961, pp.53-66.
8. Jesani, *A Size of Private Sector in Health Care Delivery System in India*, Medico Friend Circle Bulletin, July-Aug,1991,p.10.
9. *Health Information of India, 1991*, Central Bureau of Health Intelligence, Govt.of India.
10. *Health Information of India, 1992*, Central Bureau of Health Intelligence, Govt. of India.
11. *Health Information of India,1994*, Central Bureau of Health Intelligence, Govt.of India.

12. *Health Information of India, 1993,* Central Bureau of Health Intelligence, Govt. of India.
13. Mary Jo Bitner, *Service Capes : The Impact of Physical Surroundings on Customers and Employees*, Journal of Marketing, April 1992, pp. 57-71.
14. Christian Gronroos, *A Service Quality Model and its marketing Implications*, European Journal of Marketing, Vol.18,No.4,1984, pp. 36-44.
15. Kotler Philip, Paul N.Bloom, *Marketing Professional Services*, Eagle WoodCliffs, NJ, Prentice Hall, 1984.
16. Satyanarayana P, *Total Quality Management in Hospitals*, Hospital Administration, Vol.32 (3&4), Sept-Dec,95, pp. 41-46.
17. Michel Hamer, James Champy, *Re-engineering the Corporation*: A Manifesto for Business Revolution, Harper Collins, New York, 1993, p.32.
18. John H.Dobbs, *The Empowerment Environment* Training and Development Journal, Feb. 93, pp. 55-57.

13

TOTAL QUALITY MANAGEMENT IN HOSPITALS

Ch. H.K.S. Kumar* and **Dr. Talluru Sreenivas****

It is widely accepted by now that the contribution of service sector as against the traditional manufacturing and agricultural sectors to aggregate output is significant across the countries including our own country. What is equally significant to note is that the quality of the customer service rendered has not perhaps been a top priority with the Indian manufacturing/service sector. Quality has thus gained a focal point in strategy crafting and implementation at the organizational level. It has in fact become part of the vision and mission statement of every economic organization in the society today. Quality was one of the differentiators among the providers till the other day. But today, with the increased buyer power in the market, customers have reached a stage where they start assuming that quality of service/product is a big given and looking for other attributes that make a big difference among the offerings in the market place. Medical sector, being one of the important service sectors in the economy, is not an exception to this phenomenon. Quality of the medical service rendered has become a challenging task to the hospital administration, as the patient-expectation of the health service is increasing exponentially with increased health awareness on his part on the one hand increased

* Asst. Prof., Dept. of Science & Humanities, Al Habeeb College of Engg. & Tech., Hyderabad.

** Reader, Dept. of Management Sciences, RVR & JC College of Engineering, Guntur.

income levels on the other. The implementation of the concept of Total Quality Management in the Management of health care sector in our country will go a long way in improving its operating efficiency, resulting in efficient resource allocation for optimum advantage, minimum wastage of the available resources and significant improvement in the quality rendered, all leading to considerable value addition to the end user of the hospital service i.e. the patient. The hospital has a primary obligation, and a moral and legal responsibility to see that the quality of care meets acceptable standards and that the interests of the patients are well protected. Total Quality Management in a hospital encompasses a set of four principles – delighting the patient, people-based Management, Management by fact and continuous improvement. It can be implemented by putting into practice suitable Total Quality Management Method. One of the approaches to Total Quality Management is the adoption of the ISO 9000 Series of quality standards, systems and procedures.

Introduction

A large number of contemporary organisations across the globe have adopted *Total Quality Management* (TQM) to satisfy customers through quality products and responsive services in order to gain competitive advantages. TQM first took its roots in improving quality of physical products, as the measurement of quality performance of such products was easier. Subsequently, TQM found its strongest root not merely in improving the quality performance of products, but in Organisational transformation–specifically in bringing about a cultural change, in improving employees morale and in facilitating an empowering working climate for retaining excellent human performance.

The philosophy of TQM is as important to any organisation as is to manufacturing because competing more effectively for profound growth and sustaining more consistently in the context of continuous changes and ever-expanding competition have become overwhelming and all pervasive concerns for all types of enterprises. TQM focuses on the integration and coordination of all activities in a work process and aims at continuous improvement in quality. Quality means not merely the quality of end products but the quality of all kinds of means such as data, information, decision, objectives, strategy, people materials, machinery, systems etc.

A country's economic development evolves through a three stage process from agriculture to manufacturing to services. The service sector contributes to the economy by absorbing surplus labour released from the agriculture and manufacturing sectors due to automations.

The service sector plays a positive role in maintaining the economic stability and such a sector is growing at a very rapid rate. The sector covers many organisations such as health care, education, banking, insurance, hotels, transport, tourism, municipalities, power supply and distribution, police, telecommunications, judiciary, professional societies, consulting companies etc. only to name a few, and involves a number of people engaged in the variety of work processes providing innumerable types of services both tangible and intangible. The service as a function makes direct interaction with a variety of customers.

The varieties of customers are characterized by social, cultural, economic, religious backgrounds etc. and thus differentiated in their expectations about the performance of the service. The needs and priorities put forward by the customers and efforts taken by the service providers/system under the same category to meet these needs also vary both spatially and temporally. As the society becomes more matured both educationally and culturally, the societal demands for quality services increase. Therefore, today, we observe that a large number of organisations engaged in providing services are implementing TQM. To implement TQM effectively in service organisations requires an analysis of the unique characteristics of the service operations, the role of clientele of services as well as that of the providers of services; and the application of appropriate quality management concepts, tools and techniques.

Quality Defined

"The totality of characteristics and features of a product or process, which facilitate, realisation of given requirements."

German Standard DIN 55350

TQM ??????

TQM defines quality as "conformance to correctly defined requirements that satisfy user needs". The definition emphasizes the ultimate goal of quality products and services that meet customer needs and expectation at a cost that represents the best value. Quality is viewed in recent years as a system having many elements that contributes to a specific purpose. TQM has been defined in a variety of ways; meaning a quest for excellence, creating the right attitudes and controls to make prevention of defects possible and optimizing customer satisfaction by increased efficiency and effectiveness.

Features of Total Quality Management

1. Continuous improvement embodies the fundamental principle of TQM. Both incremental and breakthrough improvement are encouraged by using improvement tools and techniques and learning from within the organisations and through external benchmarking. Education and training reinforce this role for everyone in the organisation.

2. TQM blurs the boundaries between the organisation and the external customers and suppliers. Customers and suppliers are considered as part of the work processes. Customer needs drive the key processes, while supplies assume an important role in the organisational goal of satisfying the customers.

3. TQM focuses every aspect of the organisaiton's activity towards a customer-oriented, right-first-time approach. The entire organisation understands the internal working relationship and the interdependence of each individual and process as "Customers and Suppliers".

4. TQM calls for pro-active and systematic reviews and measurement of key processes that add value.

5. TQM is a management philosophy to guide a process of change and starts at the top. TQM ensures that quality be recognized as a corporate strategic priority, along with financial and other priorities.

6. TQM is about achieving results by process-based approach and focuses on the customer.

7. TQM recognizes internal customer-supplies relationship and considers suppliers as part of the organisation's processes.

TQM–Major Elements

1. Leadership
2. Leadership Commitment
3. Recognition and Rewards
4. Education and Training
5. Customer Orientation
6. Team Work and Employee Empowerment
7. Feedback Mechanism
8. Statistical Process Control

Growth and Significance of Service Sector

The service sector is expanding rapidly across the world and today represents the largest segment of the economy in all countries. A service economy is one in which more than half of the country's workforce earns its income from employment in service functions. The following table indicates the growth rate of the value-added service sector because of globalization and diversification in some select economies.

Table1: Growth Rate of Value-Added Services (% per amount)

Region/ Country	*1981-1990 (Avg)*	*1991*	*1994*	*1996*	*1997*
India	6.8	4.7	6.0	6.4	7.0
Korea	17.7	10.5	8.4	8.0	7.3
Indonesia	7.5	9.3	7.5	7.7	7.2
China	12.4	10.0	8.2	10.0	12.0
Thailand	7.7	6.1	8.5	6.4	6.2
Kazakhstan	5.2	19.0	3.1	1.2	7.5

An article on *The Reserve Bank of India – Currency and Financial Report* presents statistics demonstrating how the share of the service sector in the real GDP has surpassed that of agriculture and industry in India. The following table shows the details of this growth.

Table 2: Service Sector Growth in India

Share in GDP

Time Period	*Agriculture*	*Service*	*Industry*
1980-81	38.1	41.0	20.9
1984-85	35.9	41.0	22.9
1990-91	30.9	43.7	28.4
1995-96	26.0	47.0	26.7
1996-97	28.0	49.9	22.0
1997-98	26.4	51.2	22.3
1998-99	26.8	51.2	22.0

Service Quality

Most service quality definitions are customer led and have an external focus. Quality is defined as consistently meting or exceeding customer meeting expectations. This approach relies on the ability of the organisation to determine customer requirements and then meet these requirements. A "Customer-led" definition implicitly encompasses the "Supply-led" approach. This is because the customer's requirements are built into the service at the design stage, but it is at the transformation stage that the degree of conformance is determined. This approach, therefore, is suitable for organisations offering "high contract", "skill and knowledge based" or labour intensive services such as healthcare, law, education, leisure and hoteliering.

Berry et al have identified the principal dimensions customers use to judge service quality.

These are:

- Reliability
- Responsiveness
- Assurance
- Empathy
- Tangibility

In the view of above, an organisation can practice a set of programs which can allow the organisation, a methodology to make a beginning. The requirements of a Service Quality Program are presented here.

Table 3: Requirements of a Service Quality Program

Task Boundaries	*Customer Requirements*	*Process Control Requirements*	*Organisational Requirements*	*Quality Requirements*
Cross-functional approach	Assurance	Measurements tools	Top management commitment	Timelines
Operational option	Reliability	Evacuation tools	Education and training	Integrity
Behavioural option	Empathy	Improvement tools	Defining roles & responsibilities	Customer satisfaction
Vendor option	Durability	Information system	Recognition & reward system	Zero defects
Delivery option	Responsive-ness	Resource allocation	Team work	Total satisfaction and delight

Service Quality Model

Defining and measuring service quality is a challenging task. In fact, service quality is the most researched topic in the services marketing field. Since every organisation today is potentially a service provider, both to internal and external users, an organisation that ignores the validity of service quality does so at its own peril. There are several conceptual models that the managements in service organisations can deploy in pursuit of quality improvement. The conceptual models enable managements to identify quality shortfalls and plan the launch of a TQM program. A model attempts to show the relationships that exist between salient variables. Models developed by researchers are almost invariable simplified versions of reality. They suggest that there are simple relationships between complex phenomena and that systems operate by rules of cause and effect.

The following are few important conceptual models; all focused on different stand points.

1. The Gronross Service Quality Model
2. The Servqual Model
3. Moore's Service Quality Model

4. Service Journey Model
5. Behavioral Model
6. Service Delivery Model
7. Haywood-Farmer's Attribute Service Quality Model
8. Customer Perception Model
9. P-C-P Attribute Model

ISO 9000 Series

The ISO 9000 consists of five primary parts numbered as 9000 to 9004. If we were to display them on continuum of an operating firm, the series would range from design and development through procurement, production, installation and servicing. While ISO 9000 and 9004 only establish guidelines for operations, ISO 9001, 9002 and 9003 are well-defined standards.

Quite a bit or work and expense may be needed for a firm to be accredited at ISO 9001, which is the highest level. Furthermore, some firms may not need ISO 9001 accreditation at all. For example, ISO 9003 covers quality in a production's final inspection and testing. A firm can be accredited only at this level of final production. This would essentially guarantee the firm's quality of final output and it would be attractive to customers. A broader accreditation would be ISO 9002, which extends from purchasing and production through installation.

There are 20 elements in the ISO 9000 standards that relate to how the system operates and how well it is performing. These are contained in section 4 of the ISO 9000 guidelines. Each of these elements applies in varying degrees to the three standards, 9001, 9002 and 9003 (ISO 9001 contains all of them).

ISO 9000 is somewhat vague, but intentionally so. A firm interprets the requirements as they relate to its business. From a practical and useful standpoint for business, ISO 9000 is valuable to firms because it provides a framework, using which they can assess where they are and where they would like to be. In its simplest terms, it is sometimes stated that ISO 9000 directs you to "document what you do and then do as you documented".

While this is true to some extent, ISO 9000 is much more than that since it promotes awareness and continuous improvement. The

International Organisation for Standardization intended the 9000 series to be more than a standard, reflecting a well-organised operation with trained, motivated people. It is proposed as the new challenge, with firms that adopt it quickly enjoying the benefits of being a leader, and those that delay losing business.

ISO 9004, Part 2–About Quality

ISO 9000 is set up as a guideline to select and apply quality management STANDARDS (ISO 9001 – 9004). It also contains recommendations relevant to the adaptation of quality management to specific contractual situations. ISO 9001 contains a model describing the structure of a quality management system in all pahses of the complete "production" process, i.e. development, production, construction and service. ISO 9002 and 9003 refer to single phases, respectively. ISO 9004 contains criteria and guidelines to select relevant quality management elements. Unlike ISO 9001 – 9003, it is intended for internal use only.

ISO 9004, part 2, comprises recommendations for establishing a quality management system in service industries. All processes necessary to perform a certain service are included – marketing, design and service delivery. Permanent communication between the customer and vendor as well as evaluation by the customer is supposed to ensure constant improvement of service quality by influencing all elements of the quality management system.

Within the marketing process, the quality of market research and analysis has to be assured. Information about customer needs, legal regulations, innovations, changes in market forms and sizes have to be analyzed. If, based on these data, the decision is made to offer a certain service, a specification has to be drawn up, containing the requirements necessary to satisfy customer requests and the company's duties. In addition, the quality of advertising and service management has to be subsumed under the marketing process.

Within the design process, the service to be performed, means and methods of delivery have to be defined, based on the specified requirements. The first refers to the features of the service and the extent to which they have to be fulfilled in order for the service to be acceptable. The service delivery specification contains methods for delivery, requirements concerning necessary means and acceptance criteria for various service features. Both parts are actively intertwined during the entire design process.

Within the service delivery process, means and methods that are necessary for delivery are employed. To determine internal and external quality, the process also contains the assessment of service quality through customers and suppliers.

TQM–in Hospital System

During the last several centuries, the healthcare system has been spectacularly successful in increasing the human life span. The primary reason for this is the setting up of numerous quality controls on a wide variety of activities, products and systems, all relating to human health. In the new age of healthcare, the need is to shift the medical paradigm away from the traditional perception that the accepted standard is just to deliver healthcare in a scientific and caring manner.

Healthcare systems are of fundamental interest to all societies. As societies become more advance and standards of living rise due to economic development, quality of life improvements become more predominant. Eventually, increasing importance and reliance are placed on total quality healthcare systems. This rising importance is also reflected in the increasing percentage of national resources both private and public) allocated to healthcare systems. Healthcare systems revolve around their customer, the patients. The most important organisational and individual outcomes are comprehensive and durable changes in the mental and physical well being of people. This human centered purpose defines the fundamental nature of quality in healthcare systems.

Hospitals and other healthcare organizations across the globe have been progressively implementing TQM to reduce costs, improve efficiency and provide higher quality care. Contrary to popular belief, the TQM movement was not the start of concerns about quality in healthcare. The roots of quality assurance initiatives in healthcare extend at least as far back as the time of Florence Nightingale's work during the Crimean War (1854 – 1856), when the introduction of nutrition, sanitation and infection control initiatives in war hospitals contributed to a reduction in the death rate from 43 to 2 percent.

TQM can be an important part of a hospital's competitive strategy. Hospitals in competitive markets are more likely to attempt to differentiate themselves from their competitors on the basis of greater service quality. Thus, TQM, which places a heavy emphasis on improved customer satisfaction, offers the prospect of greater market share and profitability.

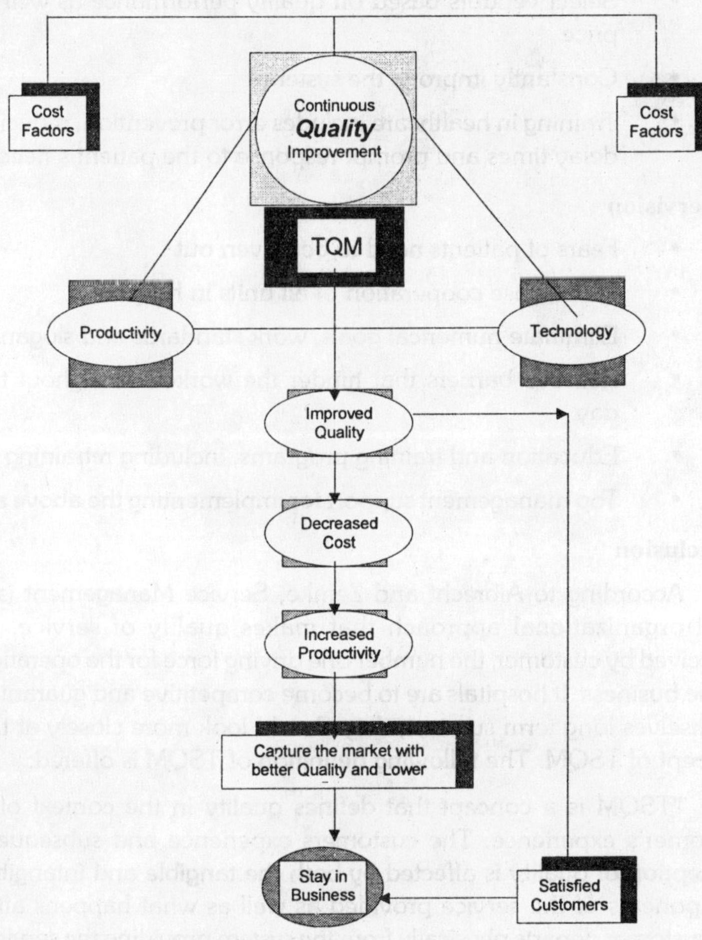

Deming's Principles–Application to Healthcare Systems

- Acceptable quality health service to patients at an affordable price
- Avoid mistakes, which may prove fatal and costly
- Insist on zero defects, eliminate inspections through proper quality control on vendors
- Select vendors based on quality performance as well as price
- Constantly improve the system
- Training in healthcare includes error prevention, reducing delay times and prompt response to the patient's needs.

Supervision

- Fears of patients need to be driven out
- Enlist close cooperation of all units in hospital
- Eliminate numerical goals, work standards and slogans
- Remove barriers that hinder the worker throughout the day
- Education and training programs, including retraining
- Top management support for implementing the above all.

Conclusion

According to Albrecht and Zemke, Service Management is a total organizational approach that makes quality of service, as perceived by customer, the number one driving force for the operation of the business. If hospitals are to become competitive and guarantee themselves long term survival, they should look more closely at the concept of TSQM. The following definition of TSQM is offered:

"TSQM is a concept that defines quality in the context of a customer's experience. The customers experience and subsequent perception of quality is affected by both the tangible and intangible components of the service provided as well as what happens after the customer departs physically from the system providing the service. TSQM begins with TOP MANAGEMENT'S COMMITMENT and must be instituted at all levels of organization".

Road Map for the Implementation of TQM

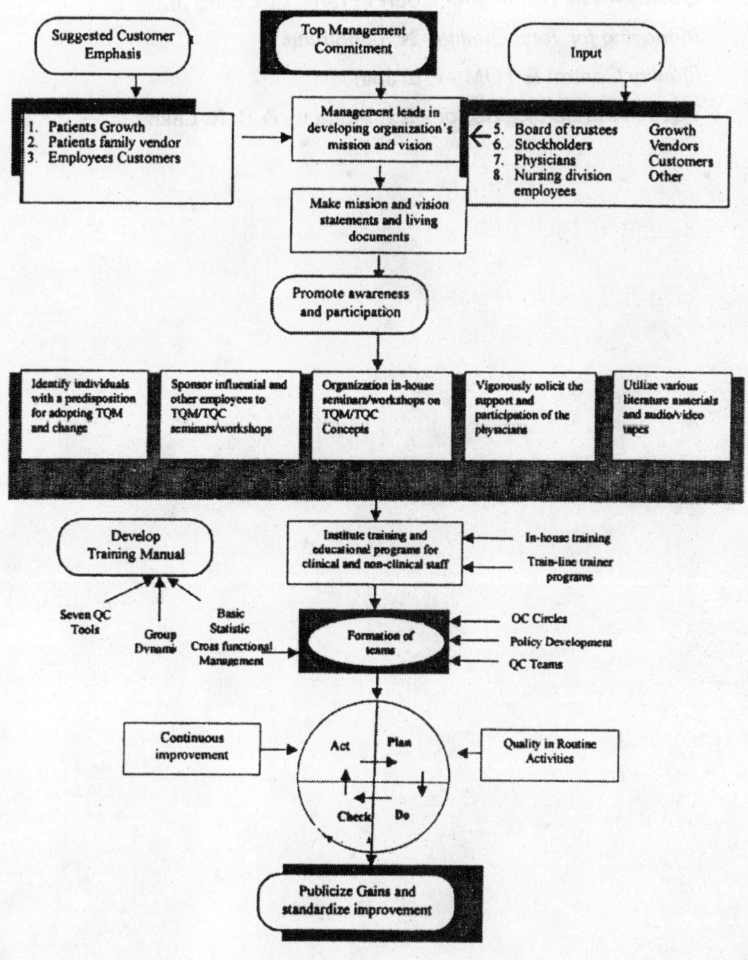

REFERENCES

1. *Total Quality Management* - Dale H. Besterfield et al
2. *Quality – The Ball in your Court* - Frank. C. Collins Jr.
3. *Managing for Total Quality* - N. Logothetis
4. *Quality Control & TQM* - P. L. Jain
5. *TQM in the Service Sector* - R.P. Mohanty & R. R. Lakhe

14

ETHICS AND VALUES
A STUDY OF HEALTH CARE SERVICES

Dr. Talluru Sreenivas* and **Professor G. Prasad****

For the last few decades there has been a tremendous progress in the field of medicine, be it in the ancient forms like Ayurvedic or Homeopathic or in the modern form of Allopathic medicine. Wonder drugs and new systems of curing are being innovated and today's patient is getting excellent attention because of the continuing research in this field. Increasing literacy rate, Information availability through print and electronic media, globalisation process, Increased resources have changed the mind-set of patient and his attendants considerably. In fact, the patient of yesterday showed more interest on the type of medicines and the quality of doctors, but today, it is very well known fact that the patient is demanding for the timely reaction of the nursing staff, para-medical staff and other auxiliary services. In view of this, Hospital Management has become an extremely dynamic, demanding and challenging field, requiring modern management expertise.

Now a days, the tertiary care hospitals are able to create such an environment whereby the medical and non-medical experts combiningly redefined the meaning of health treatment. They are mainly responsible for changing the concept of hospitals and are able

* Reader, Dept. of Management Sciences, R.V.R.& J.C.College of Engineering, Guntur.

** Dept. of Commerce & Business Administration, Acharya Nagarjuna University, Guntur.

to mix up medical treatment, clinical facilities, hospitality services, technology and management in the administration of hospitals. Irrespective of their achievements in the medical field, these hospitals are being criticised for non-follow up of medical ethics while doing the business of health. Conducting unnecessary tests, Corruption, favoritism, unhealthy competition and unethical advertisements are some of the important issues on which these hospitals are subjected to criticism. This paper tries to evaluate the reasons for performance decline in large hospitals in India from ethical point of view and tries to analyse the major criticism against these hospitals. Finally, the paper also suggests certain measures for bringing value-oriented holistic approach in the management of these hospitals.

Introduction

The importance of state of health of the people can scarcely be over- emphasised. The ultimate objective of all socio-economic development is to bring about a meaningful and sustained improvement in the well- being and welfare of the people, and there is no better index of the well- being of the people than the state of their health. Investment in industry, agriculture and education finally would have impact on health. The importance of direct investment in the health sector to improve health status of the people and the contribution of a healthy population to socio-economic development is too obvious to need any elaboration. Distinguished economist like Professor Amartya Sen, Noble laureate, has been advising on the need for increasing investment in the health sector and reengineering of the present management of health sector in India.

The Concept of Hospital

The word hospital is derived from the Latin word 'hospitum' which means a place where guests are received. Hitherto, the concept of hospital is that it is a diagnostic and treatment centre, incidentally providing boarding, lodging, medical care and continuous nursing care for cure of disease, illness or injury. The concept of hospital today is different from that of the past. Earlier, a hospital was regarded as a curative organisation and performed traditional custodian functions. But now it has undergone many radical changes and it is being recognised as a social institution, in addition to a curative one. A hospital develops its own individual character by providing services to the society at large. Now a days, hospitals are considered as a patient-focussed centres instead of provider-focussed centres. Let us examine a few definitions of the term hospital.

According to the directory of hospitals in India, 1988, "A hospital is an institution which is operated for the medical, surgical and/or obstetrical care of in-patients and which is treated as hospital by the Central/State Government/Local body or licensed by the appropriate authority."[1]

Goyal, R.C. evolved a comprehensive definition for the hospital: "A modern hospital is an institution which possessed adequate accommodation and well-qualified and experienced personnel to provide services of curative, restorative and preventive character of the highest quality possible to all people regardless of race, colour, creed or economic status, which conducts educational and training programmes for the personnel particularly required for efficacious medical care and hospital service, which conducts research assisting the advancement of medical science and hospital services and which conducts programmes on health education."[2]

With the passage of time, it is natural that a change in perception is visible. Yesterday, the hospitals were considered as alms houses. They were set up as a charity institutions to take care of the sick and poor. Today, it is a place for the diagnosis and treatment of human ills, for the education, for imparting training, for promoting healthcare activities and to some extent a centre helping bio-social research. The view-points expressed in the WHO document have enlarged the functional areas for modern hospitals. It is against this background that the hospitals rekindle new hopes and aspirations to the people of the society. The WHO documents further consider a hospital as a complex organisation. It is complex in the sense that multi-faceted developments in the society have made the people of the society more conscious of their rights. Today, they demand modern and best possible means of medical care and health education. They want everything not only within the four-walls of the hospital but at their door-step or in the vicinity of living places. Thus hospital is a major social institution for delivering healthcare, offering considerable advantages to both patient and society. It is considered to be a place for the diagnosis and treatment of human ills and restoration of health and well-being of those temporarily deprived of.

Role of Hospitals

Broadly the role of modern hospital has two major aspects viz. the curative and preventive aspects.

The Curative Aspect: The curative or restorative function of the hospital remains its most important and best appreciated service. This involves firstly diagnosis as an out and in patient service. Early diagnosis and prompt treatment is having prime importance not only for the individual patient but also for the general health and medical care system as well. The curative function includes apart from diagnosis and treatment, rehabilitation of patients. Rehabilitation means helping the physically and mentally handicapped to resume their normal roles as useful members of the society.

The Preventive Aspect: In a developing country like India, with a large population, the importance of preventive aspect of healthcare cannot be undervalued. The preventive aspect includes health education, maintaining hygienic conditions, immunisation, etc. In developing countries the bulk of preventive work needs to be decentralised and carried out by health centres situated at the periphery of health services as majority of the population lives in rural areas. The role of modern hospital in this context would be to act as a referral base for health centres.

Functions of a Hospital

The modern hospitals have a full range of important functions such as diagnostic and treatment services to in-patients. Within this broad function there will be many sub-functions such as medical, surgical, obstetrical, pediatric and other special forms of care. Secondly, there should be services to outpatients, with an equally wide range of specialties and technical modalities. Thirdly, there should be professional and technical education. The fourth function includes the medical research and fifth concerns prevention of diseases and health promotion in the surrounding population.The main function of a hospital is to promote health of the community which it serves.

Changing Concept of Hospitals

The major changes in concept of hospitals can be divided into different periods such as trusteeship period, physician period and administration period. Trusteeship period began with the origin of hospitals. Trustees funded most hospitals during this period. The economic and political environment had little influence on hospitals. Hospital employees worked primarily on humanitarian grounds rather than for financial rewards. During physician period, therapy progressed and laboratory medicine developed. Ancillary hospital services were provided. Political environment began to affect the hospitals. Labour unions gained power. Rural hospitals were established. During this period hospitals were not viewed as a charitable service. In team and administration period, Hospital services were the result of teamwork. Various services were expanded considerably. Many hospitals tried to adopt various strategies to meet the competition. There was a time when hospitals were in the sellers' market and not in the buyers' market and hence most hospitals in the absence of any competition, managed to survive, even flourish, despite a care-less attitude. During the last few decades, with emergence of corporate hospitals, the scene is fast changing. Quality patient care is the key word in most corporate hospitals today backed by professionally qualified specialists. Once patients and their attendants used to depend on mercy of the doctors and other supporting staff, but today the patient is demanding for clean-environment, time management, quality of auxiliary services in addition to the medical attention.

Growth of Corporate Hospitals in India

In India, the history of medicine and surgery dates back to the earliest of ages. But hospitals as institutions to which a sick person could be brought for treatment were of much later origin. In 6th century BC, during the time of the Buddha there were a number of hospitals to look after the poor. King Ashoka was responsible for building outstanding hospitals. During 17th century, the European doctors employed by the East India Company played an important role in the introduction of modern medicine in India in its present form. Allopathic medicine became dominant during 19th century. By 1920, foundation has been laid for contemperary hospital system. By 1960, health institutions like other industrial organisations became common. Most of the hospitals during this period, are administered by the traditional system of promoting the senior-most physician in the institution as a Director. By and large he does not posses any formal training in Hospital Administration. Lack of training in the modern management techniques and human behaviour services, principles of general Business Administration or budgetary procedures, has adversely effected the medical service provided to the patients. Today, Hospital Management has become an extremely dynamic, demanding and challenging field, requiring modern management expertise. To fill the existing gap, Corporate hospitals are emerging for provision of medical assistance to the public.

The development of the corporate hospitals is the most important development in the private health sector in the eighties. The pioneer in the field was the Apollo Hospital in Chennai. This multi-crore hospital with the latest diagnostic and therapeutic facilities and established with money raised from the capital market has set the trend. The Apollo Hospital was set up in 1983, and was followed by diagnostic centres of the United Group, Standard Medical Group, Surlax Diagnostic Ltd., etc. Within a period of just two years, between 1984 and 1986, Rs.200 crores were invested in these corporate ventures. This rapid expansion is due to the high profitability of such ventures. For example, the United Group recovered its investment on a brain-scanner within two years[3]. The non-resident Indian doctors have also linked themselves with this trend. For example, Kovai Medical Centre and Hospital in Tamilnadu has been promoted by a group of NRI doctors. This company has set up a 250 bed hospital complex at Coimbatore[4]. The public sector institutions are helping these ventures. For example, the Andhra Pradesh State Financial Corporation has lent Rs.7.35 crores for the Delhi Administration to buy 26% of equity-shares in a joint sector company – Indraprastha Medical Corporation Limited – in Delhi, with the Apollo Group[5]. After the Apollo hospital, nine more corporate hospitals involving an investment of around 120 crore rupees are in the pipeline in Hyderabad city alone.

The following Table gives the information relating to corporate hospitals established in Indiain the span of one and half decade.

Corporate Hospitals in India between 1979-1994

Sl. No.	Organisation name	Year of establishment	Place
1.	Appolo Hospitals Ltd.	1979	Madras
2.	United Diagnostics International Ltd.	1981	Bombay
3.	Deccan Hospitals Ltd.	1982	Hyderabad
4.	Seahorse Hospitals Ltd.	1982	Tiruchirapalli
5.	Tamilnadu Hospitals Ltd.	1984	Madras
6.	Surlex Diagnostic Ltd.	1985	Bombay
7.	Kovai Medical Centre&Hospitals Ltd.	1985	Coimbatore
8.	A.D.S.Diagnostics Ltd.	1985	New Delhi
9.	C.D.R.Healthcare Ltd.	1986	Hyderabad
10.	Regency Hospitals Ltd.	1987	Kanpur
11.	Noida Medicare Centre Ltd.	1988	New Delhi
12.	Medwin Hospitals Ltd.	1989	Hyderabad
13.	G.I.L.Hospitals Ltd.	1989	Baroda
14.	Malar Hospitals Ltd.	1989	Madras
15.	Sharma East India Hospitals and Medical Research Ltd.	1989	Jaipur
16.	Devaki Hospitals Ltd.	1990	Madras
17.	Secunderabad Healthcare Ltd.	1991	Secunderabad
18.	Lokmanya Industries Ltd.	1982	Bombay
19.	Ishwar Medical Services Ltd.	1992	Thane
20.	Dolphin Medical Services Ltd.	1992	Vijayawada
21.	Medinova Diagnostics Ltd.	1993	Hyderabad
22.	Dr. Agrawal's Eye Hospitals Ltd.	1994	Madras

Achievements of Corporate Hospitals

The corporate hospitals are able to create an environment where in the medical and non-medical experts combinedly redefined the meaning of health treatment. They are mainly responsible for changing the concept of hospitals and are able to mix up medical treatment, clinical facilities, hospitality services, technology and management in the administration of hospitals.

Corporate Hospitals are giving treatment in a way, an Indian patient could never have dreamt of never have dreamt of two decades back. These hospitals are able to provide proper guidance at the registration counters to avoid misunderstanding and efforts are being initiated by these hospitals to minimise the waiting time and long queues. These hospitals are providing world class facilities in health care. The environment is so created that the patient feels at home. The admission process is so streamlined that it causes minimum amount of inconvenience to patients. This helps in determining the humanity in the hospital. Research and Development was a forgotten area before emergence of these Corporate Hospitals in India. These hospitals are able to bring capable doctors' teams under one roof. The authorities of these hospitals are able to establish links with the hospitals of other countries. These hospitals have grown to an extent whereby they are able to bring International experts in specific fields in less than 24 hours. These hospitals are able to provide adequate physical facilities with a good functional layout. Provision of adequate waiting areas, toilets, drinking water and refreshment facilities are some of the unique characteristics of modern corporate hospitals.

The patients are being provided with clean and well-ironed linen along with good communication system, which helps the patients in many ways. These hospitals are maintaining state of the art equipment (both surgical and electronic). Maintenance of the operation theatres, ICUs, Casualty are excellent. These are well manned, equipped and organised to deal with any type of situation. Corporate hospitals are striving to render quality services. All levels of staff are committed to render quality patient care. The management of various corporate hospitals is continuously emphasiging on quality patient care and efficiency in the care of patients. Waiting period of receiving specimens at the lab counter, X-ray and ECG etc. is kept to a bare minimum. Specialists are serving food that is hot and hygienic. Another remarkable achievement made by these corporate hospitals is introduction of scientific management for its administration. These hospitals are able to appoint experts in the fields of Management, organisational behaviour, Marketing, Financial Management, Management of Hospital Information Systems, and advanced techniques like sequencing, transportation, assignment, linear programming in order to optimise the various resources and services.

Irrespective of their achievements, Corporate hospitals are being criticised by many due to the following reasons.

Criticism Against Working of Corporate Hospitals

The cost of medical care in these profit-oriented corporate high-tech hospitals is, of course, beyond the means of ordinary citizens. Now healthcare has become sheer business. Heavy investments in the health business make them profit-oriented and hence they tend to unnecessarily hospitalize patients. Quite often expenses of high tech equipment are at the cost of patients by subjecting them to unnecessary investigations. There are many instances where even for common illness the helpless patient has to undergo a list of tests. For example, at a corporate hospital, a person, despite presenting classic clinical symptoms of T.B. was asked to undergo numerous tests including C.T. Scan before in normal, inexpensive X-ray, sputum or montoux test getting done. The specialists apparently are carried away by the manuals of the machines and forget to do the standard tests. But some consultants say that it is difficult to prove that many of these investigations carried out are unnecessary. For example, it is 'normal' during a master checkup to have an ECG done and instances of patients suggested to undergo the treadmill test is a matter of rule rather than exception, according to senior consultants. The treadmill being only a fifty percent specific pointer to the existence of heart disease, the patient is again advised a coronary angiogram.

1. The commercialisation undermining medical ethics is now well known. The nexus between the doctors and the medical Industry is well established. Similarly a nexus exists between the drug stores, pathology laboratories, diagnostic centres and doctors. That is why excessive and unnecessary investigations are carried out and drugs used on patients – all as a means of augmenting profits. All this naturally adds to the cost of medical care in the private sector.
2. Commercialisation breeds unhealthy competition as also unethical advertisement. The code of ethics does not prohibit institutions, and hospitals from advertising their services. But it does clearly forbid doctors from doing so. However, even doctors' skills are being given as advertisements in the form of news paper inserts or by giving interviews in the media about their specialised skills.

3. In corporate hospitals, huge investments are made on sophisticated and costly equipment and there are complaints that patients are made to pay for services involving use of equipment, irrespective of whether such services are necessary in a particular case. Though a person may afford to get admitted to a hospital there is no guarantee of getting proper care and attention. In recent years, the media has highlighted numerous instances of reckless attitude and malfeasance on the part of the members of the profession[6].

4. Assistants employed in this sector, except in few big hospitals, are under-qualified. Given their low educational qualifications and the very superficial training given by the doctors, most assistants cannot cope with the responsibilities they have to handle. The quality of care thus suffers. Owing to long hours of work and poor wages, poor avenues of progress, the staff is dissatisfied and this, in turn, adversely effects the quality of their work.

Ethical Issues Involved

A doctor or a hospital cannot divorce himself/itself from social realities and moral dilemmas. Medical ethics is a discipline concerned with establishing standards of ideal human conduct in providing health care to a community. Medical ethics is understood to be a code of conduct acceptable and normal within the medical profession. A health care professional has access to privileged communication and resources to enable him to care for and maintain the health of a society. Health care professionals must therefore have definite guidelines to solve ethical problems, which may arise in the course of their practice. A professional code of ethics and legal sanctions thus attempt to lay down permissible standards of conduct. The general principles in medical ethics include Truthfulness (patient is entitled to know the truth), Beneficence (responsibility to do good to the patient), Non-malfeasance (do no harm), Justice (concerned with the equitable distribution of benefits and burdens), Confidentiality (limiting access to patients' records). The actual application of these four principles is not uniform – codified rules are determined by the extent of social progress made by the concerned society and the emergence of a consensus on this matter within the society and the profession. Further, situations can arise in which two principles might come into conflict while rendering care to the patients.

The new code of Ethics, 2002 (See Appendix) issued by the Medical Council of India came into force from 6th April,2002. The code specifically stated certain acts of physicians as unethical. The broad items of these acts include - advertising, patient and copy rights, running an open shop (Dispensing of Drugs and Appliances by Physicians), rebates and commission, secret remedies, human rights and euthanasia. The code of Ethics also included certain acts of commission or omission on the part of Physician as 'misconduct', leading to disciplinary action by the Council. The code of Ethics is applicable to the doctors personally and not to the Corporate Hospitals as institutions.

However, the Corporate Hospitals as social institutions cannot escape from the responsibility of safeguarding the Indian ethics and human values. They must consider the social and ethical implications of their decisions as the survival and growth of any enterprise depend upon its acceptance by the society and its environment.

Conclusion

For the last few decades there has been a tremendous progress in the field of medicine, be it in the ancient forms like Ayurvedic or Homeopathic medicine or in th modern form of Allopathic medicine. Wonder drugs and new systems of curing are being innovated and today's patient is getting excellent attention because of the continuing research in this field. Increasing literacy rate, Information availability through print and electronic media, Globalisation process, increased resources have changed the mindset of consumer considerably. Once the patient used to ask for mercy of the doctor and their supporting staff but today, it is very well known fact that the patient is demanding for the timely reaction of the nursing staff, para-medical staff and other auxiliary services. Our hospitals, today, are well-equipped with all the facilities and equipment and can proudly claim the presence of well qualified doctors with commitment and dedication. Yet they are not ready to face the present radical changes particularly in the area of patient centered care. The change in the doctors and other staff is not real. It is only half-hearted. Doctors are unable to come out from their own psychological set up. What they are saying to the out side world is not being implementing in the real life situations. Paramedical staff is becoming strong and envious of doctors and the Institution and unable to come up to the expectations of the top administration. Another problem quoted in the study is cost of medical care. One should not ignore the Indian conditions. In India, most of the population is below the poverty line. These masses cannot afford to pay luxurious facilities. These corporate hospitals are becoming pro-rich. Following ethical principles necessary for any organisation. The services of these hospitals should be economical and professionally managed. Unethical advertisements, advertisements are to be curbed with heavy hand. Doctors should not forget the Indian code of medical ethics, which is given to each applicant at the time of their registration to take a pledge to dedicate their lives to the service of humanity.

REFERENCES

1. Directory of hospitals, New Delhi, Central Bureau of Health Intelligence, Ministry of Health and Family Welfare, 1988.
2. Goyal R.C. Handbook of Hospital Personnel Management,New Delhi, Prentice-Hall International Inc., 1993, pp.3-4.
3. Bhaskar R.N., The Corporation of Medicare; Business India, Dec.-Jan 1986-87,p.79.
4. Anantharam Saraswathy, Corporatisation of Health-Care in India, FRCH Newsletter, Vol-IV No.4, p.6.
5. ibid.
6. Saraf, D.N., Genesis of COPRA, Health for the millions,December, 1992, Vol.18. No.6

APPENDIX

Following are the Code of Ethics, 2002 (Regulations published in part III, Section 4 of the Gazette of India, dated 6th April, 2002) issued by Medical Council of India that every medical professional has to keep in mind.

Unethical Acts

A physician shall not aid or abet or commit any of the following acts which shall be construed as unethical -

Advertising

1.1 Soliciting of patients directly or indirectly, by a physician, by a group of physicians or by institutions or organisations is unethical. A physician shall not make use of him/her (or his/her name) as subject of any form or manner of advertising or publicity through any mode either alone or in conjunction with others which is of such a character as to invite attention to him or to his professional position, skill, qualification, achievements, attainments, specialities, appointments, associations, affiliations or honours and/or of such character as would ordinarily result in his self-aggrandizement. A physician shall not give to any person, whether for compensation or otherwise, any approval, recommendation, endorsement, certificate, report or statement with respect of any drug, medicine, nostrum remedy, surgical, or therapeutic article, apparatus or appliance or any commercial product or article with respect of any property, quality or use thereof or any test, demonstration or trial thereof, for use in connection with his name, signature, or photograph in any form or manner of advertising through any mode nor shall he boast of cases, operations, cures or remedies or permit the publication of report thereof through any mode. A medical practitioner is however permitted to make a formal announcement in press regarding the following:

1. On starting practice.
2. On change of type of practice.
3. On changing address.
4. On temporary absence from duty.
5. On resumption of another practice.
6. On succeeding to another practice.
7. Public declaration of charges.

1.2. Printing of self photograph, or any such material of publicity in the letter head or on sign board of the consulting room or any such clinical establishment shall be regarded as acts of self advertisement and unethical conduct on the part of the physician. However, printing of sketches, diagrams, picture of human system shall not be treated as unethical.

2. *Patent and Copy rights:* A physician may patent surgical instruments, appliances and medicine or Copyright applications, methods and procedures. However, it shall be unethical if the benefits of such patents or copyrights are not made available in situations where the interest of large population is involved.
3. *Running an open shop* (Dispensing of Drugs and Appliances by Physicians): - A physician should not run an open shop for sale of medicine for dispensing prescriptions prescribed by doctors other than himself or for sale of medical or surgical appliances. It is not unethical for a physician to prescribe or supply drugs, remedies or appliances as long as there is no exploitation of the patient. Drugs prescribed by a physician or brought from the market for a patient should explicitly state the proprietary formulae as well as generic name of the drug.
4. *Rebates and Commission:*

    4.1 A physician shall not give, solicit, or receive nor shall he offer to give, solicit or receive, any gift, gratuity, commission or bonus in consideration of or return for the referring, recommending or procuring of any patient for medical, surgical or other treatment. A physician shall not directly or indirectly, participate in or be a party to act of division, transference, assignment, subordination, rebating, splitting or refunding of any fee for medical, surgical or other treatment.

    4.2 Provisions of para 4.1 shall apply with equal force to the referring, recommending or procuring by a physician or any person, specimen or material for diagnostic purposes or other study/work. Nothing in this section, however, shall prohibit payment of salaries by a qualified physician to other duly qualified person rendering medical care under his supervision.
5. *Secret Remedies:* The prescribing or dispensing by a physician of secret remedial agents of which he does not know the composition, or the manufacture or promotion of their use is unethical and as such prohibited. All the drugs prescribed by a physician should always carry a proprietary formula and clear name.

6. *Human Rights:* The physician shall not aid or abet torture nor shall he be a party to either infliction of mental or physical trauma or concealment of torture inflicted by some other person or agency in clear violation of human rights.

7. *Euthanasia:* Practicing euthanasia shall constitute unethical conduct. However on specific occasion, the question of withdrawing supporting devices to sustain cardio-pulmonary function even after brain death, shall be decided only by a team of doctors and not merely by the treating physician alone. A team of doctors shall declare withdrawal of support system. Such team shall consist of the doctor in charge of the patient, Chief Medical Officer/Medical Officer in charge of the hospital and a doctor nominated by the in-charge of the hospital from the hospital staff or in accordance with the provisions of the Transplantation of Human Organ Act, 1994.

Misconduct

The following acts of commission or omission on the part of a physician shall constitute professional misconduct rendering him/her liable for disciplinary action

1. Violation of the Regulations: If he/she commits any violation of these Regulations.
2. If he/she does not maintain the medical records of his/her indoor patients for a period of three years as per regulation 1.3 and refuses to provide the same within 72 hours when the patient or his/her authorised representative makes a request for it as per the regulation 1.3.2.
3. If he/she does not display the registration number accorded to him/her by the State Medical Council or the Medical Council of India in his clinic, prescriptions and certificates etc. issued by him or violates the provisions of regulation 1.4.2.
4. Adultery or Improper Conduct: Abuse of professional position by committing adultery or improper conduct with a patient or by maintaining an improper association with a patient will render a Physician liable for disciplinary action as provided under the Indian Medical Council Act, 1956 or the concerned State Medical Council Act.

5. Conviction by Court of Law: Conviction by a Court of Law for offences involving moral turpitude/Criminal acts.
6. Sex Determination Tests: On no account sex determination test shall be undertaken with the intent to terminate the life of a female foetus developing in her mother's womb, unless there are other absolute indications for termination of pregnancy as specified in the Medical Termination of Pregnancy Act, 1971. Any act of termination of pregnancy of normal female foetus amounting to female foeticide shall be regarded as professional misconduct on the part of the physician leading to penal erasure besides rendering him liable to criminal proceedings as per the provisions of this Act.
7. Signing Professional Certificates, Reports and other Documents: Registered medical practitioners are in certain cases bound by law to give, or may from time to time be called upon or requested to give certificates, notification, reports and other documents of similar character signed by them in their professional capacity for subsequent use in the courts or for administrative purposes etc. Such documents, among others, include the ones given at Appendix-4. Any registered practitioner who is shown to have signed or given under his name and authority any such certificate, notification, report or document of a similar character which is untrue, misleading or improper, is liable to have his name deleted from the Register.
8. A registered medical practitioner shall not contravene the provisions of the Drugs and Cosmetics Act and regulations made there under. Accordingly,
   (a) Prescribing steroids/ psychotropic drugs when there is no absolute medical indication;
   (b) selling Schedule 'H' & 'L' drugs and poisons to the public except to his patient;

   in contravention of the above provisions shall constitute gross professional misconduct on the part of the physician.
9. Performing or enabling unqualified person to perform an abortion or any illegal operation for which there is no medical, surgical or psychological indication.

10. A registered medical practitioner shall not issue certificates of efficiency in modern medicine to unqualified or non-medical person.

    (**Note:** The foregoing does not restrict the proper training and instruction of bonafide students, midwives, dispensers, surgical attendants, or skilled mechanical and technical assistants and therapy assistants under the personal supervision of physicians.)

11. A physician should not contribute to the lay press articles and give interviews regarding diseases and treatments which may have the effect of advertising himself or soliciting practices; but is open to write to the lay press under his own name on matters of public health, hygienic living or to deliver public lectures, give talks on the radio/TV/internet chat for the same purpose and send announcement of the same to lay press.

12. An institution run by a physician for a particular purpose such as a maternity home, nursing home, private hospital, rehabilitation centre or any type of training institution etc. may be advertised in the lay press, but such advertisements should not contain anything more than the name of the institution, type of patients admitted, type of training and other facilities offered and the fees.

13. It is improper for a physician to use an unusually large sign board and write on it anything other than his name, qualifications obtained from a University or a statutory body, titles and name of his speciality, registration number including the name of the State Medical Council under which registered. The same should be the contents of his prescription papers. It is improper to affix a sign-board on a chemist's shop or in places where he does not reside or work.

14. The registered medical practitioner shall not disclose the secrets of a patient that have been learnt in the exercise of his/her profession except –

    (i) in a court of law under orders of the Presiding Judge;

(ii) in circumstances where there is a serious and identified risk to a specific person and/or community; and

(iii) notifiable diseases.

In case of communicable/notifiable diseases, concerned public health authorities should be informed immediately.

15. The registered medical practitioner shall not refuse on religious grounds alone to give assistance in or conduct of sterility, birth control, circumcision and medical termination of Pregnancy when there is medical indication, unless the medical practitioner feels himself/herself incompetent to do so.

16. Before performing an operation the physician should obtain in writing the consent from the husband or wife, parent or guardian in the case of minor, or the patient himself as the case may be. In an operation which may result in sterility the consent of both husband and wife is needed.

17. A registered medical practitioner shall not publish photographs or case reports of his/her patients without their permission, in any medical or other journal in a manner by which their identity could be made out. If the identity is not to be disclosed, the consent is not needed.

18. In the case of running of a nursing home by a physician and employing assistants to help him/her, the ultimate responsibility rests on the physician.

19. A Physician shall not use touts or agents for procuring patients.

20. A Physician shall not claim to be specialist unless he has a special qualification in that branch.

21. No act of invitro fertilization or artificial insemination shall be undertaken without the informed consent of the female patient and her spouse as well as the donor. Such consent shall be obtained in writing only after the patient is provided, at her own level of comprehension, with

sufficient information about the purpose, methods, risks, inconveniences, disappointments of the procedure and possible risks and hazards.

22. Research: Clinical drug trials or other research involving patients or volunteers as per the guidelines of ICMR can be undertaken, provided ethical considerations are borne in mind. Violation of existing ICMR guidelines in this regard shall constitute misconduct. Consent taken from the patient for trial of drug or therapy which is not as per the guidelines shall also be construed as misconduct.

23. If a physician posted in rural area is found absent on more than two occasions during inspection by the Head of the District Health Authority or the Chairman, Zilla Parishad, the same shall be construed as a misconduct if it is recommended to the Medical Council of India/State Medical Council by the State Government for action under these Regulations.

24. If a physician posted in a medical college/institution both as teaching faculty or otherwise shall remain in hospital/ college during the assigned duty hours. If they are found absent on more than two occasions during this period, the same shall be construed as a misconduct if it is certified by the Principal/Medical Superintendent and forwarded through the State Government to Medical Council of India/ State Medical Council for action under these Regulations.

15

BIOMEDICAL WASTE MANAGEMENT

Dr. Venkateswara Rao Malapati*

Wherever we go in India over the length and breadth of the country, we find accumulated garbage along the roads, unclean environment and hazardous disposal of waste. The scene is not different even in metros, cities, towns. In villages there is no organized system of disposal at all. In fact, majority of the Indians do not bother about surroundings. Strangely, even those that keep their houses clean throw the waste on the road or in front of the neighbour's house.

Falling in line with the general situation, we find certain public places like hospitals, vegetable, fish and other market places, Railway Stations, Bus stands, Parks and Cinema Halls are maintained unhygienically contributing to the spread of infectious diseases. It is wonder how the elite like doctors and higher officials who work in such public places and spend major part of their day time in these places are callous to the environment. Particularly, hospitals generate an enormous amount of dangerous waste. The amount of solid waste generated by hospitals has been increasing rapidly in developing countries like India. Hospital waste has increased to such proportions that it can no longer be ignored. Increasing concern for community health standards and pollution control requirements demand that the huge mass of infectious waste be rendered as harmless as possible before it is disposed.

* Professor and Head, Dept. of Chemical Engineering, RVR & JC College of Engineering, Chowdavaram, Guntur - 19, A.P.

Introduction

Man is the most dominant being in the biosphere. A unique combination of certain physical and mental abilities has made him more powerful than other living beings. With the accumulation of knowledge and increase in the sophistication of artifacts and machines, man has acquired the capacity to change the environment to suit his needs. Human needs and greed coupled with short-sightedness have disturbed the delicate ecological balance by depleting and degrading the vital life supporting systems such as air, water and land – which rightfully belong to the generations that succeed us. The biosphere is rapidly changing from a naturally self-sufficient system to a system of resources for just one of its inhabitants – MAN. The present day man is plundering the environment as though he is the last to inhabit the earth.

Environment is the Surroundings in which an organisation operates, including air, water, land, natural resources, flora, fauna, humans and their inter relations. Surrounding in this context, extend from within an organisation to the global system. Basic functions of environment are to support life, provide material and energy, and absorb and recycle the toxins and wastes. Impact of human activity on environment is either positive or negative, improving or degrading, polluting the atmosphere and resulting in possible damage to plant and animal life.

All over the world, there is an exodus of people from villages to cities, partly for education and employment and partly because agriculture has become less and less profitable. It is estimated that 65% of the world's population will live in cities by 2030.The infrastructure required for this lop-sided growth of the cities is resulting in mountains of garbage collecting in the unplanned extensions in larger cities, because of poor conservancy services and lack of civic amenities. It is estimated that the domestic garbage produced per day in Mumbai is of size of an eight stored building coplux. The quality of air in the surroundings of the cities is so poor that it is estimated about two million children under five die each year from respiratory infections

Preserving the environment, which is essential for survival of humanity, is the biggest problem faced by India. By nature, environmental preservation and development of urban and rural infrastructure are two things that do not always go hand -in- hand. Development of urban infrastructure and irrigation facilities invariably reduce the forest areas and the greenery in the urban areas producing dangerous waste material of unmanageable proportions

Further, the growth of chemical industry with dangerously toxic effluents let out into open areas and nearby rivulets and establishment of large hospitals and health care units that create infectious and hazardous wastes is the greatest problem to be surmounted by Environmentalists and civic authorities.

The dilemma of the problem is that one cannot be sacrificed for the other. Sustaining the development and protecting the environment is a difficult balancing act, which the civic authorities have to perform. Invariably, it is a compromise, but to what extent? On the one hand, development is essential for the economic growth and on the other a clean environment is as much essential for the survival of the humanity

Health-care activities like immunizations, diagnostic tests, medical treatments, and laboratory examinations, protect and restore health and save lives. But what about the wastes and by-products they generate?

Of the wastes generated by health-care activities, almost 80% is the general waste comparable in safety to domestic waste. The 20% of wastes are hazardous materials that may be infectious, toxic or radioactive. The wastes and by-products cover a diverse range of substances and materials.

The amount of solid waste generated by hospitals has been increasing rapidly and ranges from 2-5 kg/bed/day in developed countries and 0.5-2.0 kg/bed/day in developing countries like India. Of course, the total amount of waste produced in a hospital each day depends on the type of specialization and the standard of the hospital. Cities consume 75% of the planet's natural sources and at the same time discharge equal percentage of waste. For instance, Delhi hospitals alone produce more than 30 tons of biomedical waste every day. Hospital waste has increased to such proportions that it can no longer be ignored.Increasing concern for community health standards and pollution control requirements demands that the mass of infectious waste be rendered as harmless as possible before it leaves the hospital. It is imperative that the problem of ever increasing garbage, toxic and bio-medical wastes has to be tackled in an efficient and effective manner, so that the fruits of development and the nature's gifts of clean air and water are both enjoyed by the people.

Against this background an attempt is made in this paper to discuss the problem of disposal of wastes in Indian hospitals and suggest a few measures for the effective management of waste disposal.

Hospital Waste(bio-medical Waste)—Environmental Pollution

It is matter for concern that even hospitals, like other public places-Railway stations, Bus complexes or Fish markets-are very unhygienically maintained: it is a wonder that people who should know better, the Doctors and other officials who spend most of their time in these surroundings, are insensitive to this issue. Particularly Hospitals generate an enormous amount of dangerous waste. The amount of solid waste generated by hospitals has been increasing rapidly in developing countries like India. Hospital waste has increased to such proportions that it can no longer be ignored. Increasing concern for community health standards and pollution control requirements demand that the huge mass of infectious waste be rendered as harmless as possible before it is disposed.

It has been established beyond doubt that improper management of hospital waste has been responsible for spread of infectious diseases among the general public. Hospital employees, patients and the attendants are susceptible to diseases due to infected tissues, biological fluids, and infected materials of patients. The patients themselves are at the risk of cross infection, if adequate precautions are not taken.

It has been observed that many hospitals and nursing homes dump the waste at the garbage collection site from where garbage is cleared away by the vehicles for final disposal. The sites are visited by rag pickers looking for disposables may get infected while handling infected items. The greater danger is that items picked are often cleaned and sold in the market and may find their way back to the hospitals. For instance used needles, syringes, gloves, discarded drugs etc. get recycled increasing the risk of infection.

Categories of Bio-medical Waste

According to Bio-medical waste (management and handling) rules,1998 (amended in 2000),based upon the Environmental (protection) Act 1986,the categories of bio-medical waste are as follows.

1. *Human Anatomical Waste*: Human tissues, organs, body parts
2. *Animal Waste:* Animal tissues, organs, body parts, carcasses, bleeding parts, fluid, blood and experimental animals used in research, waste generated by veterinary hospitals, colleges, discharge from hospitals, animal houses.
3. *Microbiology & Biotechnology Waste:* Wastes from lab. cultures, stocks of specimens of micro-organisms, live or attenuated vaccines, human and animal incineration cell culture used in research and infectious agents from research and industrial laboratories, wastes from production of biological toxins, dishes and devices used for transfer of cultures.
4. *Waste Sharps:* Needles, syringes, scalpels, blades, glass etc. that may cause puncture and cuts. This includes both used and unused sharps.
5. *Discarded Medicines & Cytotoxic drugs:* Wastes comprising outdated, contaminated and discarded medicines
6. *Soiled Waste:* Items contaminated with blood, and body fluids including cotton, dressing, soiled plaster casts, lines, beddings, other material contaminated with blood
7. *Solid Waste*: Waste generated from disposable items other than sharps such as tubings catheters, intravenous sets, etc.
8. *Liquid Waste*: Waste generated from laboratory and washing, cleaning house-keeping and disinfecting activities
9. *Incineration Ash:* Ash from incineration of any bio-medical waste
10. *Chemical Waste*: Chemicals used in production of biologicals, chemicals used in insecticides etc.

11. Left-over food in patients and visitors plates, fruits waste
12. *Blood bank waste:* Discarded, expired, infected blood or its products

Wastes from Health-Care Activities-WHO Classification

1. Infectious wastes — cultures and stocks of infectious agents, wastes from infected patients, wastes contaminated with blood and its derivatives, discarded diagnostic samples, infected animals from laboratories, and contaminated materials (swabs, bandages) and equipment (disposable medical devices etc.)
2. Anatomic-recognizable body parts and animal carcasses. Infectious and anatomic wastes together represent the majority of the hazardous waste, up to 15% of the total waste from health-care activities.
3. Sharps — syringes, disposable scalpels and blades etc. Sharps represent about 1% of the total waste from health-care activities.
4. Chemicals — for example solvents and disinfectants; and
5. Pharmaceuticals – expired, unused, and contaminated, whether the drugs themselves (sometimes toxic and powerful chemicals) or their metabolites, vaccines and sera. Chemicals and pharmaceuticals amount to about 3% of waste from health-care activities.
6. Genotoxic waste – highly hazardous, mutagenic, teratogenic1 or carcinogenic, such as cytotoxic drugs used in cancer treatment and their metabolites; and
7. Radioactive matter, such as glassware contaminated with radioactive diagnostic material or radiotherapeutic materials;
8. Wastes with high heavy metal content, such as broken mercury thermometers. Genotoxic waste, radioactive matter and heavy metal content represent about 1% of the total waste from health-care activities.

Health Impacts

The status of poor waste management currently practiced poses a huge risk towards the health of the general people, patients, and professionals, directly and indirectly through environmental degradation. Communicable diseases like gastro-enteritis, hepatitis - A and B, respiratory infections and skin diseases are associated with hospital waste either directly as a result of waste sharp injuries or through other transmission channels. The hosts of micro organisms responsible for infection are entero-cocci, non-haemolytic streptococci, anaerobic cocci, clostridium tetani, klebshella, HIV and HBV.

Health-care waste is a reservoir of potentially harmful micro-organisms which can infect hospital patients, health-care workers and the general public. Other potential infectious risks include the spread of, sometimes resistant, micro-organisms from health-care establishments into the environment. These risks have so far been only poorly investigated. Wastes and by-products can also cause injuries, for example radiation burns or sharps-inflicted injuries; poisoning and pollution, whether through the release of pharmaceutical products, in particular, antibiotics and cytotoxic drugs, through the waste water or by toxic elements or compounds such as mercury or dioxins.

The potential risk to health care workers comes from the handling of infected sharps; 60 percent of them sustain an injury from sharps knowingly or unknowingly during various procedures. The practice of re-sheathing the needle after use is the major factor for needle stick injuries. Through poor waste management practices, all health care workers (nurses, doctors, lab technicians), service personnel, rag pickers and the general public are at risk of contracting infections while handling storage, and treatment. Incinerators operating at sub-optimal conditions are an added environmental and health hazard.

Sharps

Throughout the world every year an estimated 12,000 million injections are administered. And not all needles and syringes are properly disposed of, generating a considerable risk for injury and infection and opportunities for re-use.

Regarding injection practices, public health authorities in West Bengal, India, have recommended a shift to re-usable glass syringes, as the disposal requirements for disposable syringes could not be enforced.

Hazards occur from scavenging on waste disposal sites and manual sorting of the waste recuperated at the back doors of health-care establishments. These practices are common in many regions of the world. The waste handlers are at immediate risk of needle-stick injuries and other exposures to toxic or infectious materials.

Vaccine Waste

In June 2000, six children were diagnosed with a mild form of smallpox (vaccinia virus) after having played with glass ampoules containing expired smallpox vaccine at a garbage dump in Vladivostok (Russia). Although the infections were not life-threatening, the vaccine ampoules should have been treated before discarding.

Radioactive Wastes

The use of radiation sources in medical and other applications is widespread through the world. Occasionally, the public is exposed to radioactive waste, usually originating from radiotherapy treatments, that has not been properly disposed of. Serious accidents have been documented in Goiània, Brazil in 1988 in which four people died from acute radiation syndrome and 28 suffered serious radiation burns. Similar accidents happened in Mexico City in 1962, Algeria in 1978, Morocco in 1983 and Ciudad Juárez in Mexico in 1983.

Risks associated with other fractions of health-care wastes, in particular blood waste and chemicals, have been relatively poorly assessed, and need to be strengthened. In the meantime, precautionary measures need to be taken.

Bio-medical Waste Treatment and Disposal

Sl. No.	*Waste category*	*Treatment and Disposal*
1.	Human Anatomical Waste, Animal Waste	Incineration and deep burial
2.	Microbiological and Bio-technology Waste	Autoclaving/micro-waving
3.	Waste Sharps, Needles, Syringes, Scalpels, Blades, Glass etc.	Chemical disinfection autoclave/micro-waving and mutilation/shredding
4.	Discarded Medicines and Cytotoxic drugs	Incineration/destruction and drugs disposal in secured landfills
5.	Soiled Waste	Incineration/autoclave micro-waving
6.	Solid Waste	Chemical disinfection autoclave/micro-waving and mutilation/shredding
7.	Liquid Waste	Disinfect-chemically and discharge into drains
8.	Incineration Ash	Disposal in municipal landfill
9.	Chemical Waste	Chemically treated disinfection and discharge of drains for liquid and secured landfillfor solid

- Chemicals treatment using at least 1% hypochlorite solution or any other equivalent chemical reagent would ensure disinfection.
- Mutilation/shredding must be such so as to prevent unauthorized reuse.
- There will be no chemical treatment before incineration. PVC shall not be incinerated.

The Central Pollution Control Board has recommended two types of incinerators:

- Incinerators or individual hospitals/nursing homes/medical stablishments.
- Common incinerator to handle waste from a number of hospitals/nursing homes/pathological laboratories etc.

Risks Associated with Waste Disposal

Although treatment and disposal of health-care wastes aim at reducing risks, indirect health risks may occur through the release of toxic pollutants into the environment through treatment or disposal.

Landfilling can potentially result in contamination of drinking water. Occupational risks may be associated with the operation of certain disposal facilities. Inadequate incineration, or incineration of materials unsuitable for incineration can result in the release of pollutants into the air. The incineration of materials containing chlorine can generate dioxins and furans 3, which are classified as possible human carcinogens and have been associated with a range of adverse effects. Incineration of heavy metals or materials with high metal contents (in particular lead, mercury and cadmium) can lead to the spread of heavy metals in the environment. Dioxins, furans and metals are persistent and accumulate in the environment. Materials containing chlorine or metal should therefore not be incinerated.

Only modern incinerators which are able to work at 800-1000°C, with special emission-cleaning equipment, can ensure that no dioxins and furans (or only insignificant amounts) are produced. Smaller devices built with local materials and capable of operating at these high temperatures are currently being field-tested and implemented in a number of countries.

At present, there are practically no environment-friendly, low-cost options for safe disposal of infectious wastes. Incineration of wastes has been widely practised, but alternatives are becoming available, such as autoclaving, chemical treatment and micro-waving, and these may be preferable under certain circumstances. Landfilling may also be a viable solution for parts of the waste stream if practised safely. However, action is necessary to prevent the important disease burden currently created by these wastes.

In addition, perceived risks related to health-care waste management may be significant. In most cultures, disposal of health-care wastes is a sensitive issue that has ethical dimensions too.

Personnel involved in final disposal of waste may be at risk due to improper wrapping or loose pathological waste.

Personnel handling waste that contains blood-soaked material from patients in dialysis units need protection against Hepatitis B infection.

Injury by infected sharp can cause HIV infection, sometimes

Legislations Relating to Disposal of Bio-Medical Waste

Hospitals should act not only as 'healer' but also prevent spreading diseases. The responsibility to ensure that the hospitals not only attend to the health needs of patients but also maintain an acceptable hygienic condition squarely rests on the hospital authorities. Scientists in search of new products for mankind have succeeded in making products of convenience. The entrepreneurs and industrialists in turn engage in mass production of these products. The Supreme Court took the initiative and entrusted the Ministry of Environment and Forests to come out with suitable guidelines for the proper disposal of medical waste. The Central Government has framed the bio-medical waste (management and handling) rules 1998 (amended 2000) making use of section 6,8,and 25 of the Environmental(protection) Act 1986.This gives clear guidelines for segregating, handling, transporting and disposal of biomedical waste.

Environment (protection) Act,1986

Objectives

- Protection and improvement of environment (water, air, land)
- Prevention of hazards to all living creatures (human, plants, animals) and property
- Maintenance of harmonious relationship between human beings and their environment.

Important Sections

Section 3 & 4 empower the Central Government to constitute authority or authorities for the purpose of exercising or performing such of the powers and functions, appoint a person for Inspection, for analysis of samples and for selection or notification of environmental laboratories.

Section 5 gives power to the Central Government to issue directions in writing to any person or officer or any authority to comply.

Section 6 empowers the Government to make rules to achieve the objectives of the Act.

Section 8 requires the persons handling hazardous substances to comply with procedural safeguards

Section 15 provides the information relating to the penalty for contravention of the provisions of the act, rules, orders, and directions.

Section 16 fixes the criminal liability on the directors and the principal officers of a company where an offence is committed.

Section 17 gives authority to fix criminal liability on the heads of the departments of Governments where an offence is committed by the concerned department.

Section 25 delegates the powers to the concerned authority for carrying out the purposes of the proposed legislation.

Biomedical Waste (Management and Handling) Rules, 1998 and Amended in 2000

Through the powers confirmed by section 6, 8, and 25 of the Environment (Protection) Act 1986, the Central Government has made the Bio-medical Waste (Management & Handling) Rules,1998 and amended in 2000 to safeguard the public and health care workers from the risk arising due to bio-medical Waste. These rules apply to all persons who generate, collect, receive, store, transport, treat, dispose, or handle bio-medical waste in any form

Rule 2 covers all persons responsible to generate, collect, receive, store, transport, treat, dispose or handle biomedical waste in any form.

Rule 3 clarifies the meaning of biomedical waste, biomedical waste treatment and operator of a biomedical waste facility. Biomedical waste means any waste, which is generated during the diagnosis, treatment or immunization of human beings or animals or in research activities or in the production or testing of biological application. Biomedical waste treatment facility means any facility wherein treatment, disposal of biomedical waste or processes incidental to such treatment or disposal is carried out. Occupier in relation to any institution generating biomedical waste means a person who has control over that institution. Operator of a biomedical waste facility means a person who owns or controls or operates a facility for the collection, reception, storage, transport, treatment, disposal or any other form of handling of biomedical waste.

Rule 4 stresses the responsibility of an occupier of an institution. It shall be the duty of every occupier of an institution generating biomedical waste which includes a hospital, nursing home, clinic, dispensary, veterinary institution, pathological laboratory, blood bank, by whatever name it is called, to take all steps to ensure that such waste is handled without any adverse effect to human health and the environment.

Rule 5 states that biomedical waste shall be treated and disposed of in compliance with the standards prescribed. Every occupier shall setup requisite biomedical waste treatment facilities and ensure requisite treatment of waste at a common waste treatment facility.

Rule 6 says that biomedical waste shall not be mixed with other wastes. It shall be segregated and stored in containers at the point of generation. Untreated biomedical waste shall be transported only in such vehicles as may be authorized. No untreated biomedical waste shall be kept stored beyond a period of 48 hours.

Rule 7 provides authority to the Governments of every state for establishing a prescribed authority.

Rule 9 states that Government of every state has to constitute an advisory committee. It includes experts in the fields of medical and health, environmental management, municipal administration and other non-governmental organizations. This advisory board shall advise the state government.

Rule 10 stresses on the responsibility of every occupier regarding submission of annual report by January 31st every year. This report should include information about the categories and quantities of biomedical wastes handled during the preceding year.

Rule 11 specifies that every authorized person shall maintain records related to generation, collection, reception, storage, transportation, treatment, disposal and handling of biomedical waste. These records should be ready for inspection and verification at any time.

Rule 12 states that accident occuring at any institution or facility or any other site where biomedical waste is handled or during transportation of such waste, the authorized person should report.

Environmental Awareness

The Indian macro environment consisting of demographic, economic, technological, political, legal, physical and socio-cultural environments have been changing very rapidly resulting in changes in every walk of life of Indian people. The doctors or the patients did not bother that much about the physical environment prevailing in the hospitals. They show greater interest about the curative aspects than the cleanliness and beauty of the surroundings. There is tremendous change in the attitude of the doctors as well as patients. In Corporate Hospitals, separate departments are being maintained for in-house maintenance and interior decoration. These hospitals, almost all built and arranged like five star hotels, take care in the management of all types of wastes. In fact, they have professionals to destroy or manage not only biological wastes but also for providing cleanliness and interior decoration. Unfortunately, the managers of the public hospitals are unable to upkeep the environment at satisfactory levels. The doctors including the specialists, para-medical staff, IV class employees, patients and the visitors are even today responsible for the bad management of the wastes and environmental pollution.

Probably the first change we have to bring about in the functioning of majority of the hospitals in India is not on the matters relating to the curing process or the equipment which is fairly satisfactory but the maintenance and cleanliness of these hospitals. The hospital managements have to meticulously plan the sanitation system as this is of primary importance to avoid infections. Good occupational health and safety measures include:

- Proper training
- Protective clothing and equipment
- Effective occupational health programmes including immunization (against hepatitis B) and post exposure prophylaxis along with medical surveillance
- Conveniently placed washing and bathing facilities.

Environmental Education

Present situation of formal Environmental education in India: several educational Institutions and Universities are offering Degree or Diploma programmes covering all aspects of environmental Sciences and Engineering. Technical Institutions are offering M.E., M.Tech., and Ph.D programmmes in environmental engineering in the Departments of Chemical and Civil Engineering. Following the directive of the Supreme Court, the UGC has taken the necessary steps to introduce a course "Environmental Science" at under graduate level. The syllabus prescribed for the above course covers various types of diseases like HIV/AIDS due to the improper handling of hospital waste, Environment and human health, value education, public awareness, environmental Acts and Laws. Hence by maintaining the proper environment in and around Hospitals, we can avoid diseases caused due to wastes produced in hospitals

Non formal education: Majority of the population that still do not have adequate access to formal education are visiting the Government Hospitals where improper unhygienic conditions prevail due to waste which is not properly handled or treated before it dispossess. Hence Government organizations like Central Pollution Control Board, State Pollution Control Boards, Media and Non Government organizations like IMA and voluntary organisations have to educate the people, particularly patients, by conducting eco development camps, exhibitions, nature camps, mobile exhibitions, audio visual presentations, seminars, workshops, and poster presentations etc. The environmental education should be a continuous process

Suggestions for better Management of Waste in Hospitals

Attitudinal Change: Management of hospital waste requires diligence and care from a chain of people starting from the ward attendant, nurse, doctor, labour staff, persons transporting waste, persons handling mechanical and technical aspects. If need for safe disposal is stressed, cooperation for segregation, storage, disinfection will not be difficult.

Truly speaking, an attitudinal change is required at the level of top management. Waste disposal should be a management's policy. Chief Executive Officer or the Doctors are to be held responsible. Employees at all levels must be trained and motivated.

The hospitals cannot be disease generators. The general public also should be their concern, not those patients who contribute to their revenue. It is desirable to specify job responsibility. If there are failures or problems, proper communication will sort out the same and decide on better alternatives.

The risk due to occupational hazards is the highest for the staff themselves.

Waste disposal involves expenditure but it is not an area to look for saving on expenditure. After all the expenditure does not go beyond 0.2 to 0.5% of the total running cost of the hospital.

Surveillance: The following steps are to be taken to help rag pickers

- Emphases on dangers of handling infected waste and recycling
- Train rag pickers in acquiring recyclable waste
- Public awareness about segregation of waste and role of rag picker's activities, must be created.
- Establishment of linkages between formal system and rag pickers
- Medical assistance and health education for rag pickers and their families.
- General public must be convinced about reducing the quantity of garbage by utilizing reusable and recyclable items.

Staff Training: Those who handle garbage are often not aware of the risk and hazard of the activity. They are also not aware of the importance of their contribution. Training of the staff is therefore necessary. The goals of training should be

- Information on all aspects of hospital waste policy
- Information on the role and responsibilities of each hospital staff members in implementing the policy
- Technical instructions, relevant for the target group, on the application of waste management practices
- Clarify the components of the waste management system
- Explain the assigned roles and responsibilities to the personnel involved
- Educate and ensure proper use of the protective equipment
- Information regarding the procedure to be followed for a needle stick or other exposures

- Get an honest feedback from the workers
- Suggest preventive remedies to their problems, if required

Waste Management Committee: The most important factor in successful implementation of medical waste management lies in the cooperation of the hospital staff and medical personnel. Proper management of hospital wastes calls for a well-coordinated approach and the role that the administration plays in this is of vital importance.

Ideally a hospital should form a waste management committee representing the following Departments, which has the responsibility to design and implement a policy.

- Administration
- Clinical services
- Hospital infection control committee
- Nursing
- Housekeeping
- Maintenance
- Microbiology
- Accounts

REFERENCES

Books

1. Spiro Thomas G, *Chemistry of Environment* (Second Edition), New Delhi, Prentice-Hall of India, 2004.
2. Richard T, *Environmental Science: Towards a Sustainable Future* (Eighth Edition), New Delhi, Prentice-Hall of India, 2004.
3. Venu Gopal Rao, *Text Book of Environmental Engineering*, New Delhi, Prentice-Hall of India, 2004.
4. Abbasi SA, *Renewable Energy Sources and their environmental Impact*, New Delhi, Prentice-Hall of India, 2001.
5. Uberol NK, *Environment Management* (Second Edition), New Delhi, Excel Books, 2003.
6. Divan, *Environmental Law and policy in India* (Second Edition), New Delhi, Oxford, 2003.
7. Barthwal, *Environmental Impact Assessment*, New Delhi, New Age International Publishing Company, 2002.

8. Suresh K, Dhameja, *Environmental Engineering and Management*, New Delhi, SK Kataria & Sons Publishers and Distributors, 2003

9. Brunner RC, *Hazardous Waste Incineration*, New Delhi, McGraw Hill, 1989.

10. Jadav H , Bhosale VM, *Environmental Protection and Laws*, New Delhi, Himalaya Publishing House, 1995.

11. Project on *Health Care Waste Management Plan for Hospitals in Tamil Nadu*, Department of Health and Family Welfare. Government of Tami Nadu.

12. Trivedi RK, *Hand Book of Environmental Laws, Rules, Guidelines, Compliances and Standards, Vol I & II.*

13. Anil Kumar De, *Environmental Awareness Series: Air and Water*, New Delhi, New Age International Publishing Company, 1990.

14. Jugal Kishore. Joshi TK. *Biomedical Waste Management*. Employment News 2000. Government of India. Feb 19-25.

15. The Gazette of India. *Biomedical Waste (Management & Handling) Rule 1998.* No 460, July 27th 1998 and Amended No. 375, June 2nd 2000.

Journals

1. *Environment Science and Engineering*, Enviro Publishers Private Limited, Chennai

2. *Journal of Institute of Engineers (India):* Environmental Engineering Division, Kolkatta

3. *Journal of Environmental Science & Engineering* (Formerly Environmental Health), National Environmental Engineering Research Institute (NEERI) Publications, Nagpur, India.

16

MARKETING PRACTICES IN CORPORATE HOSPITALS
AN APPRAISAL

K. Deepthi* and N.S. Ramakrishna**

The success of a plan of the National Economy rests on the health and well being of its human resources apart from educational skills. The development of health care facilities is influenced not only by the opening of hospitals but more so by their management. The corporate hospitals of developed countries over the last one-decade have developed a marketing culture in their set up which has enabled them to scale new heights in their ventures, developing countries the need is being felt just now. Marketing hospital services is the least understood and felt as being not very urgent by many health professionals today. Inflation, globalization, liberalization, privatization, decrement in interest rates have complicated the tasks and necessitate the application of marketing principles in hospital establishments. It is in this context, the study tries to probe into the details of marketing aspects of corporate hospitals in general and Medwin hospital in particular and tries to provide suitable suggestions to strengthen these hospitals.

* Research Scholar, Dept. of Business Management, Bharatiar University, Coimbatore.

** Cotton Corporation of India, Guntur.

Introduction

Human resources are most precious endowment in a country. The success of a plan of the National Economy rests on the health and well being of its human resources apart from educational skills. This focuses attention on the health services. The development of health care facilities is influenced not only by the opening of hospitals but more so by their management. In the recent past, corporate sector entered health care sector and opened hospitals with super specialization. This makes it necessary to apply the principles of Marketing to public and private hospitals for their successful functioning. The application of marketing strategies is considered essential as it makes possible a fine fusion between the user's and provider's interests. The users expect world-class services and the providers naturally want a reasonable return. The concept of marketing hitherto used in commerce only, has brought about dynamic changes in the health-care delivery system. In brief this can be explained as follows :

(i) Organizations typically become aware of marketing when their market undergoes a change. When buyers (patients), funds and other resources needed by the organization become scarce, the organization becomes concerned and receptive to non-traditional solutions such as marketing.

(ii) Health care settings run in the model of 'cash and carry'. The organizations that fit this model have always had to attract the Market's usage in order to generate revenue. As a result, they have often tended to be more sensitive to marketing.

(iii) The cost of services can be optimized through application of marketing principles in a hospital.

(iv) Marketing principles helps in increasing health consciousness.

(v) Marketing principles brings about behavioural changes in providers that satisfied the users of the hospital services.

(vi) It helps in generating internal sources.

(vii) As Marketing principles concentrates on transmitting the information from one to another, communication gaps can be filled in.

These hospitals in India are facing severe problems and the reasons are multi-dimensional. Giving weightage to the marketing principles gives the best possible outcome. Hospitals can provide many extra services-let us call them Service Plus of Care Plus-which are not directly concerned with the professional care of patients, nevertheless, add to the quality of care as well as comfort and satisfaction of patients. It calls for some imagination, concern and understandings on the part of hospital authorities to provide these extra services which will support the hospital's marketing effort and enhance its value and success.

Product, place, price and promotion are the important aspects to be covered in external marketing. By using the information taken from research and analysis phase one has to decide what the product should be. The main products of hospitals are medical services. The nature of the hospital, the changes in environmental conditions, technology and global competition govern the product mix of a hospital. After developing the initial product description, one has to identify the positioning strategy. It is describing the product in terms of each target group of patients. Sometimes the product will be the same but the way it is positioned may be different. It is essential that the decision-makers give weightage to the factors influencing the medical care, medical education, training and research facilities. While formulating product mix one has to give importance to the task of satisfying the users. The marketing strategies should satisfy the users with the help of refined services. As explained earlier, while formulating product mix one has to consider the environmental factors, the doctors, paramedical staff and other supporting staff.

The Study

The corporate hospitals of developed countries over the last one-decade have developed a marketing culture in their set up which has enabled them to scale new heights in their ventures. In developing countries the need is being felt just now. Marketing hospital services is least understood and felt as being not very urgent by many health professionals today. Inflation, globalization, liberalization, privatization, decrement in interest rates have complicated the tasks and necessitate the application of marketing principles in hospital establishments. It is inthis context, the study tries to probe into the details of marketing aspects of corporate hospitals in general and Medwin hospital in particular and tries to provide suitable suggestions to strengthen these hospitals.

Present State of Corporate Hospitals

Middle class urban patients rely heavily on private providers for both ambulatory care and in-patient services. There has been a steady growth of private hospitals since 1978 both in terms of institutions and bed-strength. It suggests that the late seventies and eighties were the substantial growth years for the private sector. During the seventies, the private bed-strength was less than that of the public sector across the states. During nineties, in Andhra Pradesh, the bed-strength in the private sector was higher than that of the public sector. This can be seen from the following Table.

Ownership Status of Hospitals and Beds

Year	*Hospitals*			*Hospital Beds*		
	Govt.	*Private*	*Total*	*Govt.*	*Private*	*Total*
1974	28.32 (81.4%)	644 (18.6%)	3476 (100%)	211335 (78.5%)	57550 (21.5%)	268885 (100%)
1979	3735 (64.7%)	2031 (35.5%)	5766 (100%)	331233 (74.2%)	115372 (25.8%)	446605 (100%)
1984	3925 (54.6%)	3256 (45.4%)	7181 (100%)	362966 (72.5%)	137662 (27.5%)	500628 (100%)
1988	4334 (44.1%)	5497 (55.9%)	9831 (100%)	410772 (70.0%)	175117 (30.0%)	585889 (100%)
1991	4379 (40.2%)	6522 (59.8%)	10901 (100%)	415628 (69.7%)	180386 (30.3%)	596014 (100%)
1992	4411 (39.5%)	6763 (60.5%)	11174 (100%)	416868 (64.4%)	230235 (35.6%)	647103 (100%)
1993	4579 (33.4%)	9113 (66.6%)	13692 (100%)	385216 (62.6%)	230507 (37.4%)	615723 (100%)

Source: (1) Jesani.A, Size of Private Sector in Healthcare Delivery System in India, Medico-Friend Circle Bulletin, July-Aug,1991, p. 10.

(2) Health Information of India, 1991, 1992, 1993.

The development of the corporate hospitals is the most important development in the private health sector in the eighties. The pioneer in the field was the Apollo Hospital in Chennai and was followed by diagnostic centres of the United Group, Standard Medical Group, Surlax Diagnostic Ltd., etc. Corporate houses in India are joining this attractive business one after another. Within a period of just two years, between 1984 and 1986, Rs.200 crores were invested in these corporate ventures. This rapid expansion is due to the high profitability of such ventures.

Some of the strengths of these corporate sectors include the fact the needy people receive quality services under one roof with the use of high technology utilizing doctors' specialized expertise. Some of the weaknesses of corporate sectors include: Basically, an average Indian citizen is not in a position to go to corporate hospital because of affordability. Middle-income group and low-income group are not in a position to use this facility. Reasons include high treatment cost, unnecessary tests are being done by the staff as a precautionary measure, lack of continuing medical education and research facilities to the staff, lack of social responsibility feeling, concentrating more on the areas where they are getting maximum profits, high expertise exodus. In this competitive environment, in order to get success, one has to concentrate on structural transformation. The application of marketing principles would pave the way for rationalizing and standardizing the services.

History of the Sample Hospital—Medwin Hospitals, Hyderabad

Medwin hospital was established in Hyderabad in 1987 under the name of Jay diagnostic & Research centre Limited. The diagnostic centre of the company has commenced its operations from 30-06-1989, the cancer department started its operations from 31st December 1989 and some of the in-patient departments were opened from January,1990 onwards. Medwin hospital is equipped with the most modern and sophisticated state of the art technology,managed by highly skilled and internationally renowned doctors extending better services and sober treatment both in Medicare and health care systems. Medwin hospital has international reputation for its apt treatment and professional excellence. The successive increase in the number of patients for treatment is an evidence of the standards and the confidence of the patients Medwin hospital enjoys.

Major Findings of the Study

In this section, an attempt has been made to provide how marketing activities are being followed in Medwin hospitals. The findings are categorised in the form of marketing mix.

Product Decisions: It is found that the hospital is giving priority to the core and supportive services and due weightage to the auxiliary services. It is paying considerable attention on creating mass awareness. Medwin hospitals is providing peripheral services which makes the stay and visit of patients and attendants comfortable and convenient. The seating arrangement, provision of drinking water, sanitation, transportation and communications, the entertainment facilities, the cafeteria are being maintained by the hospital. The hospital is undertaking risky surgeries from time to time.

Pricing Decisions: The hospital is taking cost of providing those services in the scientific way. But, it is observed that for some of the services hospital charges are arbitrary. They are following what prevails in the other hospitals in the region. The hospital is concentrating on determination of total costs. The major components of these costs include fixed and variable. Fixed costs are constant for each procedure. These include equipment and administrative costs for each procedure. The variable costs vary from procedure to procedure and include cost of supplies and labour needed for the procedure.

Place (Distribution) Decisions: Medwin Hospital have clean and neat surroundings. Beautification of the surroundings is the extra attraction to the hospital premises. The Management selected a hospital location in such a way that it is very near to all infrastructural facilities like transportation, communication, electricity etc. It was located in the heart of the city only ¼ KM from the railway station. The hospital is giving due weightage to the disposal of wastages. Which plays vital role in maintaining cleanliness in the premises.

Promotion Decisions: The hospital uses promotional tools such as advertising, publicity, personal selling, public relations, lobbying and word-of-mouth aimed at promoting and selling goods and services. The hospital is organizing a press kits such as table talk, press conferences and it is distributing write ups to the press people which contains complete information regarding the hospital activities. Hospital is organizing speeches of eminent people in their field of study, and it is also organizing seminars, workshops inviting patients, attendants, industrial customers. Hospital is preparing annual reports as natural phenomena mentioning the financial position of the hospital. Hospital is developing rapport with the leading industrial organizations and business magnets evincing interests in the promotion of social welfare. Hospital is sponsoring for a programme 'lifeline' in the local language to educate the masses.

People Decisions: The Medwin hospital is succeeded in formulation of a sound people mix with professionally sound people, personally committed people and value based people. By keeping the another objective of cost effectiveness, the hospital is engaged in promoting research and innovating the diagnostic and treatment measures. Hospital personnel are being trained to enrich the quality of biomedical equipment, apparatus, instruments, machines, infrastructural facilities. Hospital is motivating the employees by using carrot and stick approach. Carrot approach includes both financial and non-financial incentives. To encourage the 'Quality' in people, the hospital is using both participative and autocratic leadership styles. Managers are being trained through developmental techniques such as classroom teaching, in basket training, conferences etc. In the hospital, authorities are giving due importance to the concept of New People Management.

Processes in Medwin Hospitals: The hospital is paying due attention for process i.e. arrangements in sequential manner such as cash counter, admission, registration, investigation reports, reception. While processing the issues, hospital is giving a fresh look on the channelization of services. The hospital is giving due weightage to the behavioural profile of personnel because a large number of complaints will be found against the behavioural profile. Hospital is conducting training classes to the front line staff like receptionists, nursing staff, paramedical staff.

Physical Evidence: The hospital staff are using uniforms. This dress narrates the culture of their hospital for which they work. While selecting the dress, the hospital is taking professional requirements, situational limitations, circumstantial compulsion, cultural barriers. There exists variation in the dress used by technocrats, corporate executives, doctors. Apart from core services, hospital is maintaining peripheral attractions which acts as aesthetic.

Finally, one should not forget the most important element of marketing – the consumer who is in the centre of the total package. In point of fact, the starting place for effective marketing is the consumer. In other words, the emphasis in marketing is not centered on things, it is largely concerned with people and their wants. Successful marketing concentrates on creating goods of value that satisfy potential consumers' needs.

Suggestions

The following are some of the suggestions made to the administrators and policy makers of hospitals. It they are implemented. The present crisis in the hospitals may be resolved to a great extent.

Suggestions for Strengthening Product

LDRP Suites: The hospital has to design a set of elegant LDRP suites where a mother-to-be can have the entire birthing process – labour, delivery, recovery and postpartum care – in her suite decorated In stylish family-like settings with sleeping accommodation for the father, and convertible chairs/beds for siblings. Here the expectant mother enjoys the best of both the worlds – the warmth, comfort and cheerful atmosphere of her home and the security of the hospital setting.

Same Day Surgery: The hospital has to introduce same day surgery in order to reduce hospitalization costs. All tests or investigations would have been completed on an outpatient basis long before the day of surgery.

VIP Lab: Hospital can design a V.I.P. room where a busy, has-no-time-to-wait-in-the-queue businessman can have his blood drawn for testing in a couple of jiffy, and the result communicated to him at his home or office within an hour or two.

Five-Star Hi-Tech Hospital: In a five-star hi-tech hospital, befitting the life-style of the rich and the famous, where guest relations programme operates at its best, the service the hospital offers is so well packaged that the patient feels that he is treated like a V. I. P. guest.

Suggestions for Strengthening Location

Location of a hospital is another crucial decision to be taken by the administrator. It should have neat and clean surroundings. In addition, it is also important that the policy-makers should make all possible efforts for the beautification of the surroundings and premises. While selecting a suitable site for the location of the hospital, the management should be careful to the availability of infrastructural facilities like the transportation, communication, electricity etc. The place should improve the quality of services. The financial involvement on the beautification of premises and surroundings is nominal but its impact on the hospital output is of high magnitude. The hospital authorities have to give due weightage to disposal of wastages, as this plays vital role in maintaining cleanliness in the premises.

Suggestions for Strengthening Distribution

Speeding up Service: Many hospitals have what is variously called Prompt Care, Emergency Health Card, Speed Health Card and Quick Admit, to enable holders of the card, the size of a plastic credit card, to speed up admission process and receive quick medical attention without going through the cumbersome formalities of the admission procedure. The hospital has to establish a such sophisticated admission mechanism which helps the hospital and the patient in many ways.

Cutting down Distribution Cost: The marketing department of a company provided fine customer service so that it could maximize sales. Its declared policy was that customers should receive their goods at the shortest possible time. This required a rather large inventory resulting in increased inventory cost which the department did not grudge. The distribution department, trying to cut down its cost, was ordered by its chief that they should hold orders from customers who ordered relatively small quantities of goods at random intervals until enough of them accumulated for a truckload.

Suggestions for Strengthening the Promotion

The last step in creating the marketing mix is developing promotional strategies. In addition to the positioning strategies developed for each target group, specific promotional strategies also should be developed. The main purpose of promotional strategy is to convince the target group and compete with similar institutions. Promotion can be both personal and impersonal. Personal promotion can be person to person where as impersonal promotion can be through advertising, publicity and sales promotion. Advertising is important to contract avenues for a multiplication in the number of users of the services. In promotional activities, there is great need for creativity, sensitivity and accessibility. It is also important that, through promotional strategies the general masses should get information regarding the treatment facilities which are available in the hospital. Another promotional strategy is providing health care packages for a fixed price to fast-growing health conscious customers. Still another strategy is achieved through regular means, which includes word of mouth publicity. Hospitals can adopt insurance tie-ups with insurance companies. Yet another strategy is to publish magazines, which give information about various services. Hospitals can arrange frequent public lectures, seminars and workshops to spread awareness about health care. As a promotional strategy hospitals can adopt master check-up at reasonable prices. The prices should depend on economic levels of the population and should attract the general masses. Some other suggestions include-

In Relation to Public and Patients

Signage System, Name Boards, Landscape, etc: Lack of a good signage system is one of the serious problems for patients in finding their way through the complex maze of hospital buildings. An effective and easy-to-follow signage system should be provided. All rooms should be numbered. There should be large boards bearing the names of specialists displayed prominently in conspicuous place(s). Floor plans (layout) of the building should be displayed in strategic places. Beautiful landscape, pleasing interior and warm and cheerful facilities provide patients a homely atmosphere which psychologically help them and their relatives who are fearful of hospital surroundings to relax and get well sooner. It has been found that in such a congenial environment, employees are motivated to work better and more productively. They take pride in their place of work.

Car Rental, Taxi, Ambulance Service, etc: Transportation can be arranged for a fee for out-of-station patients and their relatives from and to the airport, railway station, etc. and for local patients from and to their homes before and after the day surgery and on discharge. This can be an effective public relations and marketing programme.

Centralized Patient Service Centre: This is a powerful marketing tool which is more than a mere info desk. The friendly, knowledgeable patient service representatives give the hospital a personality, a decided advantage in the market place, and a public relations plus.

Executive/VIP Suites: while taking care of needy patients, hospitals should not ignore rich patients. Special amenities like choice menu, fresh flowers, newspapers, personalized get well card from the CEO, etc. may be provided.

Gift and Florist's Shops, Book Shop, Public Telephone, Coffee Shop, Assisted STD and ISD call Facilities, Vending, Machines, etc: For the benefit of patients, their relatives, visitors and staff.

Medical Insurance Programme: This can be either hospital's own insurance scheme or the one linked to insurance companies. Careful thought should be given to the scheme so that it does not become a liability to the hospital. With the insurance sector, under the liberalization scheme, promising to open up to other players outside the national insurance companies, healthcare industry appears to be poised to play a bigger role in this area.

In Relation to Staff

Recruitment strategy: If the hospital wants to develop a team of competent staff, the right place to begin is in selection. If the authorities exercise proper care and judgement in choosing the people, they will gradually assemble the kind of team that they want. If the institution is to operate efficiently, each position must be filled by a person who is not only best qualified but also the most suitable to fill it.

Human Resource Development Programmes: All staff, from the top management to housekeeping, however qualified, need to be given orientation, training and development programmes to enhance understanding of their jobs, job skills and ability to perform at a high level, make them responsive and level up to the requirements of their jobs. An employee who is not equal to his job and cannot perform satisfactorily can be a source of great trouble to the organization. The following are some of the programmes aimed at achieving high quality performance.

In-service and Continuing Education Programme: For all Staff: Knowledge is power. Staff must continue to learn, enhance their skills, or learn new skills, develop professionally and keep abreast with the latest technological, medical and scientific advances.

Conclusion

It is needless to say how important the service sector has become in the national economy in the terms of its contribution to the GDP. Nearly 50% of GDP is now accounted for by the service sector. Though the service sector is gaining prominence in terms of its dominant role at the national level as an important contributor to the GDP, much thought has not yet been given by the academic in terms of introducing latest management techniques, more importantly marketing strategies, towards improving the effectiveness and efficiency of the hospital system, in providing service. Whether the hospital is large or small it should deal with a facility wide marketing plan. Marketing of hospital services is needed to educate large numbers of people. There is a need for marketing the hospital services in order to provide the right kind of information and education and to cure the ailments of the patients in the best possible manner. It is in this context, this attempt is made to study the state of the art and growth of the hospital industry in India and to develop a model to market hospital services. It is presumed the fact that these concepts go a long way in improving the overall effectiveness of the hospital industry. Good Marketing Programme will build up more awareness among the public, create loyalty, establish a kind of tie-up with potential customers. Thus it may be concluded that application of marketing principles in the Indian hospitals cannot be ignored or delayed any longer.

REFERENCES

1. Philip Kotler and Roberta N. Clarke — *Marketing for Health Care Organizations.*
2. G.D. Kunders – *How to Market Your Hospital Without Selling Your Philosophy.*
3. S.M. Jha – *Hospital Management.*
4. S.M. Jha – *Services Marketing.*
5. K. Rama Mohana Rao – *Lessons on Services Marketing.*

17

PROSPECTS OF HERBAL FORMULATION AND EXPORT POTENTIAL

Vinit V. Dani*

Among various products with which India is endowed, a large variety of herbs are grown under different climatic conditions through length and breadth of this country. India is further endowed with the technical knowledge in respect of processing various herbs and other natural products into an effective blend to constitute medical preparations for a variety of diseases. We are equally proud that our country is further endowed with enormous literature transferred over countries of use on herbal preparations which include medicines, cosmetics, hair care preparations and nutraceutical supplements. In past three years India has created a real dent in the International market in terms of exporting extracts, powder and mixtures used for the preparation of pharmaceuticals etc. the WTO, UNIDO and world bank are keenly advising India to embark upon value added agro herbal products so that India will be able to achieve better balance of payments with a reasonably good surplus. A need has also arisen to get ready with market acceptable products also to evolve an effective marketing strategy. The marketing efforts of our country have to be further reinforced by our traditional knowledge and preparations of our ancient medical practitioners. The industry considered to be a sunrise industry with the highest anticipated exports turnover.

* Assistant Professor, TKR Institute of Business Management, Hyderabad.

Introduction

As the 20th Century drew to close, the past one hundred years could be defined as the renaissance century for modern science, Technology and Medicine. This was also the century that closed on the genesis of a new generation devoted to environmental awareness, a society intent on getting back to nature and one that many times perceives simple and natural as better regardless of logical scientific parameters.

Globally, there is a big shift towards herbal medicine. A large number of international companies hold patents on medicinal plants, NRI's hold some of these. There are 1866 patents related to botanicals in US patent list of 2,780,279 patents. Although many plants have wealth of data on their medicinal utility, the global focus in mainly on plants with patents. It is believed that herbals are going to be big money makers in next 10 to 20 years.

According to 1998 article published in JAMA, 42% of US populations used at least one form of alternative therapy in 1997. use was more frequent among women than men (49% vs 38%) and was most frequent (50%) in the 36-49 year age bracket. Use was higher in these with a college education (51%) and with an income over $50,000 (48%). Because of the consumber revolution that's creating the demand the size of the herbal market will increase. Refer to Annexure 1(i), 1(a) and 1(b).

New Trends in the Usage

1960-1980: mainly driven by traditional folklore usage and consumers were closely to alternative medicines but least side effects and word of mouth drew elderly patients towards herbal medicine.

In 1990-1991 the market is driven by a combination of folklore scientific research and media hype consumers have shifted to the middle classes and elderly who are looking for 'natural medicines' for maintenance of health.

New Emergence of Phytopharmaceutical, and Phytonutraceutical Products

Top selling herbs and growth rates.

European Sales $7 Billion in 1996

Asia 2.3 billions

Japan 2.1 billions

N.America 1.5 Billions

Average growth rate world wide is around 12-15% (Institute of Medical Statistics) per annum and India is vulnerable as it has core competency in this field.

Main Therapeutic Categories for Herbal Product

Therapeutic Area	*Percentage*
Cardiovascular	27.2
Respiratory	15.3
Digestive	14.4
Tonics	14.4
Others	12.0
Hypnotics/Sedatives	9.3
Topicals	7.4

Source: J.Grunwald, Herbalgram p.60, 1994.

Indian Scene

What is unique about the ISM is that it has survived the ravages of tie and the onslaught of the modern medicinal system. In India, for a vast section of the population it is still popular and for many perhaps the only facility they can access. But the system and its practitioners had suffered long years of neglect, especially during the British period.

After Independence, the government did recognize the relevance of the ISM, but no special attention could be devoted towards its development & upgradation in view of the pressing need for urgent attention to massive health care problem confronting the people at large. Lack of the necessary patronage from the Government as well as the market (constituted by the educated middle class) had hampered modernization of the ISM and its products and services.

Even today, this sector continues to suffer from lack of necessary infrastructure and financial support, and has been practically marginalized as an undependable system of medicine. What has been really ignored and allowed to suffer is vast and rich reservoir of traditional knowledge on the one hand and knowledge and skilled medical manpower on the other hand, growth and advancement has stopped in absence of R & D.

In spite of its vast span and embrace, there has been a steady erosion of credibility of ISM and practices in a world of fast changing lifestyle. It has failed to keep pace with the changing society. The focus of this sector is also found ot be shifting, leading to grater thrust on ISM products rather than medicines. Further, although there are 4 distinct wings of ISM, it is Ayurveda that dominates the total ISM market of about Rs.4,000 crores and the rest are really insignificant.

In this context, the recent initiatives of the Government of India, namely setting up a separate department of the Indian System of medicine and Homeopathy, is a welcome initiative. Since its establishment, this department has initiated a number of steps towards revitalization of this sector. A broad institutional frame work has been developed to regulate the activities in the field of ISM & H.

However, the basic problem remains – The availability of adequate resources. Revitalization of the ISM would call for necessary financial support not only at the institutional level but also at the individual level of the companies and individual practitioners. There is also need for publicity campaign in faovur of ISM although the task is gigantic. One of the problems of the ISM & H is that the system is highly organized and scattered, and reorganization of it would call for a massive effort.

Herbal Market

India has been using its rich biodiversity for healthcare for at least 4000 years through its traditional system of medicine – Ayurveda. However she has not put appropriate efforts to (1) Test the concepts as well as the products through modern biology & Chemistry (2) Characterize the products at molecular levels. (3) Develop newer products, which are far simpler, more benign and effective than the ones hitherto employed. The country's rich traditional experience and wisdom is ensconced in Ayurveda, Siddha and Unani the three traditional systems of medical practice. Thus India is rich in traditional and ingenuous knowledge, both coded and informal.

More than 4000 years ago her people developed a system of medicine called Ayurveda, which means knowledge of how to lead a healthy life. The treatment was individual oriented and hence very specific. This system is one of the most ancient systems of treatment in the world. This system of medicines is popular flourishing in India even today. This science not only thrived in India but also influenced healing practices in many countries.

Domestic

Herbs as cosmetics: The concept of beauty & cosmetics is as old as mankind and civilization. Proof of this lies in the world famous sculptures of Khujuraho and Ellora and the paintings on the walls of the Ajanta Caves, which depict adored mean and women, and medicinal herbs work at purifying blood and eliminating vitiated Doshas (mainly pitta), which play a vital role in skin disorders. The herbs, therefore clear the complexion, lend a glow to the skin and alleviate purities, Kusstha and boils.

Commonly Used Herbs As Cosmetics

Indigo	–	used as a bindi/tika
Madder root	–	to beautify lips and cheeks
Hibiscus rosa cynesis	–	to blacken hair
Aloevera	–	heals skin irritation and rejuvenation of new cells
Chandan	–	used a face packs
Haldi	–	used as face pack along with usher (vertiver)

Herbs As Oral Care Products

Betel leaf	–	Calcium Supplementation
Neem	–	toothpaste

Herbs As foods

If no claim is made on a product, then the herb is considered as a food supplement rather than a medicine. Some countries have herbal shops called botanicals selling herbs as food. Mostly food supplements or nutraceuticals are sold as OTC products targeted at health conscious people through advertising campaigns.

Ex:-	Amls	–	Chawanprash (Food Tonic)
	Spirulina	–	health supplement
	Ashwagandha	–	A vital nutritive tonic

Herbal Medicines

Though use of herbal drugs in health care is as old as the mankind itself, there has been increased interest in usage of herbal medicine for the treatment of various diseases. This usage of using herbal medicine is brought because of changed perceptions of people as "Natural is good and synthetic is bad" and penetrating marketing communication.

Commonly Used Herbal Medicines are:

Neem	–	Decoction used for fevers, liver problem
Isabgol	–	bowel problems
Cassia Fistula	–	Antibiotic Activity
Amla	–	Respiratory complaints & for preventing ageing process
Bel	–	Panacea for digestive disorders
Tulsi	–	Tonic for heart
Methi	–	Tonic for digestive, respiratory and nervous systems
Cuscus	–	Vomiting & Diarrhoea.

Reasons for Growth of Herbal Preparations

Reemergence of traditional medication has influenced increased interest and therefore usage.

1. Exposure to exotic foreign foods prepared with non local culinary herbs.
2. People increasingly are willing to 'self doctor' their medical needs by investigating and using herbs and herbal preparations. They are using it as adjuncts for treating chronic illnesses.
3. High cost of treatment and side effects with Allopathic Medication.
4. Changing lifestyle and value systems.

India's Opportunities

Number of manufacturers have already established market for their products and a niche can only be created by displacing and occupying some of the space currently occupied by them. Hardly any Indian product is available in standardized form, which is the minimum requirement for introducing a product in the western market. Standardization involves ensuring that the product is efficacious, safe and has physiochemical range falling within an acceptable band. To obtain and generate a commercial niche in the international arena in existing scenario requirements the formulation and execution of pragmatic strategy is a necessity.

Thus in future India shall have to develop knowledge based products. These products have an inherent advantage over the products, which have traditional and empirical observation as the knwoeldge base. Thus knowledge needs to be integrated in traditional products to generate superior knowledge based products. This will result in better definition of the existing products, improved understanding of the mechanism of their action, modified composition at molecular level and better understanding of interactions amongst various molecules.

Above all, earnest efforts have to be put in place (i) to consolidate the past gains of traditional knowledge base (ii) Start developing entirely new herbal preparation based on India's biodiversity and (iii) Make these products available to the international community.

Global Market

Total Global present herbal market is of size 62.0 billion US Dollar,s in this India's contribution is only one billion US Dollars. European union is the biggest market with the share 45% of total herbal market. North America accounts for 11%, Japan 16%, ASEAN Countries 19% and Rest of European Union 4.1% as given in *Annexure 1 (iii)*. Countries like Japan and China have successfully marketed their traditional medicines abroad. Their alternative therapies are well accepted in Europe & US. Product like Ginseng – the famed aphrodisiac from China is having the same property as of Ashwgandha – an Ayurvedic medicine, yet it accounts for over US$ 800 million of International Market as compared to all herbs put together (which is less than US$ 1 million). When compared to the Chinese and Japanese level of penetration in the global market, India is not at all figuring anywhere. Inspite of its vast herbal treasure.

But there are positive signals also for us in the Global Market. India has 16 Agro Climatic Zones, 10 Vegetative Zones, 15 Biotic provinces, 426 biomes, 45000 different plant species and 15000 medicinal plants that include 7000 Ayurvedic, 700 in Unani Medicine, 600 in Siddha Medicine and 30 in Modern Medicines. This makes India one amongst 12 mega bio diverse countries of the world, which despite having only 2.5% total land area, accounting for over 8% of the recorded species of the world.

The forecast is that the global Market for herbal products is expected to be US $ trillion by 2050. Herbal remedies would become increasingly important especially in developing countries. India, with its biodiversity has a tremendous potential and advantage in this emerging area.

Indian Exports

The Exports of Ayurvedic and Unani Medicine put up for retail sale to other countries have increased from Rs.17 crores in 1992-93 to 98 crores in 1998-99. In U.S.A. our exports have increased from Rs.47 lakhs in 1992-93 to 8 crores in put up for retail sale. U.S.A. has stringent rules for the imported products that are used for consumption. These medicines are not exported under the category of medicines but find their way in US markets as food supplements and herbal products. Similarly in UK the Indian exports of these products have increased from mere 5 lakhs Rs. to above 1 crore from the year 1992-93 to 1998-99. European Union is the biggest market in global herbal products. Indian products to other countries like Germany, France, Italy and Netherlands have also increased. In 1992-1993 to Germany was the Biggest importer of Ayurvedic and Unani Medicines followed by Nigeria but their importance decreased drastically in terms of share of the exports of Indian Ayurvedic & Unani Products. Russia was the biggest importer and destination market for Ayurvedic and Unani products in 1996 –97. Russia is one of the most important partners for India in the exports of Ayurvedic and Unani finished products.

The exports for Ayurvedic and Unani medicines have been increasing but nothing can be predicted from the yearly exports because that has been fluctuating. This section for not put up for retail sale constitutes of raw materials, crude herbs and other products. This requirements keeps changing from one year to other. We can conclude that USA has emerged as one of the important countries as the buyer of Ayurvedic and Unani medicines both put up for retail sale and not put up for retail sale. Among other countries South East Asian Countries have also emerged as important market and from the table we can say that India has explored these emerging market but how far is it successful and what is their percentage share in imports of these countries is yet to be answered. UAE is another country, which import from India as herbal product category. In Middle East people's choice have shifted to herbal products, - they now use more of these types of hair oil, shampoo and other cosmetics. Germany's share in the exports of ayurvedic and Unani medicines have decreased drastically but if we take European Union together their share has increased.

Herbs of Immediate Greatest Potential

Future developments needed for product licenses/efficacy studies:

- Matricaria Recutita

  Precise effects of anti inflammatory terpenoids and flavnoids.

  Applications for topical/eczema.
- Zingiber officinalis

  Confirm efficacy in motion sickness and nausea (including post operative).
- Echinacea

  Bioactivity of constituents needs to be tied up properly. Clinical trials needed to confirm treatment/prevention of flu/colds.
- Ginkgo biloba

  Establish if 24% flavonoids is the best dosage. Proper safety evaluation needs to be carried out. potential for memory enhancement/Alzheimer's disease.

- Hypericum Perforatum

  Establish mode of action. Elucidate main actives and appropriate extract etc.

Implications for the Future—The Environmental Impact

With the increasing environmental pressures for industry to use "clean technology" and to utilize sustainable sources of materials for manufacturing processes. The use of crude plant extracts, if proved safe efficacious must be encouraged. If the need for "greener" products continues to play an important role in our society, then in the future there may well be government legislation that insists on using herbal products rather than unsustainable synthetic products or highly purified natural products, which wastes raw material and increases pollution. Companies that get involved now will become market leaders in a business that is likely to become much more important in the years to come.

Strategies to Achieve Competitive Edge in International Market

1. Develop superior products
2. Develop Trimmer preparations.
3. Optimized products
4. International trading products.
5. Bioenhancers
6. Detoxifiers
7. Entirely new herbal preparations (Formulations).
8. Products based on food components and special products of traditional system.

REFERENCES

Books

1. Pandeya, Gyanendra: *System of plant nomenclature in Ayurveda.*
2. K.R. Srikanth Murthy: *Dravya Prakash*
3. Dr. Sharma R.K. , Dr. Dash Bhagwan: *Charaka Samhita* Vol. I, II, & III.
4. Prof. Singh R.H.: *Panchakarma Therapy*
5. Dr. Kumar Bhatia, *Achieving Varietal Diversity*, Hindu Survey of Indian Agriculture, 04.

6. Dr. Chandra, Babu Suresh, *More Supportive Policies* Hindu Survey of Indian Agriculture - 2004

7. Pandey, Mukesh and Tewari, Deepali, *Rural and Agricultural Marketing*, International Book Distributing Co., 2004 .

Websites

www.naturalhealthvillage.com

www.timesinfo.com

www.timesofindia.com

www.indianexpress.com

www.tandursti.com

www.thehindu.com

www.ayurvedwebline.com

www.allayurveda.com

www.google.com

www.imf.com

who&usfda websites

SECTION–IV
OTHER KEY SERVICES

18

DEVELOPED INDIA
ROLE OF THE SERVICE SECTOR

Professor G.N. Brahmanandam*

India is fast dashing towards its dream of conversion into developed country by 2020. Many of the highly paid software wizards in the globe have their origins in India, and hence the emergence of service sector has taken a steep positive slope in India. A well developed country needs a well established service sector. Hence, this paper briefly points out the role of service sector during this developing phase of India.

Introduction

Since 1960s, there has been a steady decline in the contribution of agriculture and primary sector to Gross Domestic Product (GDP), and its place has been taken by service based enterprises. Industrial development has been moving briskly, but not as fast as services in its contribution to GDP. The shift has been so significant and some refer to it as the second industrial revolution. This happened because:

1. Individuals are spending greater portion of their income in travel, entertainment and leisure, and communication services,
2. Growing complexity of banking, insurance, investment and legal services,

---

* Dean, Faculty of Commerce and Management Studies, Acharya Nagarjuna University, Nagarjuna Nagar - 522 510.

3. Growing awareness among people about health care led to the development of health care, in terms of polyclinics, corporate hospitals, etc.,
4. Greater life expectancy led to increase in entertainment, travel resorts, leisure services, old age homes, insurance products, investment and banking services,
5. Complexity of life led to the development of legal aid, tax counseling, professional services, airlines, courier services, insurance and banking services, and bank assurance,
6. Growing number of working women caused for the development of domestic services travel, nurseries, fast food restaurants, marriage counseling, retailing, personal care, beauty parlors, working women hostels,
7. Consumer affluence resulted in the development of entertainment clubs, holiday resorts, carpet, dry cleaning services,
8. Developments in Corporate world or corporate crowd are responsible for the development of legal services, management counseling, airlines, travel booking, courier services, market research, advertising services, etc.,
9. Changes in socio-economic cultural factors led for the development of supply organizations, and event management activities,
10. Unprecedented breakthroughs in Science and Technology resulted in the upgradation of infrastructure services, financial services, investment services, Banking and insurance, health care services, trading services, entertainment services, etc., In fact, technological breakthorough led for a sudden shift in the service sector which made the service sector to occupy the first place in terms of contribution to the GDP and economy. Service organizations are now able to extend instant services to the customers; at the same time they are able to extend superior services at a competitive price-showing concern for quality, promptness, and customer focus.

Thus, service sector encompasses the major areas of trade, finance, insurance, communications, public utilities, transportation, health care, education, business and personal services. Economies of advanced countries like USA, UK, Germany, Japan, Canada, and Australia have changed from goods dominated to services dominated. In several countries including India, the service sector accounts for more employment in comparison to other sectors.

Country	% of GDP Manufacturing	% of GDP Services	% of Employment in Service Sector
USA	21	74	80
Japan	29	58	60
UK	32	69	77
Australia	22	72	75
Canada	24	70	79
India	29	47	60

The Trends Indicate that the Future Belongs to the Service Sector

The service sector in the Indian Economy accounted for 28% of GDP in 1960-61, 31% in 1970-71, 37% in 1980-81, 47% in 1999-2000 and 56.1% in 2002-03. Service sector has been the major beneficiary from the falling share of agricultural sector which accounted for 45.8% in 1960-61 to 22.1% in 2002-03. Contribution of Manufacturing sector has been fluctuating around 25%,28%,30%, 27% and during 2002-03 is 21.8%. There is a need for improving the excellent health, education of masses in rural areas. There are excellent health, and education, transport and communication services in the metropolitan cities, but these are quite inadequate in rural areas. High rate of growth in service sector should follow high growth rates of agriculture and industry, if the growth has to generate everlasting benefits.

There is a tremendous growth achieved by the Indian Economy in service sector. The excess growth achieved in service sector may temporarily benefit the economy by providing employment opportunities to millions of people. But experts opine that high rate of growth in service sector at the fall of growth rates in agriculture and industry is not good enough in the long run. Growth in agricultural sector is also very important to our economy as we cannot leave millions of people for hunger and starvation. Manufacturing sector is a tangible sector over which any developing country like India should hold a strong grip. Hence, high rate of growth in the service sector should follow high growth rates of agriculture and industry, if the growth has to generate everlasting benefits to the developing Indian economy. Further, the benefits of growth are not passed on to the low profile income common men in the country. Almost all the services are not within their reach and many do not access have to the above services in rural areas.

Conclusion

Our overall concern, therefore should be that suitable policies and strategies be evolved and adopted to achieve sectoral congruence aiming at balanced growth among all the sectors, and the high growth rates achieved be passed on to the low profile income common men and rural people in the country to get India developed as per the expectancies of millions of people.

19

EMERGENCE OF SERVICE ERA AND SERVICE QUALITY

Dr. Y. Srinivasulu* and **Dr. B.K. Surya Prakasha Rao****

We are living in the age of service. The service era has not arrived by accident, it is part of the evolutionary process of the society for millenia most people in the world worked the land. For the last humdred and fifty years we have considerable earnings from manufacturing, making goods to sell. Now the majority of the people are involved in service business, no longer making goods but rather doing things that other will pay to have done. Human beings have needs which are great drivers or motivators. Obasic needs are for food, shelter and clothing and if we lack those, we will strive resolutely to acquire them. If our basic needs are met then more sophisticated ones energe.

As we shop, cravel, seek entertainment, use banks, buy insurance, move, house, talk holidays, eat out, visit garages, take legal advice, have goods repaired, employ builders or decorders, use libraries, health services and so on, we are expesiencing customer service. Every contact we make when we spend our money as a customer leaves us with an impression. We are all expects on it; we all know the difference between good and bad service when we experience and feel it.

* Sr. Lecturer, Dept. of Management Sciences, RVR&JC College of Engg., Guntur.

** Reader, Dept. of Management Sciences, RVR&JC College of Engg., Guntur.

Business, not only those who are in service, but also those involved in manufacturing, now have to pay very close attention to an increasingly aware and selective group of people who have the power to make or break them. Today, what is acceptable and valuable to the customer is quality but nothing else. As such the thoughts and feelings of the customer need regularly to top the board room agendas of any business seriously committed to success.

Introduction

We are living in the age of service. For millennia most people in the world worked the land. For the last hundred and fifty years we have earned our livings largely in manufacturing, making goods to sell. Now the majority of the people are involved in service business, no longer making goods but rather doing things that other people will pay to have done.

Although the service economy is growing in leaps and bounds, not everyone is rejoicing about the transformation of the economy from an agricultural/industrial economy to a service economy. Materialism snobbery reflects the attitude that only manufacturing can create real wealth, and that all other sectors of the economy are parasitic and/or inconsequential. Materialismic individuals believe that without manufacturing, there will be little for people to service. As a result, more people will be available to do less work. Consequently, the abundance of labour will drive wages down and subsequently decrease the standard of living. Ultimately these individuals believe that the shift to a service economy will jeopardise the way of life of the society. Similar concerns were voiced, when the economy was slowly shifting from agriculture to manufacturing. Infact, the shift lead to economic growth. Similarly, with advances in technology and new management practices, the need no longer exists to have as many people in manufacturing as we had earlier. Manufacturing is not superior to Services, the two are interdependent. Infact, half of all manufacturing workers perform service – type jobs.

"Opportunities must be recognized and seized;

Risks must be understood and evaluated"

The service era has not arrived by accident, it is part of the evolutionary process of the society, human beings have needs which are great drivers or motivators. Our basic needs are for food, shelter and clothing and if we lack those, we will strive resolutely to acquire them. If our basic needs are met then more sophisticated ones emerge. We then strive for more secure environments and more stability in our circumstances. Given this sense of physical well-being we are still unlikely to be content. Our needs then are for acceptance and recognition, which, if we receive them, promote our sense of worth, our positive self esteem, which underpins and emergises so many facets of our life. We want to be linked and appreciated and respond positively to signs that we are. For the last hundred years, not only the individuals but societies have worked through this hierarchy of needs. From recession and economic deprivation in the 1930's, through the very destructive war and years of reconstruction which followed, our priorities were the basics, food, shelter and clothing along with security. Now we are beyond the basics. With rebuilt economics most people take for granted a relatively high standard of living. TVs, personal vehicles, all kind of domestic appliances, houses and holiday trips are now unremarkable. Our needs have moved beyond merely 'having', we are now in pursuit of something more sophisticated.

"The Future belongs to People who see possibilities before they become obvious"....Theodore Levitt

Continually, as we shop, travel, seek entertainment, use banks, buy insurance, move house, take holidays, eat out, visit garages, take legal advice, have goods repaired, employ builders or decoraters, use libraries, health services and so on, we are experiencing customer service. Every contact we make when we spend our money as a customer leaves us with an impression. Sometimes however, as a customer, the way we are treated falls below our expectations. If we are ignored, treated rudely, some how cheated or dealt with unfairly, then we emerge with negative feelings of anger, frustration or disappointment. We will be keen not to do business again with anybody who has made us feel like that. On other occasion, however the attention we receive as a customer seems some how special. The person dealing with us is warm, friendly and attentive; he/she treats us courteously, takes some trouble on our behalf, and appears knowledgeable about the offer (product). After such a contact we emerge feeling good about that experience, we are pleased appreciative and no doubt ready for more of the same.

"Quality is Remembered Long after Price is Forgotten"
.....Jan Carlzon, Scandinavian Airlines

We want very much to be treated as though we matter, we want to be valued, recognized and respected. We are all experts on it: we all know the difference between good and bad service when we experience and feel it. The meaning for good and bad service is so simple. Giving customer a little more than they expect is good service and giving even a little less than the customer expect is bad service.

What Customer Receive	is less than	What Customer Expects	result is 'Bad Service"
What Customer Receive	is more than	What Customer Expects	result is 'Good Service'

We all, as customers carry round expectations about the way things should be. We have ideas about the way we, or other people, ought to be treated, about standard of hygiene, about common courtesies, about fair play and value for money, about how long things decently ought to take and about many other things. We are not usually conscious of those expectations until they are either not met or exceeded.

The secret of business is to exceed what the customer expects. The old pursuit used to be customer satisfaction (delivering equivalent to expectations), should now be that 'little bit more' which results in customer pleasure or delight. Remember, this year's little bit more becomes next year's norm. Good service educates the customer and establishes new standards, which raises the challenge of continuous improvement.

Businesses, including those involved in manufacturing, now have to pay very close attention to an increasingly aware and selective group of people who have the power to make or break them. As such, the thoughts and feelings of the customer need regularly to top the board room agendas of any business seriously committed to success.

"Service is like Love ... it is not the Word that matters, it's the Actions!"

....Dr.Barrie Hopson and Mike Scally Life Skills
Communications, UK

The changes that are taking place in technology, mainly the Information Technology and Reengineering combine to change customer expectations of service. The union of two major trends-information technology and reengineering of work processes – are resulting in customer service break throughs that significantly alter customer expectations. Reengineering which involves changing the processes and assumptions by which work gets accomplished, is facilitated by technology that includes electronic mail, video conferencing, laptop computers, car faxes, cellular phones, personal computer networks, and hand held wireless terminals. These information technologies increase the speed of processes such as billing, handling of customer complaints, solving of customer problems, etc. Many managers still see Service Quality as cost rather than as a contributor to profits, partly because of the difficulty involved in tracing the link between service quality and financial returns. Detrmining the financial impact of service quality parallels the age-old problem of finding the connection between advertising and sales. Service Quality's results – like advertising results – are cumulative, and therefore evidence of the link may not come immediately or even quickly.

"Marketing can catch the customers, Service Quality keeps them"

As the customers are hungry for the 'quality' treatment which is a central theme of the service era, all businesses now have to be able to provide for sophisticated, discerning customers who want to have 'experiences' rather than mere physical objects.

As a matter of globalization fragrance, now the customers are more discerning and sophisticated, those who serve them (the marketers) have to have those things also. The immediate need of the marketer is the ability to 'read' the customers, to look at the business, and the customer contact/interaction points through the eyes of the customers. This lead to a situation that the services marketer should have an established system of information for ensuring 'quality' in the service deliveries, which resulted the emergence of A Service Quality Information System".

The task of improving service quality in organizations is complex. It involves knowing what to do on multiple fronts, such as technology, service systems, employee selection, training and education, and reward systems. It involves knowing how to implement these actions and how to transform activity into sustainable improvement. Genuine service improvement requires an integrated strategy based on systematic listening. The quality of listening has an impact on the quality of service. Firms intent on improving service need to listen continuously to three types of customers: external customers who have experienced the firm's service; competitor's customers who the firm would like to make its own; and internal customers (employees) who depend on internal services to provide their own services. Effective leaders are information gatherers who listen to their subordinates and to sources outside the organization, especially customers. The customers are around and available, not remote and unapproachable. They read. They develop wide information networks. They share and disseminate information appropriately with the organization. Service leaders, in particular, are typically "deeply and personally involved in the customer service function of their business. They personally read complaint logs and letters, took phone calls, and were highly visible and available to the rank and file. Sam Walton, the late founder of Wal-Mart, highly successful discount retailer, once remarked, "Our best ideas come from delivery and stock boys". Bill Marriot, Jr.,visits most of the company's hotels to listen to customers and employees, and he eats at company restaurants as often as five times a week. When listening to customers and employees becomes a habit in an organization, when all employees understand the service improvement priorities – then it is clear that the organization is systematically using information to improve the quality of service.

"Knowledge is power. In post capitalization, power comes from transmitting information to make it productive, not hiding it".

.... Peter.F. Drucker, in HBR, May – June, 1993, p.120

REFERENCES

1. Michael E.R. Aynor, *After Materialism* Across the Board, July – August 1992,pp.38-41.

2. *Wealth in Services, The Economist*, February 20, 1993,p.16.

3. Leonard L.Berry and A.Parasuraman; *Listening to the Customer, The Concept of a Service – Quality Information System; Sloan Management Review,* Spring 1997.

4. Loke et.al., *The essence of Leadership.*

5. W.H.Davidow and B.Uttal, *Total Customer Service.*

6. Stephen Koepp, *Make that Sale, Mr. Sam*, Time, may 18, 1987.

20

MANAGING INSURANCE SERVICES IN THE NEW MILLENNIUM *(A CASE STUDY OF UNITED INDIA INSURANCE COMPANY LIMITED)*

Dr. Talluru Sreenivas* and **D.L.K. Ratna****

Insurance Business is facing intensified competition all over the world, including India. Economic reforms brought private players into the battlefield. Age-old methods, which are being practicing by our Public Sector Insurance Agencies, may not give in the long run overwhelming results. The change should be brought in all directions starting from product design to employee attitude. It has to find ways to decrease the overall costs while continuing to provide maximum benefits to the customer. Application of modern Management principles would pave the way for rationalizing and standardizing the services. Insurance companies have to formulate facility wide marketing plan. An attempt has been made in this study to present the state of the art and Growth of Insurance Industry with particular reference to United India Insurance Company Limited. The paper displays the relevant strategies to develop the Marketing activity in Insurance Business. Attempt has also been made to explain innovative concepts like Telesales, Banc Assurance, and also suggests formulation of Risk Management Consultancies, Appointment of Rural Agents, Printing of attractive single page literature etc.

---

* Reader, Department of Management Sciences, R.V.R.& J.C.College of Engineering, Guntur-522 019, A.P.

** Executive Director, Mahatma Gandhi College, Guntur.

Introduction

Insurance Marketing is becoming increasingly competitive all over the world and India is no exception. After 1990, in the emerging scenario of liberalization, competition is coming from the private players also. Under these circumstances, age-old methods may not give us long run results. It is the need of the hour to use some innovative techniques to sell their products. There should be change in all directions while selling our products starting from attitudes of the employees to features of the product. Specifically, Insurance Companies have to find ways to decrease their costs while continuing to provide the maximum possible benefits to the customer. The application of modern Marketing principles would pave avenues for rationalizing and standardizing the services. Every one of us know that Marketing concept is a recognition that the objectives of an organization can best be reached by identifying the needs and wants of the customers who make up the target market and meeting those needs and wants through an integrated, efficient, organization- wide effort. The four pillars that support the Marketing concept are customer orientation, profit, total company effort, and social responsi-bility. The Insurance Corporations with the help of innovative Marketing strategies would be efficacious in achieving the organizational goals. In order to promote the business and to visualize the increased satisfaction index, it is essential that the product mix is redesigned or a number of new policies be introduced, keeping in view the changing needs and requirements of potential investors. Channeling the insurance funds and the promotional policies for expanding the business are found important. It is also believed that an innovative marketing approach would be successful in redressing the grievances of customers.

Insurance Business—A Bird's Eye View

The business of insurance is related to the protection of the protection of the economic values or assets. Every asset is an economic source and has value. Earlier, if the asset got lost, being destroyed or made non-functional, through an accident or other unfortunate event, the owner and those deriving benefits therefrom, suffered. Such possible occurrences are called perils. Fire, floods, breakdowns, lightning, earthquakes, etc are perils. The damage that these perils may cause the asset is the risk that the asset is exposed to. Insurance is a mechanism that helps to reduce such adverse consequences. Conceptually, the mechanism of insurance is very simple. People who are exposed to the same risk are brought together. Insurance companies collect in advance and create a fund from which the losses are paid. The share, which is collected, is called a "premium". Insurance business is broadly classified into two groups.

1. Life Insurance &
2. Non-Life (or) General Insurance

Life insurance deals with all insurances covering human lives. Non-life or general insurance deals with insurance covering non-human objects like animals, agricultural crops, goods, factories, cars, etc. Sickness and accidents to human are classified as non-life insurance in India but as life insurance in many countries. Non-life insurance also covers losses through individual behaviours like fraud, burglary, non-fulfillment of promises (in the case of repayment of mortgage loans), professional negligence by doctors etc. Non-life Insurance polices are mostly for short periods of one year. The claim has to arise in that particular year.

Insurance Business—Historical Perspective

Insurance is said to have commenced with Marine Insurance, covering goods sent on ships, against the risks of piracy and storms. The Lloyd's coffee house in London, where the traders used to gather and from where the first insurance risks were under written still exists and continues to be the centre of insurance activity. Life and other insurances were developed later. The first life insurance policy is issued in 1583 in England. Life Insurance came to India from England as far back as in 1818. The first Insurance Company on Indian soil, namely Oriental Life Insurance Company was started in Culcutta in the year 1870. At the end of 1955 there were 245 Insurance Companies operating in 97 centres in India, but the development of insurance companies was however marked by many malpractices, deficiencies and frequent liquidation of insurance companies, shaking public confidence and depriving policy holders of their savings and security.

With the promulgation of an ordinance on January 9, 1956, all 245 Life Insurance Companies were nationalized and LIC of India came to existence. Shri C.D. Deshmukh, the then Finance Minister is the man behind the nationalization of insurance business in India. At that time, Insurance Companies started with motto 'Yogakshemam Vahamyaham' which means 'your welfare is my Responsibility'. The business of Non-life Insurance was nationalized in 1973. 107 Indian and Foreign companies were integrated into four insurance companies all of which were subsidiaries of the General Insurance Corporation of India (GIC). The total premium income rose from about Rs.200 crore in 1973 to over Rs.9982 crore in the year 1999-2000. The total assets of the G.I.C. and the four subsidiaries, aggregate to about Rs.25,000 crore. Insurance coverage has extended to the farmers and the rural economy, giving it some stability in the wake of vagaries of weather and disease.

General Insurance Corporation of India

The Corporation is the holding company, separate and distinct from the subsidiary companies. The Corporation does not write any direct insurance business except the aviation insurance business of Air India, Indian Airlines, Hindustan Aeronautics and crop insurance. It receives by way of reinsurance, 20% of all the direct business written in India by the subsidiary companies.

The Subsidiary Companies: The functions of the companies are to underwrite all types of General Insurance business both direct and by way of reinsurance in India. The companies also operate in overseas territories. The companies are autonomous with their own Boards of Directors and Management. The Head Offices of the four companies are located in the four metropolitan cities National Insurance Co. Ltd., - Kolkata; The New India Assurance Company Ltd., - Mumbai; The Oriental Insurance Co. Ltd., - New Delhi and United India Insurance Co. Ltd., - Chennai.

The Head Offices of the companies are responsible for overall planning, direction and control of Indian and foreign business. The Head Offices are also concerned with final accounts, investment, reinsurance and other specialist functions. Each Head office functions with the help of Regional, Divisional and Branch offices.

Table 1 presents the information about organizational set up of GIC of India and its Market share. From the table it can be said that

New India Insurance Company have highest number of offices with market share of 31.83% and National Insurance Company is running with 962 Branches with Market share of 20.98%.

Table 1: Organizational set up and Market Share of Insurance Companies in India as on 31.03.2001

Company	*H.Off*	*R.Off*	*D.Off*	*B.Off*	*Total*	*Market Share %*
GIC	01	–	–	–	–	–
National	01	20	272	670	962	20.98
New India	01	26	394	730	1123	31.83
Oriental	01	21	311	638	970	21.94
United India	01	25	360	737	1112	25.25
Total	**05**	**92**	**1373**	**2738**	**4177**	**–**

The following table depicts business of four subsidiaries during 1998-2001 along with the GIC of India. Through the table, it is clear that the business of all branches is improving considerably during all the years.

Table 2: Business procured by GIC and the four subsidiaries from 1998 to 2001

Rs. In millions

Company	*1998-99*	*1999-2000*	*2000-01*
GIC	55.7	79.9	280
National	1853.5	2042.1	2227
New India	3017.6	3306.5	3493
Oriental	1969.9	2166.5	2247
United India	2260.8	2390.5	2524
Total	**9157.5**	**9982.2**	**10771**

Table 3 gives data relating to Human Resources of all subsidiaries along with GIC. The number of employees is highest in the case of New India among the subsidiaries and National Insurance stood last.

Table 3: Human Resources of GIC & Its subsidiaries as on 31.03.2001

Company	*Class I*	*Class II*	*Class III*	*Class IV*	*Total*
National	3892	2782	9917	2338	18928
New India	4975	3839	11943	2782	23539
Oriental	4086	2932	9618	2375	19011
United	4652	2947	10953	2313	20865
GIC	273	–	316	110	699
Total	**17878**	**12500**	**42747**	**9918**	**83042**

Source: Insurance Times, Kolkata.

Threats/Problems Encountered by GIC of India

The threats to the non-life insurance companies from the impending competition are :

(a) Superior products and services offered by the international companies outweigh the existing products offered by state owned companies.

(b) Present procedures are long, manual and cumbersome.

(c) Entry of Corporate Houses like Tatas, Reliance, Bajaj may lead to the loss of their accounts from the existing insurers.

(d) Presently Banks are making efforts to enter into Insurance Business. As these have lot of network, it becomes threat to existing players.

(e) There will be flight of trained and experienced personnel from the existing companies to the new companies.

(f) The density of insurance per capita in India shows that the existing distribution channels have not been effective.

(g) Technology-driven system and processes will give cost effective distribution channels and generally have high standard of productivity. This is a threat to the present companies.

Apart from the above threats, the following problems are also to be faced by the public sector insurance companies.

Management Expenses: After the passing of the Broker's Bill in the parliament, the new scenario will be most beneficial to the private players and they will exploit the situation fully as they have very small manpower and network to operate. They can operate within the stipulation of 19.5% of management expenses to the premium income since their management expenses will be reduced with the introduction of Broker system.

High Claim Ratio: During the last decade, the public sector general insurance companies have suffered underwriting losses aggregating to Rs.6209 crore. They have made marginal investment profit because of high claims ratio especially in the motor insurance. The premium is not increased to match the outgo as there is a stiff resistance from the transport lobby. Due to poor road conditions the number of own damage claims for vehicles is also increasing.

Claims Settlement: The statistics show that 80% of the claims are settled. Almost 99% documents cleared. Still the public perception is that the service of the general insurance company is poor. Genuineness of the claims is not appreciated. They claim that the same yardstick is applied in all the claims and Claims pass through several hands causing delay. Documents are asked in piecemeal and ultimately, the customer is unhappy even though claims are settled but with delay. On the other hand, the employees are afraid to take commercial decision because of audit and vigilance.

Excessive Man Power: After nationalization with an objective of providing employment and also developing the network, the general insurance companies have recruited officers and other clerical staff and adopted reservation policy for various sections. Because of no expansion, offices are being closed or merged. As a result, the companies have come to the situation of excessive manpower.

Product Development: The public sector companies grown in a protected environment and with no competition are in a monopolistic situation all these days. They have neglected the customers' needs and expectations. No great effort has been made to evolve tailor made policies to fulfill the customers' expectations.

Application of Marketing Principles in Insurance Business

Many of the Insurance service organisations all over the world, developed a marketing culture in their setup in the last decade, which has enabled them to scale new heights in their ventures. In advanced countries, marketing has taken deep roots whereas in the developing countries, like ours, the need is being felt just now. Marketing of Insurance services is the least understood and felt as being not very urgent by many professionals today. Many of us still prefer to be victims of established rules, ethical codes, social constraints and spiritual laws. There is an inbuilt tendency to think that services will be sold out automatically and money will flow if an office is started. Administrators are keeping other issues aside as secondary and focusing their attention on upgrading their infrastructure. But unfortunately, Marketing, which is very essential for survival of any service organisation, is being almost ignored. Technological sophistication has raised the cost of services.

The following points justify the application of marketing principles in the Insurance services:

1. In the present day context, society and Insurance system are out of touch with each other and are not communicating. Marketing brings the two together again. Marketing tries to convert Insurance agencies into consumer oriented enterprises.
2. Marketing tries to correct the imbalances between the society and Insurance system.
3. The emphasis on marketing today is no longer centered on goods and things; it is largely concerned with people and the satisfaction of their needs. Marketing tries to assess the needs of certain segments of the population and acts as basis in creating new products or services.
4. Through application of marketing principles in Insurance Corporation, one can optimize the cost of services. It is particularly important in the developing countries like India where the users are unable to bear the burden of costly policies.
5. Marketing principles would minimize the cost of services by expanding the scale of operation. It helps in promoting increasing safety consciousness.
6. Marketing principles bring about behavioural changes in providers that satisfy the users of these services.

7. Another strong justification for applying the marketing principles in the Insurance services is related to the financial soundness. It provides avenues for generating internal resources.

The significance of marketing in Insurance services is supported by the fact that promotion strategies like advertisement and publicity will increase the number and the revenue, consequently.

Now, let us take the example of United India Insurance Company and we will probe into the Marketing activities that are being implemented by this subsidiary and based on the conclusions we derive, try to suggest some suitable measures for effective functioning of the non-life Insurance Companies.

United India Insurance Co. Ltd., - A Profile

It is a flag company in South India with its head office in Chennai. It has 25 Regional Offices, 360 Divisional Offices and 737 Branch Offices under its control for effective penetration throughout the country. General Manager-Marketing looks after the marketing functions of the company. United India Regional Office, Vizag was formed in the year 1987 with its Divisional and Branch Offices located in the coastal Andhra Pradesh. At present, it has control over 14 Divisional Offices spread over the nine coastal districts of Andhra Pradesh. Deputy Manager-Marketing looks after the Marketing functions of entire Regional Office under supervision of Regional Manager.

Table 4 presents Year-wise performance of Regional Office from 1995 to 2000 by showing year-wise operational results.

Table 4: United India Insurance Company Limited Year-Wise Performance at a Glance

	1995-96	*1996-97*	*1997-98*	*1998-99*	*1999-2000*
Target	450000	570000	700000	750000	800000
Premium	453695	552118	605195	689000	724847
Incurred Loss	320289	607833	982847	612853	654210
Underwriting Loss/Profit	126395	-64397	-391178	61399	70637
Expenses of Management	103256	128262	128338	147322	154432

Table 5 provides year wise operational results. These results gives the impression that growth rate is not constant and needs consolidation. By 2000, the results need careful analysis.

Table 5: United India Insurance Company Ltd. Year-Wise Operational Results

	1995-96	*1996-97*	*1997-98*	*1998-99*	*1999-2000*
Growth Rate	18.31	21.69	9.61	13.85	5.19
Target Realisation	100.8	96.86	86.46	88.33	90.61
Incurred Loss Ratio	70.6	110.09	162.4	88.94	90.25
Expenditure Ratio	22.76	23.23	21.2	21.38	21.58

Marketing of Non-Life Insurance Products in Prevailing Scenario

Product: Presently the number of policies promoted in the non-life insurance sector exceeds nearly 160 in number. It is a moot point to ask whether the marketing force is aware of the existence of the various product lines. Though customer benefit is the prime concern, the concept gets diluted slowly and steadily as it percolates down from the corporate level to operating level. Recent example is "Janarogya Beema Policy", "Rajarajeswari Mahila Kalyan Yojana" and so on. They have faced infantile death and relegated to 'decline' stage of product life cycle.

Pricing: Due to high level of intangibility, price determination is very difficult for insurance covers, especially in case of customer-oriented products. Though Market regulates the prices, when price revision becomes inevitable, prudent strategies are not introduced.

Promotion: The promotion strategies are lackluster indeed. The products are promoted mainly by personal selling, incurring huge amount of management expenses; it appears they only aim at enhancing the social status of the marketing force rather than aiming to reach the target customers and a vast untapped market. Advertisements in mass media are very occasional. Though the advertisements are effectively designed so as to reach the target group, frequency of such advertisements is irregular. Vast majority of even literate population is unaware of the existence of non-life insurance companies. Even publicity campaigns for popularizing some of the products targeted at the rural segment, turn out to be mere rituals with no follow up action.

Place: In almost each district, there is an office of one or the other general insurance companies. The public sector insurance companies score an advantage over their perspective competitors in this aspect. Still, the Marketing force in such offices has restricted their operations to traditional segment only. Due to lack of professional and managerial approach towards Marketing, right from the top to bottom, the concept of general insurance remains to be popularized as yet.

Physical Evidence: The physical evidence element comprises of Peripheral and Essential evidence. Peripheral Evidence is actually possessed by the buyer as evidence of purchase of service namely policy formats and claim forms. Due to the monopoly enjoyed by the nationalized companies designing of policies or packaging aspects were not paid desired attention. Essential Evidence is with respect to the infrastructure facilities possessed by the companies. Very little efforts have been put in for strengthening this aspect as these are public sector entities.

Process: The system by which delivery of the service is done constitutes the process element. Though automation is introduced, it has not reduced the service delivery time – be it issuing of policies or claim settlement. In fact because of poor training at the operating level, poor quality of computers and lack of adequate infrastructure required for automation have augmented the delay involved in rendering customer service in many places.

People: Though it is an important constituent of services marketing, it is accorded least importance because of lack of professional approach at the operating level and the bureaucratic procedures followed by the top management. Recruitments were made more as a deed than to fulfill a need.

Strategies for Marketing Insurance Services

The following are the some of the suggestions for strengthening the Marketing activity.

Product

- Package policies could be designed in unique way to prevent comparison with competitor products.

- Tailor-made policies to cover losses normally encountered according to the choice of the customers segment.
- Combination of two or more related schemes like Motor Insurance with Personal Accident coverage, health care insurance with personal accident cover. An element of discount may be embedded into the combination covers, to increase the volume of sales.

Price

- Easy payment plans.
- Offer long-term policies to save premium.
- Introduce maturity refund schemes on long-term policies, depending upon claim history.
- Group discounts.
- Offering discounts to the regular customers their sustained patronage.

Promotion

- Establishing a brand image in order to create value to the product. It increases consumer awareness, improves chances of the repeat purchases, inculcates an image for the product and helps adoption of new products.
- Advertisements should be affective enough to create the demand.
- Whenever new schemes are introduced, after identifying the profitable segment, Direct Mailing method can be followed.
- Opening of point of purchase outlets at Airports, Railway Stations, and Major Hospitals.
- Publicity campaigns in association with business organizations, sponsoring sports events, health checkups etc.
- Personal selling through qualified and trained agency force.

Place

- Insurance players can have access to the untapped rural market through cooperative sector. By imparting insurance knowledge and awareness in the midst of rural populace they can be made insurance friendly.

- *Banc assurance:* For insurers it is an additional distribution channel. Banc assurance can be either restricted to being a more distributor of insurance products or extended to running a separate subsidiary of insurance. Banc assurance offers a more complete range for the customers, facilitating the customers to deal with one firm for all their financial services.

People

- Formulation of risk management consultancies in major cities, employing persons with technical as well as marketing flair, to guide the customer to choose the right cover and render required service in claim settlement.
- Appointment of Rural Agents, preferably choosing opinion leaders, respectable citizens and land lords as they will ensure a large following, and inculcate insurance awareness among the rural population.

Physical Evidence

- Tangible representation of the services – by providing distinct looks of the policy document by adopting suitable and attractive packing – like the policy document filed in a docket, or laminated with an opening at the top to take out the document etc.
- Providing attractive single page literatures with list of holidays and the year calendar to keep beneath the glass slat on an executive's table.
- Creating a brand image by incorporation of brand name either as a suffix or a prefix of an insurance scheme.
- Emphasize on essential evidence by locating the office appropriately adapting professional interior decoration in tune with the changing trend.
- Creating a suitable logo to identify easily, keeping in mind the overall image which the organization wishes to project to the customers.

Process

- Issuing over the counter immediately upon payment of premium by the insured.
- Convenient claim processing formalities.
- Transparency in claim settling process by providing opportunities to the insured to seek clarification.
- Reducing the time gap between reporting and settlement of claims, by utilizing the services of claim settling agents, immediately on receipt of intimation of loss or damage.

Conclusion

Service sector has become an important contributor in building the national economy. Nearly 50% of GDP is now accounted for by the service sector. Though the service sector is gaining prominence, much thought has not yet been given by the academia in terms of introducing the latest management techniques, more importantly marketing strategies. More specifically, Insurance Companies should formulate facility-wise marketing plan. Marketing of Insurance services is needed to educate large numbers of people. This is an attempt to study relevant marketing tools, which improves the overall effectiveness of the Insurance Industry. State of the art and growth of the Insurance Industry with particular reference to United India Insurance Company Limited is covered. Relevant strategies to develop the marketing activity in Insurance Company are discussed. The study seeks to explain innovative concepts like Telesales, Banc assurance; and it also suggests formulation of risk management consultancies, appointment of rural agents, printing of attractive single page literature etc.

21

INSURANCE SERVICES IN INDIA

U. Ravi Kumar* and **Dr. R. Sivaram Prasad****

All over the world, the service sector of the economy is going through a period of almost revolutionary change in which established ways of doing business continue to be shunted aside. At the begining of a new millenium, we are seeing the manner in which we live and work being transformed by a new developments in services. Innovators continually launch new ways to satisfy our existing needs and to meet needs that we did not even know we had (How many of us, 10 years ago, anticipated the personal need for e-mail?). The same is true of services directed at corporate users.

According to recent estimation, forecastimation, it was visualized that by March–April, 2004 the contribution of service sector to the India's GDP would be at 48%. This makes clear that we are living in 'Service Imperative Era'. The enormous growth potential in the service sector has lead to the great visualization of 'Developed India-2020' by many Indians. Among all the service oriented organisations, Insurance Industry occupies a prominent place. The insurance industry is one of the cornerstones of any economy. Liberalization of the insurance industry in India has helped in bringing out several positive developments including the expansion of the market size, introduction of new products and development of new channel distribution in the market.

* MBA Student, R.V.R.&J.C. College of Engineering, Guntur.

** Faculty Member, Dept. of Computer Science & Engg., Acharya Nagarjuna University, Guntur.

Unfortunately, today, only 3.5% of the Indian population, i.e., 35 million in one billion, is insured. From this one can draw inference that there exists a hidden market in insurance, which remains to be tapped. It is in this context, an humble attempt has been made by the authors to present the concept of Insurance, its history, present day problems, prospects with a special reference to its market potential in Rural India.

Introduction

The term insurance is not a different animal altogether. The concept of insurance has been taking its shape for the last 300 years in the world. Life insurance made its debut in India well over a hundred years ago. Today life insurance is widely accepted as one of the most attractive financial instruments in an individual's portfolio that provides an insurance of security with attractive returns. Life insurance plays an important role in mitigating life's uncertainties. There are innumerable types of life policies which provide cover against a variety of illness, accidental death etc.

Insurance industry is one of the cornerstones of any economy in the world. In the present dynamic environment, insurance has become one of the core sectors in deciding a country's prosperity. It is an industry where excellence is driven by competition. This is why the entry of foreign insurers, as minority partners in domestic joint ventures, has brought the hope that the market will reach a new level.

Need for Insurance

The purpose of insurance is to safeguard against misfortunes by making good the losses of unfortunate few, through the help of the fortunate many, who were exposed to the same risk but saved from misfortune.

Thus the essence of insurance is to share losses and substitute certainity by uncertinity. Life is full of uncertainities about the occurrence of a disaster, and insurance is based on uncertainities. If there are no uncertainities about the occurrence of a disaster, the concept of insurance will cease to exist.

Insurance Industry Prior to Liberalization

Before 2001 when the insurance sector was opened up LIC was the sole provider of life insurance in India. LIC had taken responsibility and left no stone unturned in taking insurance to every nook and corner of the country.

LIC with its

2,048 Branch Offices,

100 Divisional Offices and

7 Zonal Offices

Covered every possible corner of the

North-East,

North, West, South and even at

Andaman and Nicobar Islands.

In 1999, when the insurance sector was in the hands of the Government owned insurers, premium as a percentage of India's GDP was at 1.3 %, a marginal figure compared to the international standards of the countries like the USA, Japan and the UK as given below:

Country	*Premium as a percentage of GDP*
India	1.3
U.S.	7
Japan	8.87
U.K.	10.30

Prior to the liberalization of the Indian insurance industry in spite of the tremendous efforts made by the LIC, the contribution of insurance the growth of the country was very marginal.

Insurance Industry after Liberalisation

The primary objectives of liberalisation of the insurance sector are....

- to enhance the market
- to widen the insurance coverage

Pursuant to the Malhotra Committee's report, the insurance sector was opened and the monopoly of LIC and GIC and its subsidiary companies for transacting life and general insurance business, respectively, was taken away by insertion of section 30 A in LIC Act 1956 called Insurance Regulation and Development Act 1999. The Act established a Regulatory and Development Authority (IRDA) in 2000 to regulate, promote, and ensure orderly growth of the insurance industry.

The Act objectively seeks to open the insurance sector to private and foreign investors. As per the Act, new entrants, who must be Indian, will be granted license to transact insurance business only if they contribute a minimum capital of Rs. 100 crore for life and general insurance business and Rs. 200 crore for reinsurance business. Foreign collaboration will also be allowed but foreign investment is capped at 49 % of the total capital.

Liberalisation of the isurance sector has helped in bringing about several positive developments including the following.

- Expansion of the market size
- Introduction of new products
- Development of new channel distribution
- Superior Customer Responsiveness.

The total FDI in India in the insurance sector today stands at Rs. 812.50 crore. The total premium income of the Indian insurance industry, both life and non-life for the year ending March 31, 2003 stands at Rs. 71,376.11 crore out of this the share of life insurance premium is 78 % i.e., Rs. 55,738 crore and general insurance premium is 22 % i.e., 15,638 crore.

Progress of Private Insurers

Insurance industry once upon a time was a quiet and dormant industry but now it is becoming today's hottest business, as on January 2003, 12 players have entered the life insurance market and 8 players have entered the non-life insurance market. To name a few ICICI Prudential Life insurance, Birla Sun Life, HDFC Standard, Max New York, SBI Life, Om Kotak, Tata AIG, ING Vysya, Met Life, Allianz Bajaj etc., have been doing extremely well with a number of innovative strategies by giving at most importance to rural areas.

The share of private sector in life insurance cake has increased from 0.02 to 1.99 % in the last two years, while the share of private sector in general insurance cake has increased from 0.07 to 9.00 %. The total sale of all private companies is around 5 % of the total insurance business in the country.

New Distribution Channels

Traditionally, the life insurers have been banking solely on the agency distribution force. On the contrary, the general insurance business has depended totally on the Development Officers(Dos).The new age private insurers are adding more channels of distribution in the Indian market parallel to existing one. Innovation and Diversification are the two buzzwords in the business.

The various new distribution channels in the insurance industry today are as follows.

- Direct Marketing through dedicated sales force.
- Bancassurance
- Corporate agents/ Brokers
- Independent financial advisors
- Tele Marketing

Changing Scenario

The emerging economic scenario has thrown up the challenges which threaten the insurance business in India. Most individuals view life insurance as an integral part of their finance portfolio. This is a significant change from the earlier attitude when insurance was purchased as a tax-saving tool.

The major factors which affect the insurance market today are as follows:

- Changing Customer Behaviour
- Deregulation & Government intervention
- Competition, technology, distribution networks, automation etc.
- Technological advancement
- Client relationship and quality
- New service standards

Radical changes are taking place in customer profile due to changing life style, and social perception, resulting in erosion of brand loyalty.

Some other developments worth mentioning are as follows.

- Flexible packages have become the order of the day
- Higher customer aspirations lead to new expectations
- Higher ratio of return, much more efficient and ready-on-demand service expectations.
- Customer Orientation has become the 'New Mantra'.

Future Challenges in The Indian Insurance Industry

The global life insurance market stands at $ 1521 billion, while non-life insurance market is placed at $ 922 billion. India takes 23rd position with $ 9.33 billion annual premium collections having only 0.41% share. Today only 3.5 % of the Indian population, i.e., 35 million in one billion, is insured. All these indicate that there is a huge untapped potential in the Indian insurance market.

Although the growth rate of the economy has been quite impressive in the last decade, the insurance industry still has low penetration.

According a recent survey, the contributions of premium incomes to the GDPs of different countries in both life non-life and life insurance segments are as given below

Country	*Premium as a share of GDP (in %)*	
	Non-life	*Life*
India	0.56	1.50
U.S.	5	5
U.K.	3	9
Japan	3	9

It is very clear from the above statistics that India still has low penetration levels in the insurance industry when compared to any other developed country like US, UK and Japan. The per capita premium in India is also below the level of advanced countries. India which accounts for 8 % of Asia's GDP, constitutes for only 2% and

1% respectively of Asia's non-life and life-insurance business. All these indicate that there is a huge untapped potential in the Indian insurance market.

According to the projections by CII expert group, the volume of life insurance premium, which stood at Rs. 215.81 million in 1998-99, will more than double to Rs. 592.51 billion by 2004-05 and rise nearly five times by 2010. In general insurance too, the CII expects premium income to double by 2004-05.

Potentiality in Rural India

Though rural India represents around 74% of the population, it leaves a lot to desire when it comes to insurance coverage. The life insurance buyers in rural India are growing at the rate of 18 % compared to 3.9 % in cities. The share of rural business according to recent statistics in policies and sum assured are 50.25% and 45.2% respectively. IRDA statistics show that out of 12 private insurers, HDFC-Standard topped the list in terms of the total premiums from the rural and social sector with a total of Rs. 3.5 crore in 2003.

Reasons for Low Penetration Levels in Rural India

- The mindsets of rural Indians
- The lack of awareness
- Problems related to logistics
- Paying capacity (premium)
- Spread of risk
- No tax benefit motivation as most of the agricultural income is tax free.

The welcoming markets, customer's willingness to buy insurance, huge product base, wide array of distribution channels and the regulations are waiting for the insurer's active participation in rural India. The ball is in the insurer's court, to explore rural India and enable reduce the divide between urban and rural insurance markets, thereby making India a developed country in the world.

INDEX

C

H

I

Q

R

S

X

Y

Z

□□□